Soul Models

Transformative Stories of
COURAGE & COMPASSION
That Will Change Your Life

ELIZABETH BRYAN & **ANGELA DAFFRON**

Health Communications, Inc.
Deerfield Beach, Florida

www.hcibooks.com

Library of Congress Cataloging-in-Publication Data

Daffron, Angela.
   Soul models: transformative stories of courage and compassion that will change your life. / Daffron, Elizabeth Bryan.
     pages cm
     ISBN-13: 978-0-7573-1786-6 (Paperback)
     ISBN-10: 0-7573-1786-3 (Paperback)
     ISBN-13: 978-0-7573-1787-3 (ePub)
     1. Courage   2. Compassion.   3.Conduct of Life.   I.Bryan, Elizabeth.
   II. Title
   BF575.CSD34 2014
   170'44—dc23

                                                  2014012313

Publisher: Health Communications, Inc.
          3201 S.W. 15th Street
          Deerfield Beach, FL 33442–8190

Cover art: Painted by Elizabeth Bryan, co-designed by artist Byron Keith Byrd and web designer Marcella Smith, Paradigm Design.
Interior design and formatting by Lawna Patterson Oldfield

To David Brenner,
your brilliance and talent live on
through our three sons, our grandson, and
the laughter you brought to millions of people.
Thank you for inspiring me to dream bigger
than the entire universe. From there,
this book was born. My wish is that *Soul Models*
continues your legacy and helps everyone
who reads it to believe in the power
they hold to transform this world.

—*Elizabeth Bryan*

To my first Soul Model, my dad,
thank you for teaching me
to be like you!

—*Angela Daffron*

CONTENTS

Acknowledgments vii

Introduction 1

All Roads Lead Back to Craig's List Elizabeth Bryan 5

Be the Change Angela Daffron 9

Behavior Savior Dina Zaphyris 21

The Heart of a Giant Eli Manning 31

This Is Their Story: Parts One and Two
Deanne and Ally Breedlove 41

Leap and the Net Will Appear Kim Barnouin 59

Every Mother Counts Christy Turlington Burns 71

Living for Love Ibu Robin Lim 93

The "Mother of Movements" Candace Lightner 107

Operation Beautiful Caitlin Boyle 121

Play it Forward Marcus Mitchell 129

Everyone Needs Magic David Copperfield 143

Love Means Making Something Grow Temple Grandin 151

Love Does Not Draw a Line in the Sand Mary Griffith 161

Taking in the Good Rick Hanson, Ph.D. 173

It's Not What Happens—It's How You Heal with It
Elizabeth Bryan 185

**Embracing Life—and All That
Comes with It** Dawn Averitt 197

A World Without Cancer Margaret I. Cuomo, M.D. 213

Accomplishing the Impossible Ken Kragen.............................225

The Calling Marty Gruber...239

Passport to Life Eve Branson 249

Love Unplugged Roseanna Means, M.D...................................257

Life is good Steve Gross..269

The Real Life of Lieutenant Dan Gary Sinise............................281

Turning Broken Bones into Dancing Edith Eva Eger, Ph.D. 295

Soul Selfie Seikou Andrews...303

ACKNOWLEDGMENTS

From Elizabeth Bryan

*S*oul Models has been a journey of miracles that could never have happened without the love and support of many people. Thank you to my mom for being my best friend, biggest fan, and fabulous editor; to my dad for always being there. To my amazing sons, Cole, Slade, and Wyatt for being the reasons I never give up, to Michelle for being so grounded and giving us Wesley. To John Mittelman for your never-ending love and support, to Byron Keith Byrd for being my best friend and creative cohort, to Monica Ord for always helping, to Natalie Caine for your love and nurturing in the eleventh hour. To our editor Christine Belleris for being so *good* at what you do, to everyone at HCI for making this happen, to Bob Jacobs for your caring and guidance, to David Mathison for always being there, to Candace Bahr and Ginita Wall, for being my personal *Soul Models* and lighting my path to purpose.

To the amazing *Soul Models* in this book: you've *all* kept me going through the ups and downs of life. A few of you, in particular, have changed my individual world. To Angela, for inspiring *Soul Models*, to Candace Lightner for your astonishing resilience and guidance, to Mary Griffith for your miraculous spirit, to Edith Eger for surviving Auschwitz and being a brilliant therapist, to Marty Gruber for being there for my sons, to Roseanna Means for showing me true sisterhood, to Dr. Margaret Cuomo for keeping me healthy, to Steve Gross for reminding me to play. To Deanne, Ally, Shawn, Jake, and Ben Breedlove: thank you so much for being in my life and reminding me of my faith when I needed it the most.

To Nancy Farnsworth: your love, bravery, friendship and outrageous brand of wisdom helped get me through it all.

From Angela Daffron

Thank you to the Soul Models in this book, as well as those we interviewed for future editions! Each one of you taught me something unique and life changing. I am confident everyone reading this book will find their own lessons in your stories, too. Your experiences and achievements are amazing and I am honored you shared them for this project.

Thank you Dad! Thank you for always giving me such sound advice and support while teaching me the strength to overcome the toughest of challenges. You taught me to be a rock, and while I may get weathered, I can withstand the harshest of conditions! Your words "Take it slow and think it through," echo in my ears and guide me through each challenge life throws at me.

Elizabeth, this has been quite the journey as we both overcame personal challenges throughout the process of writing this book. Thank you for always finding the silver linings!

Thank you to the countless friends, colleagues, and family members, who listened to ideas, read samples, listened to my raves/rants, and encouraged me throughout the process of developing this project! I am lucky to have all of you in my life! You are all Soul Models!

We saved the room in this book for sharing Soul Model stories, but please visit our site at *www.SoulModels.net* for more acknowledgements and "lessons learned" from the Soul Models.

INTRODUCTION

Soul Models are individuals who touch the hearts, minds and souls of everyone they meet. They are the role models of today, whose journeys showcase the power we each have to discover purpose in challenge, and use what we find to better the world. Everyone can be a Soul Model— including you.

You are holding a powerful gift—not just the words on these pages, but inside of your heart. Maybe you've never felt quite smart, strong, thin or successful enough to really believe this is true. Maybe you've experienced hardships that have weakened your spirit or self-esteem. Maybe your life is pretty smooth most of the time, but you find yourself searching for deeper meaning. How do we understand what makes us special? How do we discover our purpose? What's the secret to overcoming challenge and just being happier, regardless of circumstance? Most importantly, how do we *step* up when we feel like *giving* up?

Part of this answer has been inside of us all along, and recent science is backing it up—*it's all about lending a hand . . . in fact, we are biologically hard-wired to help.*[1,3]

Translation? Not only can we all make a difference for another person; it feels really good and can improve our health. Compassionate action triggers the brain's pleasure center, releasing the same endorphins we get from eating—without the carbs. It's called the "giver's high," and physical benefits include boosting our immune system, lowering stress hormones, reducing heart rates, and possibly even helping us live longer.[2,4]

Giving also makes us feel better about our own lives. From the smallest hurts to the largest wounds, reaching out to others in any way helps transform our hurt to hope, and pain to purpose. The number one reason this works is because for that period of time, whether a minute or a month, the focus is off us—we get a break from our own lives! The second reason is that people really appreciate kindness—who doesn't feel good being on the receiving end of "thank you?"

The bottom line is this: when you know you've helped someone, you feel valued and connected. You understand that even the smallest actions have great meaning.

As two authors, advocates, and moms, we notice people doing this all the time. Every time we turn around, we hear about someone who witnessed or overcame a huge challenge and turned it around in an amazing way that helped other people. And, they are not just "doing it," they're *compelled* to do it, no matter the costs, no matter the odds. It has become a full-on mission—they are changing the world, and their lives have opened up in ways that we only dream about. They definitely "don't sweat the small stuff," and they seem much happier than most other people. When you come right down to it, they didn't even start out with much more than anybody else—in fact, many times, they had a lot less.

Science aside, what's the secret? How and why do all of these people do it, while working and/or raising families? What advice do they have for us? What do we have in common with them? How can we apply even some of this wisdom to our own lives?

This book was born of our desire to figure out the formula and inspire as many of you as possible to try it out yourselves.

So, we began our mission: gathering stories, conducting interviews and compiling information. We not only discovered the answers, but watched as a series of miracles unfolded that were undeniably growing out of something bigger. The more we trusted this process, the more opportunities opened up. We began to realize that we were tapping into the reciprocal energy of giving and receiving; the place where all possibility exists. One contributor led to the next, and before we knew it, all of our Soul Models were helping each other in a meant-to-be way that would make even the most doubtful person take pause.

Soul Models shares the journeys of individuals who experienced or witnessed all kinds of adversity; from illness to poverty to depression, loss, abuse, and everything in between—many were thrown a curve ball that would flatten out the best of us. Just like you, they were given a choice: *to give up or step up*. Whether out of frustration, anger, grief, or the desire to make a mark on this world, they *stepped* up; taking some kind of action that would spare another person from pain. They became advocates, founded non-profits, wrote bestselling books, fought for cures, or created campaigns that lifted spirits. Some simply made a conscious decision to help anyone in need; many realized that helping themselves was the best place to begin.

Regardless of what they did or how they did it, the result was the same: they tapped into courage and compassion that they never even knew they had. They discovered their life's purpose, transforming the world in some remarkable way.

Their journeys illustrate who they are, and what keeps them going. You will learn how their challenges directly led to their purpose. You will understand how they achieved great things with little or no money. Through their advice and "soulutions," you will also learn how you can do it, too.

The stories you are about to read will become your personal road map in discovering purpose. They will guide you in using the gifts, courage and compassion you were born with to help you overcome hardship, feel valued, and live a happier, more joyful life.

Soul Models was written to help you understand that you are extra-ordinary, and that you already have everything you need to be happy. It was written to inspire you with the knowledge that every act of kindness, big or small, is equally profound. It is testimony to the fact that we can all make a difference, and that the compassion with which we each are born is the most powerful, transformational gift we each possess.

Everyone can be a "Soul Model"—including you. Amazing things can happen, the minute you open your heart. Enjoy!

Gratefully,
Elizabeth and Angela

1. *greatergood.berkeley.edu/article/item/the_compassionate_instinct/*
2. *www.sciencentral.com/articles/view.php3?article_id=218392880*
3. *www.publicaffairs.ubc.ca/media/releases/2008/mr-08-032.html*
4. *greatergood.berkeley.edu/article/item/5_ways_giving_is_good_for_you/*

All Roads Lead Back to Craig's List

Elizabeth Bryan

"Coincidence is God's way of remaining anonymous."
—Albert Einstein

A s the mother of two adolescent boys, I realized long ago that there is something about being female that goes way beyond our ability to have children. Maybe it's genetic, maybe it's excess estrogen; either way, it's pretty clear that we are hard-wired with an innate desire to nurture and protect, the conviction to go to the wall for our beliefs, even to risk our lives to right a wrong or protect our young. It's why Harriet Tubman led her people through the underground tunnels to freedom, and it's why Rosa Parks refused to sit in the back of the bus.

It all began as I was about to launch the *Chicken Soup for the Soul: Count Your Blessings* book and game with my dear friend and business partner, Laura Robinson. "Social media" had become the new buzzword, and I was ready to speed up my learning curve. I turned to Craig's List, which was as much my "buzz" as a triple soy latte. After all, where else can you sell a pottery wheel, find a pet stain specialist, and buy a used electric amplifier, all in one day? I wanted to learn "Twitter," which seemed suspiciously related to the Japanese counting system for sushi.

I typed "social media training" into the search window, closed my eyes, and hit "enter." Three postings came up: Website development, futon repair, and Angela Daffron, who was offering social media marketing services for small companies. Bingo! Two e-mails and one day later, I was sitting in Starbucks across from Angela.

Angela is a five-foot-four-inch, curly-haired blonde, with a soft-spoken, Southern twang that instantly makes you feel as if a piece of pie is in your near future. Her giggle and energy are equally contagious. I learned that she is a married working mom with a beautiful fourteen-year-old daughter, who had recently moved from New Mexico to Nevada, where I was living. I asked her what had gotten her started in social media, and the response was so unexpected; it literally split my heart wide open, right then and there.

Angela's lifelong friend, neighbor, and babysitter for her daughter had been stalked, raped, and murdered in the tiny town of Arkansas City, Kansas, population, 12,000. Angela described Jodi Sanderholm: a beautiful nineteen-year-old, class valedictorian, never-without-a-smile, dance instructor, adored by everyone who knew her. Jodi had stopped to get the mail on the way home from dance class in the middle of the day and was never seen alive again.

This small town tragedy was worsened by the fact that the Arkansas City police had been well aware of Jodi's killer long before her death—in fact, at least four other women had filed earlier reports that he'd been stalking them, but, under the law, their complaints had not qualified as a "credible threat." Angela explained this meant that had the law been different, this man would have been off the streets long before he had the chance to kill Jodi.

Mesmerized, I urged Angela to continue. She shared how her grief had quickly morphed into anger and purpose—Jodi's death had to have some greater meaning. She needed to be sure no one else would suffer in the same way. Over our lattes she looked me square in the eyes and said, "It couldn't be that some monster just decided Jodi should die." With fierce determination, Angela set out on a mission to single-handedly change stalking laws, first in Kansas, and then in Santa Fe. She explained Jodi's Voice, the non-profit she had founded to raise stalking awareness. In 2007, as a result of Angela's work, Kansas State Law changed, enforcing harsher penalties for stalkers and offering greater protection for victims.

Angela didn't stop there—in 2009, she got the laws changed in New Mexico. She and her husband continue this mission nationwide; now it is their sole purpose in life. Jodi Sanderholm did not die in vain.

Staring in amazement at Angela, I was speechless, never imagining that this soft-spoken woman in front of me was capable of making such a mark in our world. I was humbled, moved, and most of all, incredibly inspired. I thought—who *is* this person? What makes her tick? How did she do all this and raise a family, when other women complained about things like laundry and car pool? She clearly lived a simple life, and worked hard to pay her bills—what gave her the courage to push so hard, no matter what she and her family had to sacrifice? I had to know more.

Be the Change

---

*"Strength does not come from physical capacity.
It comes from an indomitable will."*

—Mahatma Gandhi

SOUL MODEL: Angela Daffron

CHALLENGE: After a close family friend was stalked and murdered, Angela's advocacy work led to her also becoming a stalking victim.

CHANGE: Founded Jodi's Voice, a non-profit devoted to offering support for stalking victims and raising awareness, for a crime that affects more than 6.6 million people in the United States each year.

SOULUTION: You have to keep going. You cannot let the obstacles and problems in your path stop you. You have to understand tomorrow will get better and you will get through it. Challenges give us the chance to grow stronger than we ever thought we could!

Growing up in a small, ordinary, Midwestern town, I was full of questions about the world. By the age of six, I was reading everything in sight, and at ten, I began programming a Texas Instruments computer just to see if I could. I am the younger of two girls, raised by a close-knit family in Arkansas City, Kansas, in the south-central part of the state, about four miles north of the Oklahoma border. With a population of 12,000, everybody knew everyone else. Families lived here for generations and most lived within minutes of their extended families. With an artist for a mother and an engineer for a father, I seemed to have the odd combination of creativity and an insatiable desire to learn. According to my dad, I wanted what I "wanted right then and there," and had zero patience to wait for anything to happen on its own.

My impediments started very young in life. At the age of two, I was hospitalized with what doctors diagnosed as a very rare kidney disease called childhood nephrosis after I began retaining fluids. The doctors in our area could not determine a cause, so my parents took me to the nearest city. Even in Wichita, the doctors did not know much about the disease, other than the odd realization that it predominantly struck two-year-old blonde females, and was 98 percent fatal at the time. My condition was so rare that specialists came to Kansas from all over the country to consult and study my condition, but none could offer any real help or hope. They told my parents they would not be taking me home from the hospital anytime soon.

Of course, I was too young to understand the severity of what was happening. I had been in the hospital about two weeks when I woke up one morning and let my parents know with absolute conviction that I would be "getting better." When they asked me how I knew that, I replied, "The angel said I would." The very next day my kidneys began working again and I was released from the hospital with no signs of the disease. The doctor's explanation was simply that I had cured myself. These were their very words. Various people had different theories at the time, ranging from coincidence to a miracle. Whatever happened that night in 1976, it led me to believe that I was meant to make some kind of big difference in the world.

My parents have always instilled in me the belief that I could do anything. I took this to heart and always dreamed big! I wasn't sure what I would do with my life, but I knew I wanted it to help people and make the world a better place. I have always seen problems and wanted to help right the wrongs or help those who could not help themselves. It borders on an illness really. I simply cannot turn my back on problems. Maybe it is the naivety of growing up in a small town. I believed the world was a good place and everyone was basically good.

My parents divorced when I was fourteen. My sister was an adult and living on her own by then, and after the divorce, my father and I moved into a new neighborhood, next door to a family named the Sanderholms. It was then that I met and began to babysit for a two-year-old, dark-haired, brown-eyed toddler named Jodi. From the beginning, Jodi was one of the happiest children I have ever known. She had a smile that would light up a room and bring happiness to everyone around her. I babysat Jodi and her sister from an early age, and my relationship with her and her family remained close throughout the years.

Several years passed—I was twenty-one years old, married, and had a baby girl named Morgan. By this time, Jodi had grown into a beautiful seven-year-old, who was still never without a smile. After back surgery left me unable to completely care for my six-month-old daughter while I recovered, Jodi and her sister Jennifer would come to the house after school every day and play with her. Morgan loved the attention from the older girls and took to both of them from the beginning. She developed a close relationship with the Sanderholms while she visited her grandpa.

Meanwhile, I had moved to a neighboring and even smaller town, which was suffering from lack of economic development. My desire to help led me to construct an economic development program for the city. The mayor heard about my work, and appointed me to sit on city council when a seat was abandoned mid-term. From the minute I started, I found that the people who lived there had great opinions, but couldn't get their voices heard due to the small town politics. They had learned long ago to remain silent since only certain voices would be heard. I listened and encouraged others to share their opinions and changes began to happen. I continued until moving to New Mexico, never imagining that the next voice I'd be helping to get heard would be Jodi's.

In 2006, my husband and I decided to relocate to Santa Fe, New Mexico, when I was offered a marketing position there, but we still kept in very close touch with the Sanderholms. I had dreamed of living in New Mexico from the time I was a small child on my first vacation. I first visited the Land of Enchantment when I was about ten years old. The trip coincided with the International Balloon Fiesta so the ultra-blue sky was filled with these huge and amazing hot air balloons. A few days later, a large storm hit the area, and snow covered the city in a magical way I had never witnessed before.

Tufts of snow lined the adobe pueblo walls and immediately it felt like home to me.

The first few months following our move were fabulous. We settled into our new jobs, and hiked the surrounding mountains on the weekends. Santa Fe was an amazing place to live, the state capital of New Mexico, and full of extraordinary, world-class artists. But our idyllic lifestyle was about to change, in a most unexpected and horrifying way.

On January 6, 2007, I was leaving a child safety event I had hosted, and I called my dad to catch up. He told me that Jodi had been reported missing. Initially, my reaction was pure disbelief! Jodi was the most responsible teenager I have ever known and would never do anything without letting her parents know. I was positive there was some misunderstanding. After all, this was a small town where everyone knew everyone else, and nothing bad *ever* happened. As I listened to the details from my father, I looked in my rearview mirror, to the backseat where my eleven-year-old daughter, Morgan sat. As I looked into her innocent face, I wondered how I would ever tell her that the babysitter and friend she had known her entire life was missing, and that something seemed to have gone terribly wrong.

The next few days were filled with a sickening sense of worry and waiting. Memories of Jodi flooded our minds every moment. As the updates came in, the situation looked darker and darker, and the police began trying to prepare us for the worst, advising us the outcome was unlikely to be a good one. Four days later, our worst-case scenario came true. Jodi's body was found in a wildlife area near the Kansas/Oklahoma border. It is an odd moment when you are forced to believe the unbelievable. Jodi was gone. A twenty-six-year-old man had been brought in for questioning, and was being held in custody for Jodi's murder. Jodi did not know the man. Her dance team knew of him only because he had been hanging around practices. The police told us he had been accused of stalking multiple women over the last few years, but they were unable to make an arrest until now.

The realization that the police knew all along that this person was a threat but had been unable to make an arrest due to unenforceable stalking laws was unfathomable to me. Stalking is a hard crime to prove since it is compiled of activities that, by themselves, are legal. The 2007 Kansas law called for a credible threat to exist. In legal terms, credible threat is simply too vague so the laws were considered unenforceable. I was angered and shocked, but knowing that this man should have already been behind bars was all I needed to catapult me into action. No human being should ever have to die the way Jodi did. No family should ever have to suffer the loss of their loved one like that. I had never thought much about stalking. I had heard stories on the news about celebrities, being stalked, and assumed there were laws on the books to protect people from being followed and harassed. Yet until Jodi's murder, I didn't realize how loopholes in the legal system were allowing dangerous people to be out in public. Their rights were protected—but what about the victims' rights? Until Jodi's murder, I had no idea that such an inequity existed.

We were all so shaken that this could happen in broad daylight, in this tiny little town, and I was not about to let it happen again. I used my anger at the injustice of it all to fuel what would become my life's purpose: Jodi's death would have meaning. Her life ended at the hands of a monster, but her memory would save others. Statistics show that one in six women will be the victims of stalking in their lifetime. I wanted to help protect them from the same tragic fate.

I had no legal background, but I did have the marketing experience to get publicity. I never thought for a second that what I was doing wouldn't work because I knew it needed to happen. I was doing this for Jodi and others who needed protection. Keeping other people safe was the only way I could get past those feelings of helplessness and anger, and begin healing from the loss.

First, I got in touch with Kasha Kelley, the Sanderholm's representative in the Kansas State House of Representatives, who also knew the family. We began by working together to develop "Jodi's Law." This legislation that would ensure that no other person would be harmed at the hands of someone the police knew was dangerous. When the initial bill was defeated by the senate due to political push and pull, I knew it was only a temporary setback and vowed to keep pushing. I decided to create a groundswell so large that the politicians would be forced to listen. My plan was to raise their awareness first, then get them to speak up. I had long days working full time at my job, and longer nights giving myself a crash course learning the legalities of stalking and how its victims are affected. On the day the Kansas House was considering it for the second time that year, Kasha walked into the session, putting the bill in the hands of the Senate since it had been defeated in the House. All the while, I had been creating awareness on social media, encouraging everyone to call their representative, telling them to vote "yes" on the bill. I believed in my heart that the public outcry would prevail over politics, and absolutely refused to believe anything different. So many people stepped forward to have their voices heard that although the legislators were in Veto Session the bill was unanimously passed in the Senate! Jodi's story continues to receive international news coverage through major news outlets. I used this interest to communicate the need for change and a general awareness for the crime of stalking.

Shortly afterward, I got a call from Jodi's mom, letting me know that Jodi's death had not been in vain. A seventeen-year-old high school girl had gotten the protection she needed from a life-threatening stalker. All the hard work and long hours had been worth it. The trial for Jodi's murder still loomed over us, but her memory was already saving lives.

About two years after Jodi's murder, the trial finally began. The case of a beautiful teenage small-town girl, killed so heinously, captivated the media. Every horrific detail of Jodi's last five hours were discussed at length during the two-week trial. It was a relatively short trial but it seemed to last forever. I hung on every word that was said, worried that the prosecutor would leave out something important. I desperately wanted Jodi's killer to pay for his actions. Although the deliberation only last a few hours in total, the court recessed overnight. I tossed and turned and stared at the ceiling all night, scared that in some way the jury would not understand the evidence. I was terrified no justice would be served.

The next morning I received a call that the verdict was returned. My nerves had not allowed me to eat for a few days and suddenly I felt very sick. I was in New Mexico at the time, but the case was broadcast on the Internet. My co-workers crowded around my desk to offer support. What in reality took a few minutes seemed like hours as the court officers read the necessary legal jargon to announce the verdict. Then came the word we had all been waiting to hear: guilty of first degree murder. The guilty verdict did not make us miss Jodi any less, but at least it meant her killer would pay for what he put her through that cold winter day—and that was a relief.

Between the trial and the penalty phase, my life took another strange twist that I never saw coming. Along with campaigning for anti-stalking legislation in Kansas, I had also successfully pushed Jodi's Law through the legislative committees of my adopted state of New Mexico. My efforts were touching many of the right people but also some of the wrong ones. I began receiving anonymous e-mails, texts and notes on my car. The messages were not initially threatening, but hateful. A woman was angered by my awareness campaigns and became obsessed with everything I had built in my life. She wanted to live my life, have my job, and even my dogs. In some way she thought she deserved it or was entitled to it. I was in denial at first, but then realized that I was now being stalked, all because I had become an advocate for stalking victims. It was a strange irony.

The hateful messages soon escalated to threats against me and my family. The woman began leaving notes on my front door and making multiple phone calls to my workplace. At the height of it, I was receiving fifty to sixty instances of unwanted contacts and threats per day, making it nearly impossible to continue with my daily life, although my employer and co-workers were extremely understanding and accommodating. I was terrified and I also had a new understanding about how truly frustrating and frightening it was to be in this position.

Speaking with multiple survivors each week, I heard the worst of the stories from those fighting for their own safety. The stories echoed in my ears as I was stalked, and frightened me more each day. I turned the terror into a deeper passion for action to fight stalking.

Under New Mexico's Jodi's Law, the perpetrator was later arrested for felony aggravated stalking.

I am sure it was no coincidence that by this time, the support and encouragement for my work was pouring in, not just from friends and family, but from strangers as well. It was amazing; from the smallest to the biggest things, all of a sudden I was on the receiving end of getting help. My husband and I decided to relocate to another state and start over, to ensure our safety, since even after the arrest the stalking did not stop. I will never forget how neighbors who barely knew us packed up our entire moving van. I received messages of encouragement from Kansas friends I had not spoken to since relocating to New Mexico. Looking back, that support helped me to gain the strength I needed to get through the ordeal and continue helping others.

When I think about how I found my purpose, it was really more like my purpose found me, right out of the hardest thing I'd ever experienced. I think this is true for everyone: something has touched each and every person alive. When someone thinks they have no passion about something, it's only because they aren't thinking hard enough. Whether it is something that happened to them, their family, a friend or simply a story they heard that has stuck with them, our job is to follow our hearts, act on what touches us and make some kind a difference. My favorite quote ever is Gandhi's: "Be the change you wish to see in the world." Don't complain that something needs to change, just start trying to change it. It might not happen overnight, but it will *never* happen unless you try.

I also believe that everyone can make a difference in another person's life, even if it's just picking up the phone and calling them. You never know what will make someone's day. It could be as simple as holding a door open! The point is about doing *something*, because a positive and giving attitude truly does make everything better. Helping others makes our own problems seem less intrusive in our lives. I once read a saying that, "If everyone threw their problems in a pile you would fight to get your own back." I think this is true; everything is relative, and we are used to our own problems. They are no worse or easier than those of our friends, but they belong to us.

I could have never imagined that anything positive would come out of all this. Although I would give anything to go back to that cold day in January to stop those awful events from happening to Jodi, there have been many blessings-in-disguise all along the way. Everytime I hear from a victim whose life I've touched, I get an extra push to stay on track, and I know that Jodi is smiling and watching over all the stalking survivors.

My family has also gained so much perspective. Before Jodi died, our lives were all about work, and we'd gotten just as wrapped up living materialistically as the next family. In the end, none of that could buy us safety. Now we're just grateful to be alive, and my family has learned to take every day for the true gift that it is.

This experience has also opened my daughter's eyes to the realities of the world. Her innocence to the ways of the world were lost too soon. She learned how evil some can be, but also how amazing people can be in times of need. Many people have asked me how I got through it all. How did I not cave to the grief and terror? It never occurred to me that I would not get through it. When I was growing up, no matter what the problem was, my dad always had the same advice, "Take it slow, think it through, and it will get better." Caving to problems has never been an option in my life. You find the strength, you get through it, and you help others do the same.

My advice for anyone who is really passionate about getting anything done, whether it's a big or small thing, is to talk to everyone, because you never know if that one person will be the one who helps you the most. Because of this work, I've met incredible people who have helped make it happen. When you are on the right path, doors open and paths appear in places you never would have guessed.

My advocacy group, Jodi's Voice, currently reaches tens of thousands of people per year, and is growing daily. Since 2007, thousands of lives have been directly affected by the changes implemented in Kansas and New Mexico stalking laws. Because of Jodi, there is also a new level of understanding about the seriousness of stalking. Sadly, this awareness is too late for Jodi, but it is *because* of her that more lives are continually being saved.

Angela Daffron is an internationally recognized advocate, speaker, and marketer. She has effectively lobbied for legislative change for stalking victims while running a successful marketing firm and helping thousands of stalking survivors.

Behavior Savior

"All knowledge, the totality of all questions and all answers, is contained in the dog."

—Franz Kafka

SOUL MODEL: Dina Zaphiris

CHALLENGE: Losing her mom to a vicious, twenty-year battle with breast cancer.

CHANGE: Devoted her life to training medical scent-detection dogs to catch cancer in its earliest stages; founded a non-profit and has trained dogs who are 98 percent accurate in detecting cancer.

SOULUTION: When life feels impossible, sit quietly and ask yourself what's important. Your weight? Your hair . . . or your dreams? Try to sit quietly with this question for three weeks and trust you'll get the answer. Don't think about the "how"; go back to the "why"— why something makes you feel happy or good or passionate— that is where you will find the strength to go on.

A blank page. Nothing. There is nothing left of my mother except a memory. There was breath, and life, and now, nothing. Breath is life—now I understand that in a much different way.

The night before my mother passed away, she had incredibly labored breathing. It's what the hospital staff calls "whole body breathing," where the patient breathes with their entire chest heaving up, then down, with great effort, as if each breath were a marathon. The entire body seems to be gasping for breath, fighting for air. The back arches up, the chest rises, the whole body convulses expansively on the inhale; then the exhale releases life, waning, as if it were the final relief. She was suffocating, really, drowning in her own fluids. I had actually gotten used to this heavy, arduous breath in the past week—the gurgling sound of her airways fighting for space. We medicated her heavily, so that she would not feel the panic of suffocating, or her own pain. This was the battle—panic and pain versus a drugged-out dream state, which would eventually cause her heart to stop pumping.

But that morning was different. She was quiet. Her breathing was shallow with long, long pauses in between. I was holding her soft, cold, clammy hand as she took her last breath. It was a moment. There was no explosion, no sound; it was just a breath, and it was her last. It was very quiet. Time stopped, and she never breathed in again. With her last breath went her life, and her soul. She became smaller. I wept on her body like a little girl, hugging her still warm face and chest.

My mother began to die in 2010. I am her only child, and her single wish was that I would be there with her every day until she died. She was terminal, and this was the end of her 20-year battle with breast cancer. We were on the 4th floor of Enloe hospital in Chico, California, right above the room where she gave birth to me. She was there for my coming into the world, and I would be there for her as she left it.

So began the final three weeks that my mother and I would spend together. Three weeks to say everything we've ever wanted to say to each other—to laugh, to cry, to remember. Were we lucky? Or, was it more painful this way? We discussed life and all of the old times—the way we used to chase rainbows to try and find the pot of gold at the end. How we'd pull over every time we saw a cute dog and rush the poor owner, molesting the dog with kisses and pets. Most people got a kick out of it, because they love their dogs so much, and this was actual proof that theirs was the cutest after all. Some people backed away, as if a mother and young child were going to mug them. Others just had a blank stare, but we didn't care.

We loved singing Beatles' songs together and walking in the rain with umbrellas. She said she was sorry for all our fights, and for all the times she was mean to me. I said I was sorry for being such a brat and for being mean to her. She talked about her childhood, old lovers, friends, and how incredibly scared she was. She kept saying that she did not want to die yet, that she wanted to see the sun and walk on the beach again. She was not ready, but cancer was taking her body.

I felt really scared. I was going through something of a midlife crisis, and now my mom was dying.

I had been training dogs for twenty years, but my life felt meaningless. Watching my mom in the last year of her life made me understand my own mortality. I realized I wasn't doing what I was supposed to be doing. I was divorced and sad, thinking I would never meet the right person, questioning why I was even alive. I plunged into a deep depression that really threw me for a loop for several months.

Sometimes it seemed that I simply couldn't go on. I thought about going into hiding somewhere, on the top of some mountain, and never coming back. This was definitely the darkest, lowest time in my life. I kept thinking, "Oh my God, she's dying—my life has had no real purpose, and now I'm next to go."

My dad has always written me letters every week, and sometime in that last year of my mom's life, he sent me a tiny newspaper clipping about Pine Street Foundation, a non-profit in northern California with a mission of training dogs to detect cancer by smelling breath samples. Dogs have 300 million scent receptors. Humans have 5 million, which means dogs can smell up to 10,000 times better than we can! The percentage of the dog's brain that is devoted to analyzing smells is actually forty times larger than ours—they smell in parts per trillion, which is like one drop of blood, diluted into twenty Olympic sized swimming pools. This astonishing natural trait is why dogs have been used for decades to discover bodies and drugs, and to detect explosives on airplanes.

When I heard about Pine Street, something "clicked," and I called immediately. "I'll do anything if you let me work with you," I told them. "I'll clean the kennels, pick up poop, anything!"

Within a few months, I bought a trailer, drove to San Anselmo, and started studying with animal behaviorist, Kirk Turner. Pine Street was doing a study on the accuracy levels of canine scent detection on early stage lung and breast cancer, and I got to help with the training.

The minute cancer and dogs came together, I was on a mission—my depression lifted, and I felt like I was being guided by something much bigger. I knew I wasn't doing this just for me, but so other people didn't have to be afraid to die of cancer.

* * * *

My parents were married for fifty-three years, until the day my mom died. I grew up in Chico, California, the only child of a father who was also an only child. I didn't have much family and was around adults all the time. We had a lot of animals—hamsters, horses, fish and frogs ... anything but dogs (which I desperately wanted), because my mom really loved her white carpet and didn't want animals in the house.

My dad was a Greek olive farmer, and my mom stayed at home. She always made me believe I could do anything. I was into every kind of competitive sport—I jumped horses, took ballet, tap, gymnastics, and I participated in every school sport. Plus, I always did really well in school. Even though I was raised with a lot of love, my mom was overbearing and constantly pressured me to be perfect. She was from New York, and it was hard for her to live in Chico. I think a lot of that frustration came out on me, and it kind of backfired. Nothing I ever did was good enough, and we had horrible fights. She was at all the sports games, driving me around with my friends and telling everyone how great I was, but criticizing me behind the scenes.

I felt smothered; I thought I had to be perfect. As a result, my straight A's and competitive nature did not come from a good place— I was trying to prove that I was okay. I didn't really have a childhood, because I never gave myself a break. I was driven and determined, always like I had a fire under me—if I said I was going to do something, watch out!

I loved animals, and thought I would grow up to be a circus trainer or a dog trainer. We spent summers with my uncle in New York who had fifteen dogs, and ran a magazine called *Dog News*. He was big in the American Kennel Club, and we'd go to all the dog shows. He was a huge influence on me, and I really loved the way he lived his life.

I left for college in 1988 and went to University of California-Davis. One day in my junior year, my mom called. Her voice sounded so tiny, like a little doll. She said, "Well, I have breast cancer." There was dead silence on the line, and we both started crying. We thought she only had months to live, but it turned out that her cancer was very slow growing.

All through college, we managed to see each other every month and became very close. The day after I graduated, I moved to Los Angeles, determined to become an actor. I waited tables and did beach workout classes before anyone even had personal trainers. I printed cards saying that's what I was—I handed them out everywhere, took balls and weights, and headed to the beach to teach aerobics all day. At night I would wait tables and go to acting classes.

During this time, I watched my mom deteriorate—she'd have chemo, radiation, lose her hair, be violently ill, then go into remission only to find out a few years later the cancer had spread again. Instead of just being sick and dying, we watched her almost die over and over in the same vicious cycle.

A few years after I'd moved to LA, I thought, *I am finally alone and getting a dog!* The first time I saw Eugene, a chow-golden retriever mix, he was in a box with another puppy being sold on the Third Street Promenade in Santa Monica. He looked like a little teddy bear. I fell madly in love with him, and he changed my life forever. We started going to the dog park, and I thought . . . *I have to be with my dog all the time!* So, I printed new cards saying I was a dog walker. Soon, I was walking or rollerblading with fifteen or twenty dogs every day.

At the dog park, I met Richard Vye, a famous dog trainer. Richard trained the original "Lassie," and became my mentor. He took me under his wing and taught me everything about dog training. We became best friends, and worked together for six years. He was sixty when we met, and, as he got older, he started giving me his clients. From the beginning, I was working with people in film, like Nicholas Cage, Bruce Willis, and Tony Scott.

Dog training was smooth sailing for a long time. Because I have such a passion for animals, things just fell into my lap. I went to conferences and big seminars; I wrote a book and my business grew. Meanwhile, my mom's cancer kept coming back. Each time, she'd lose her hair, and there were more painkillers and vomiting from the treatments. Her attitude was amazing—she painted and traveled; I'll never forget her being bald and throwing up and still going to India. My mom never let the cancer ruin her life.

She lived like this for a full twenty years, while we watched her deteriorate. Instead of just getting sick and dying, we almost lost her five times, and each time was more horrible. She did live to get to see me graduate from college, get married, and begin to pursue my dreams.

Once I did the Pine Street cancer study in the last year my mom was alive, I knew deep down this was what I wanted to do. On her deathbed, she brought it up: "Do it, Dina, train dogs to find this damn cancer!" And so I did.

I took charge. I started making calls, founded my own non-profit, and began training dogs. There was no money, only trust and faith. I was alone with my mother for those last three weeks in a hospital room. I slept in a reclining chair by her side. My father would come once or twice a day, but mostly it was jut me, listening to my mother talk. I have a deep connection with a universal spirit and energy, so when things got really bad, I asked God to please help me. I prayed and prayed and sat deep in thought about how much I could help the world with my cancer detection dogs.

Right after my mother died, I founded my non-profit, In Situ Foundation, a 501(c)(3) dedicated to training dogs to find cancer in humans. Shortly after, Pine Street hired me to run a twelve-week study, where I trained nine dogs to successfully detect early ovarian cancer from breath samples. The dogs from the study went on to be able to detect prostate, lung, breast, brain, melanoma, and other types of cancer. I have trained dogs that are 98 percent accurate in early cancer detection, and we can save lives!

Breath sample screening, using canine scent detection provides a low cost, non-invasive, early detection screening method for cancer. As of today, there are no other non-invasive early screening methods for most cancers—we are seeking FDA approval for our process, and people need to demand to have this method available.

When I am doing the cancer detection work, I know I'm living my purpose. There is an easy, effortless feeling about it, yet it is the most rewarding thing I've ever done. I no longer worry about perfection or whether my life has meaning—I call it "being in the zone." There is no way to describe it, other than you'll know when you're there.

My mother used say, "Dina, trust that everything will be alright, and turn out for the best." Cliché or not, these words have saved my life and become a core part of me. I never thought that just by trusting, I'd achieve my dreams, but here I am. I overcame my fear of dying a horrible death like my mother by applying her words and believing that I could do something about cancer.

Every person has that "one thing" that makes them happy and keeps them smiling inside—that is authentic purpose. Going after it takes a leap of faith—you have to take that risk and jump off the edge—after that, everything else falls into place!

Dina Zaphiris is the founder of In Situ Foundation, a 501(c)(3) dedicated to training dogs to detect cancer in humans. The foundation has participated in two federally funded studies, investigating the diagnostic accuracy of canine scent detection in early and late stage lung, breast, and ovarian cancer.

The Heart of a Giant

"Don't do anything halfway—whether it's schoolwork, sports or a class play—when you commit to something, fully commit to it. Do everything you can to have it be the best of your ability."

—Archie Manning

SOUL MODEL: Eli Manning

CHALLENGE: Struggled with learning disabilities as a child; grew up as the youngest of three high-achieving brothers and a father who was a celebrated football player.

CHANGE: Eli made honor roll every year of college at the University of Mississippi and is a two-time Super Bowl MVP for the New York Giants. He helps a multitude of children's charities, spends hands-on time with children in hospitals, and supports Guiding Eyes for the Blind—a non-profit guide dog school that provided the blind and visually impaired with superior Guiding Eyes dogs, training, and lifetime support services—in raising millions of dollars for their programs.

SOULUTION: Find one thing you truly love to do—whether it's a job or a charity; choose to work on something about which you are passionate. Everyone can make a difference. Sometimes it's the little things that don't take a big commitment that can have a huge impact, for example, a phone call or visit.

I was always the quiet, shy one in the family. My older brother, Cooper, was a natural born entertainer; he, along with my other brother, Peyton, and my dad ran a lot of the conversations at the dinner table. Mom and I never did a whole lot of talking—we just enjoyed the entertainment. She took care of the household and was our biggest supporter; our family would have been lost without her.

Growing up, I had a lot of trouble learning to read, so school was really difficult. It was embarrassing and frustrating because teachers always called on students to read out loud in class. I was only about eight years old, and it was one of those situations where you're praying the whole time the teacher doesn't call on you. Reading was tough; math and the other subjects were easy. Eventually I got further and further behind, so in second grade, I changed to a smaller school with more one-on-one teaching. I knew the only way to get better was to do extra work and whatever it took to remedy the situation. My mom helped me study and stayed patient the entire time. Her laid-back attitude kept me calm. She's the one who kept telling me it would all work out—and it did! I kept working hard until I figured it out and from that point I did really well.

In eighth grade I went back to my original school. That experience gave me the motivation to constantly keep improving in everything I ever did.

* * * *

My parents met at Ole Miss, where my dad was the star quarter-back and my mom was homecoming queen. When I was three, my dad retired from pro football after playing for fourteen seasons, so I really only remember him just as a "normal" dad. He never really pushed me to play football. I was the baby—my brothers are five and seven years older than I am, so I was dragged around to all of their sporting events.

As I got older, I got into football like my brothers. I think having the discipline of practicing and being active all the time kept us out of trouble. Still, when you have three boys growing up together there are bound to be fights. When that happened, my dad would give us boxing gloves and say, "All right, you guys are going to punch this bag for three minutes straight." Of course, our arms were just dead after hitting the bag and we would all end up on the floor laughing and then would go back to having a good day—problem solved!

Things like that were what kept us close instead of competitive. We always rooted for each other in everything we did, and our parents were great role models. My dad was more the person to give advice; while my mom was always loving, supportive and there for a hug. Whether it was schoolwork or a sporting event, she was never disappointed in anything we did. I definitely got some of her personality, because not a lot of things get to me. She taught me that when something needs to be done you just do it quietly and you don't complain about it.

I believe my mom's attitude really shaped the way our whole family did things. As a young kid, I was pretty naïve to everything going on in the world. Early on, I saw my dad participating in charity events—he had one he did for cystic fibrosis for twenty-plus years. He was always making a phone call to a child who was sick or visiting a hospital and telling us about it afterward—a family might write him letters and he would share how much that meant to him. It was one of those things you just "did." It was never a matter of how much time it took or whether it was convenient or not; he saw the positive impact of doing charitable work and raised us with the same values.

As I got older, I had a better understanding of what my father did for a living and how he treated people. When people came up to ask for an autograph or asked to take a picture with him, he signed it, took the picture and talked to them. So when I was in college and was asked for my first autograph, I did exactly what he did and tried to treat people nicely.

We always played football with the neighborhood kids, and my older brothers also played on a team in school. When I was ten, I saw Peyton and Cooper being successful playing high school football, and what fun that was for them. I wanted to do the same things they were doing.

Peyton left for college when I was thirteen. Cooper was already gone, and my dad was sometimes away for work. With my brothers out of the house, I was pretty much an only child. My mom and I had a lot of time to ourselves, and we became a lot closer. Every week, just the two of us would head to dinner, and I learned so much more about her. She shared stories of growing up and her years in college. I wasn't competing with my brothers to be heard anymore and I kind of found my voice—that time with my mom helped me speak up and share my own stories, which gave me a lot more confidence.

By the time I left for college, I'd had almost five years without my brothers around and I had grown up a lot. I started out as marketing major and was playing football. The head coach started taking the team on hospital visits to see sick kids. There was a place called the Scott Center in Oxford, Mississippi where they helped children with severe mental illnesses. At first it was a little overwhelming, but at the same time it was a "trigger" for me, because I appreciated even more what a great childhood I had. I was very active outside, playing sports and I loved being with my friends. Seeing sick kids in the hospital, who had to stay there a really long time and couldn't be outside playing, really got to me.

It hit me that while I might not be smart enough to find a cure or to be a doctor, if I could toss a football or sit down with sick kids, sign some autographs or get them to smile, in some way maybe I was lifting their spirits and giving them a good day. I continued visiting the Scott Center all through college—it was one of those deals where if I had a break for thirty minutes I could drop in and say "hi" to the kids.

After college, I was the first overall pick in the 2004 NFL Draft and once I got to the Giants, everything took off from there. The Giants are an amazing organization, and I've learned a lot of important things on the road to our being the Super Bowl XLII and XLVI champions. One of them is, no matter how successful, smart or experienced you are, *everybody* needs a coach. It's truly beneficial to have someone from the outside looking in and telling you what improvements you can make and where you can grow as a player and a person.

Through football, I've learned to be my best and to trust myself, my coaches, and my teammates. Without the confidence to trust myself, I won't perform at my best, which would make it difficult for my teammates to trust me. A leader has to inspire others to trust in him or her and to give trust in return. This lesson can be applied off the field as well. In a world where people have to rely on others for almost everything, we have to work together to make things happen.

That kind of teamwork is what it takes to win any game, including a Super Bowl, and it is truly a great feeling to be part of that. Players learn that when you win a championship, it's not just you who wins; it's your family, the organization, the city for which you are playing! And it's also for the friends you played high school football with who never went on to play at a higher level. I brought a bunch of my high school buddies to a game and they were almost more excited than I was. There are millions of people involved who all feel like they're winning a championship and that's pretty special.

The success I've achieved inspires me to give back even more. I still visit the Scott Center every chance I get. It doesn't matter what I do when I'm there. I've attended Christmas plays, helped with arts and crafts, set up booths for field days, and tossed a football. It's about the time and attention the kids want and deserve. Sometimes I wonder if the joy the kids bring me is greater than the joy I bring them.

The biggest thing for me is seeing the people I'm helping and the difference it makes. This has been really inspiring in the work I've been doing with Guiding Eyes for the Blind. It is an organization that breeds, trains and partners guide dogs with visually impaired or blind adults. The dogs provide their human partners with much more mobility and freedom.

I didn't know anything about them, until one day Pat Brown Jr. called my dad and said, "The Guiding Eyes Golf Tournament is looking for a new host—would Eli be interested in helping?" Pat is a family friend, and an amazing blind golfer who worked with Guiding Eyes after becoming blind as an adult. He also happens to be champion of the U.S. Blind Golfers Association twenty-one times since 1975, and is in the Louisiana Sports Hall of Fame.

A few weeks later, I was on a plane and ran into Dick Ryan, who was Chairman of the Board for Guiding Eyes. He had the original idea for a celebrity Pro-Am that would make blind golfers the "stars" of the event. Mr. Ryan said, "If you host Guiding Eyes, I'll take you for a round of golf at Winged Foot Golf Club."

I told him, "Okay, you got yourself a deal!"

The first year I hosted completely based on faith, Pat, and knowing it was a good cause. But after years of working with them, what inspires me the most is seeing the people whose lives have been saved or greatly influenced by their guide dogs. I met a man named Omar whose guide dog literally saved his life during 9/11 by getting him out of one of the buildings.

Guiding Eyes now has its Heeling Autism program, which has paired more than fifty dogs with children with autism. The program has a 100 percent success rate in increased social acceptance and better behavior of its clients. Seeing a child smile because of his or her service dog makes me want to help out more and more. Whether it's helping an adult or child to live a normal life, or helping their parents breathe a little bit more easily, the program is amazing, and it's a huge honor to be part of it.

After Hurricane Katrina, Peyton and I mobilized a plane full of relief supplies like bottled water, diapers and baby formula for the people of New Orleans, where we grew up. We went with the plane and helped deliver the supplies ourselves. It was incredible for us to bring relief to people we had a connection with, and it was incredible for us to do that as brothers.

One of the questions people always ask about us is whether there is sibling rivalry. Sure, we had it growing up, but I was also Peyton's biggest fan. I've never tried to compete with him and I've never said I need to be better; he was the number one high school player in the country. In college, he was going to be the first pick in the draft—so if I tried to go out there and be the same or better, I would drive myself crazy. I just always thought, *I'm going to be the best quarterback I can be, and make the most out of my potential. If that's better than he is, great—if it's not, so be it.*

It's rare to have a best friend who is also your brother and also an NFL football player—he always knows exactly what I'm talking about. We speak every week, but now it's more about our kids than anything else—the activities they're doing or what new walker or toy we got them. We exchange advice and talk about what cartoons, food, snacks, or treats they like.

Since I've had my own family, I work even harder to be 100 percent committed to each thing I do. It helps a lot to separate each one and not overlap—if I'm at football practice, I'm at football practice, and totally focused on that task. When I come home, the phone is put away and I drop everything to be with my wife and daughters. Whether it's running around outside, or reading them a book, any time I can spend getting them to smile or laugh is a wonderful experience. I try to get the most out of each second with them that I can.

Helping kids in hospitals has definitely made me a better father and given me a lot of perspective. Every day I am grateful to have healthy children and grateful to have a job I love—I wouldn't want to be doing anything else. Each day is precious; you don't know when a turn of events is going to happen that will change everything. Knowing that makes you want to go out and enjoy whatever you are doing as much as you can. My wife Abby loves being involved in our charity work, too. For the last few years since we've had children, she's gone all in taking on the role of being a mother, but she wants to get back into the charity mix as soon as she has more free time.

I'm proud I've had the chance to impact people's lives and it's something I am excited to do with my family, since they are my number one passion. I built a children's clinic in Mississippi, and have received many letters and calls about how the clinic has saved a life or made someone's life easier. I'm proud of championships I've won with my teammates and the hard work we've done. All three of those things—my family, football, and my charity work are very rewarding and the reason I continue to work hard and enjoy each one.

My advice to anyone going through any difficulty is to just keep going—don't stop, don't quit or get discouraged. Success comes from struggling and working your way through it with hard work and dedication. For me, it was a combination of all the things my parents taught me. It was also overcoming my struggles with reading and my mom's attitude about never having a frown. She really taught me the importance of doing what you have to do and trying to be better at everything you do.

In football, whether you win or lose, you really deal with it the same way. The Monday afterward, you may not be as happy if you lost. But either way, you go in, watch the film, and decide what you're doing well and what needs improvement. By Tuesday, you're preparing for the next game. If you're not worried about trying to improve yourself this season, you're not getting better—you're going backwards and possibly getting worse. When you start feeling content or like you've got it figured out, that's when something usually happens to put you back in your place—that's also part of growing up. If you just keep going and work harder, you can get a step ahead of other people.

The other advice I have is to find something you truly love to do—whether it's a job, a charity or anything about which you are passionate. It will make your life better, while at the same time positively influencing and affecting the people around you. Everyone can make a difference and sometimes it's the little things, not a huge commitment, but just a phone call or a visit that can have a huge impact. Try not to have bad days when they aren't necessary. Live life to the fullest—you never know what's in store tomorrow.

Eli Manning raised nearly $3 million to build a clinic at the Blair E. Batson Hospital for Children. The state-of-the-art Eli Manning Children's Clinic provides health care to 75,000 children in Mississippi's only children's hospital.

This Is Their Story: Parts One and Two

Deanne and Ally Breedlove
Intro by Elizabeth Bryan

"Do you believe in angels or God? I do."

—Ben Breedlove

Unbeknownst to his family, eighteen-year-old Benjamin Daniel Breedlove shared those words with the world in an amazing flash card video he posted on a random YouTube channel just days before his passing on Christmas Day, 2011. "This is My Story, Parts 1 and 2" went viral: Ben's words continue to resonate in the hearts, minds, and souls of over 13 million people around the globe.

Ben already had a terrific YouTube following on his regular "Breedlove TV" channel, where he used an entertaining news format to share heartfelt and funny teen advice on issues like dating, asking someone to dance, and the latest fashion. But for some reason, he posted "This is My Story" in a place where no one ever would have thought to look.

Ben was born with a heart condition called hypertrophic cardio-myopathy, a thickening of the heart muscle. HCM keeps the heart from functioning normally, causing ongoing, and extremely disabling symptoms. In his video, Ben shared his personal journey living with HCM, including the multiple times he "cheated" death. During his last encounter, Ben had no pulse and didn't breathe for three full minutes. According to the team fighting for his life, he was already gone.

For Ben, "gone" meant a magnificent, infinite white space and an experience of overwhelming, unmatched peace, pride, love, and joy, one that was beyond human comprehension. He described his feelings upon seeing his reflection in a full-length mirror: "I was proud of my entire life, of everything I had done, and it was the BEST feeling."

That place was so beautiful that Ben never wanted to come back.

If you believe in angels and God, you have to believe that God brought Ben back one final time to share his profound message with the world. When Ben's heart gave him trouble, he called it "bumping." Whatever you believe, watch Ben's video, let your heart "bump," and decide for yourself. To see Ben's video, visit *www.benbreedloveoriginal.com*

Part One: "Grace"

*"God, I pray that my family wouldn't be sad or scared
for me anymore, because I'm not sad or scared. I pray that
they would have the same peace that I have. And I'm
okay with whatever God decides."*

—Ben Breedlove, December 18th, 2011

SOUL MODEL: Deanne Breedlove

CHALLENGE: Giving birth to and raising a son with heart disease; learning to relinquish control, honor his wishes, and his message— before and after his passing.

CHANGE: Extraordinary bravery, helping families with children who have health issues, sharing her son's message with the world.

SOULUTION: When the pain and struggle and chaos of life hits, try to be still and connect with God. Choose to be the rock by setting a good example for others, and you will find stability— you will also be helping others in chaos to stand firm.

A s we bowed our heads in family prayer a week before Ben's last day of earthly life, wc were overwhelmed by his words; he was the one who was dying, yet all he cared about was that *we* were okay. But that was Ben—he was happy and joyful and caring from the moment he came into this world. And, he was *always* smiling. I remember once when he was a newborn lying on the bed, I was videotaping him and said, "Ben, say hi to the camera!" He lifted up his tiny hand and waved at me!

Our family emphasizes faith and belief over religion. We think it is important to love and respect all people instead of trying to convince them that our way is the right way. For us, it is all about a *relationship with God.* When Ben was little, he asked, "How do I know if we get to go to heaven?" I said, "You just ask God, and he'll talk to you in your heart." From that point on, Ben had a very constant, active awareness of God—he would pray with us or by himself. He would go out to the lake at night on the dock and very honestly talk to Him like a tangible friend. We know he asked God why he had to come back, because he really just wanted to stay where he was.

Ben wanted everyone to know that they could find that same relationship. This isn't something you can teach, and I don't think it takes any special prayer or church language. I believe that if anyone takes a quiet moment to sincerely ask God questions in his or her own natural way, God will answer those questions, and that is when the relationship begins. I think the older I get the more understanding I have that spiritual timing is a process. It is so slow in our terms; if you have to wait five years for an answer, that is a relatively short time in terms of eternity.

I learned this through my own personal journey. I went to church with my family until I was about five. We quit going when my parents divorced, and I didn't think much about God again until I was about twenty-five. I should have been finished with college, all of my friends were done and starting their lives. I was just floundering, going around in a circle. I was ashamed that I hadn't done more because I had so much more potential. In addition I'd been very irresponsible and not thinking ahead. I was sincerely looking for more wholesome friends and a better path forward. I remember asking, "God, if you are there, can you help me? I need direction; can you help me find good people to help me along?" I honestly didn't think of the question the next day. Within a week, this old friend of mine called and asked me to go skiing that day—it was my husband, Shawn. He introduced me to some great people who were much more motivated. Before I knew it, there were more solid people in my life and everything was moving forward in the right direction. It didn't dawn on me until much later that I had been so authentic in my request; I am sure that's why the answers showed up. Now, I have constant, all day long dialogues with God, like, "Can you help that man over there? Can you give peace to my friends? Tell Ben I said 'hi' and can't wait to see him again!" Honestly, in most of my conversations, as a very natural thing, I am just thanking Him for the things we have. I don't know how I would have coped without that connection in my life; I can't count the number of times I prayed for God to see Ben through and to spare him from pain. And He did. Even in the end. You will see how God was there with Ben, and with us.

* * * *

Because he was diagnosed at only three months old, Ben started out very oblivious to what was happening, and he was always compliant. As he grew up and became more aware of his condition, he never wanted to dwell on it with anyone, not even with his big sister Ally or his little brother Jake. If he was feeling bad, he would be very polite and let us help him, but he never wanted to be pampered or pitied. He also never wanted extra attention—he just wanted the freedom to be himself. When he was in the hospital, his only goal was to get right back out, be a kid and be with his friends. He knew his prognosis and had such maturity about it; instead of being afraid, it made him appreciate life and really live it while he could.

When he became a teenager, his health was more of an inconvenience, like when he didn't have any energy, or when the medicine made him feel bad. But he never complained—he just became more assertive. If he said, very respectfully but firmly, "No, I don't need to go to the hospital this time," or "I don't want to take that medicine," my husband Shawn and I supported his decisions whenever possible.

As parents, his condition was heart wrenching. Because HCM is so unpredictable and can lead to sudden death at any time, our family always lived with a measure of alertness and anxiety, because we never knew when his heart would go into arrhythmia and how serious it would be. If he felt good enough to go to school, all day I would be aware that I might get a phone call to come get him. When his heart wasn't doing well, we were always striking that balance of helping him live normally and protecting him as best as we could. Then, there was the giant looming understanding that every day could be his last, so we worried even when he was sleeping. And even though (and maybe *because*) there were so many times we thought we might lose him, our family made a conscious decision to give him as close to a normal life as possible, and to live our lives to the fullest. Ben reminded us to do this all the time; he had this amazing balance of what mattered and what didn't. He was extremely compassionate, and so focused on experiencing life that he was never stressed out.

Ben also loved to entertain—he was always saying hilarious one-liners and doing crazy, noisy pranks. In his freshman and sophomore year of high school, he and a couple of his best friends were big on dressing up in gorilla and bunny costumes and going all around town like that. One time, the giant gorilla and bunny pretended to fight in the parking lot of a local grocery store in front of the main door. People were standing around staring until security came and broke it up. No one ever knew who it was in the costume! He and his friends loved to show up, do something really silly and then disappear.

The other side of Ben was the calmness he brought to every situation, with his special way of making everyone feel at ease. For him, the people in his life were always what mattered most. He was incredibly gentle with people and animals, and was extra compassionate with kids who didn't have a lot of friends. He was a great listener, and took a lot of time with Ally and Jake to really "hear" them. Ben had the gift of encouragement in a very wise way, and that was evident in all of his videos.

Ben also never let fear impede anything he did, which is an incredible lesson for a mother to get from her child. His life was truly about caring for others and not being afraid, and I want mine to be like that. I'm still working on it! Things every normal teenager could do carried a risk for him—even swimming in the lake when it was cold wasn't a good idea. Yet, he was always doing things that pushed his limits like wakeboarding, snowboarding, or going out with friends and staying up all night. He and his best friend Grant secretly bought tickets to skydive after they graduated high school, but Ben never had that chance.

Sometimes our lives felt like endless trips to doctors and hospitals, different procedures and different medicines. There were devastating episodes when we thought we'd lose him, with breaks in between, when we made the most we could out of life with our family and friends. Wherever we went, and wherever Ben was, I was always mapping out the nearest emergency facility. I can't put words to the depth of worry we lived with, but Ben's fearlessness and love of life helped ease that for us.

We were continually riding that fine line between what we "should" do as parents—what we thought was best for Ben from a medical standpoint—or letting him have a say. It's especially hard when you are deciding these kinds of things for someone else—you constantly question: Do we forego the medication and take the health risk, or opt for it, even though it makes him feel horrible? Sometimes there is just no clear answer. So, you have to make whatever seems to be the least awful decision. As Ben got older, we chose to let him lead whenever we could, whether it was not taking a medicine that made him feel bad, going on a crazy ride at Disneyland, or eating Taco Bell, which was his very favorite food, but had way too much sodium and MSG for his heart. I was constantly challenged between protecting Ben with all my might, and allowing him the freedom to be who he was and to live on his own terms.

The theme of our lives was "letting go of control." It is a process that began when Ben was diagnosed, and continued after he passed away. Sometimes it was easy; sometimes it was hard. During an ambulance ride, in my heart, I had to tell Ben, *I will let you go to God*. If he was wakeboarding, it was, *I will let you do this, so you can live your life*. I would have loved to maintain control, but it just wasn't possible.

After Ben passed away, I understood several things about what letting go meant for us. Number one: there was never a choice. Number two: I truly, deeply believe Ben is in heaven. He so lovingly helped us get to that point by letting us know he had a glimpse of it and wanted to go back, even though he loved his life. Number three, God is there and knows what he is doing, and Ben is with him. As a mom I have accepted all that, even though we completely miss having him around every day.

* * * *

Between Thanksgiving and Christmas of that last year of Ben's life, all the dynamics were changing rapidly as his health declined. Physically, things were getting out of our control. He was having arrhythmia nonstop, his medication was no longer working, and there was nothing keeping him "safe." Before, there were always different things we could try like a new medication or the defibrillator. The next level up of medications had very severe side effects like damaging his liver. One would even turn his skin bluish gray. The doctors didn't want to do anything more for him surgically, because it was too dangerous. It was very scary and emotional for us, especially because Ben was getting so discouraged. He was missing more school and falling more behind. Everything was just sliding backwards and we were powerless to do anything. Then, on December 6th, when he had his amazing vision, he discovered a very different kind of peace. He felt like, *If all these things don't work, I'm okay with it.* We weren't, because we weren't ready to say goodbye. We didn't want to treat him like he was dying, and we just wanted to love him as much as we could. We were still frantically pursuing ways to keep him here, but because he had shared his incredible vision with us, and his very selfless prayer *for* us, a different peace settled into our hearts.

Still, when Ben passed away Christmas Day, we were surprised. What happened after that was so much bigger than words.

On Saturday, December 17, we were visiting a small town about three hours outside of Austin. Ben had a very serious emergency—he had a cardiac arrest miles from help. When the ambulance arrived, Ben did not want to go to the hospital . . . again. He knew the routine. He would be admitted, then be observed for several nights, finally being allowed to go home. This time, he asserted himself and said he did not want to be admitted. He preferred to take the long drive home that night and sleep in his own bed. We convinced him to at least go to the ER to get checked out, which he did. Against the advice of all the small town doctors, and his team of doctors back home, we decided to honor Ben's wishes and drive him home that night to sleep with his family in our own home. As parents, this was extremely scary, but our newfound sense of peace made it easier to let Ben lead. Most importantly, it gave him confidence and dignity knowing that he had a say in his medical care.

It wasn't until I was writing this story that I realized that, had we gone against Ben's wishes and admitted him to that hospital, we would not have been home the next morning to have our home church, where he prayed his prayer—and, he would not have been home to quietly sneak into his room and make his video, which has since touched so many millions of lives.

We had no idea Ben had even made the video. Ally's boyfriend, Cameron, came over to be with her, and at about 3 AM, he asked her what she thought of "the video." She had no idea what he was talking about, so he showed it to her. She showed it to us the next morning, which was the day after Ben passed away. I was so overwhelmed; he wasn't *with* us anymore, but there he was, moving and smiling and just being himself. I couldn't believe what he was communicating because it was so personal, and he had always been so private about his condition. At the same time I was blown away by how amazing it was, and understood almost immediately that it was a huge gift. Had I seen that video before Ben passed, I might have thought he was clinically depressed or something and it never would have gotten out. I believe God protected it and let it be what it was supposed to become.

As devastating as it was that Ben was gone, there he was; reminding us in his own words that he was good, and exactly where he wanted to be. We knew that as much as our hearts ached and we missed him, he was at peace with God's plan for his life—and that was a huge comfort.

Outside of our home, one miracle was happening after the next—the video was going viral, and news reporters started coming over. We weren't really ready to connect with the outside world yet; we wanted to stay insulated with close friends and family, but we were astonished at how many people had been touched by the video, and we wanted to be sure Ben's message was delivered the way he meant it.

CNN called on the day of Ben's memorial and asked if I would be willing to talk on live television. I had no clue what I was going to say. When the newscaster asked what I thought about how Ben had seen his reflection in a mirror, how good he had looked, and how proud of himself he had felt, I said that we believed that Ben saw himself the way God sees him—a perfect creation with a beautiful purpose. So many people don't see themselves in true reality; they are mixed up because of what others tell them. The phenomenon of Ben seeing himself in this light resonated with so many people. Ben's experience brought forth a message that God is real, and we are so very loved by Him.

The video started to become a "call to action" for people—there was a girl from Canada who reached Ally on Facebook. She had seen it and experienced a whole new level of spirituality. It inspired another man to learn more about the Bible, and he actually was baptized in the lake behind our house, right where our own children had been baptized. A man from England e-mailed my husband and said he'd always been an atheist, but now wanted to go to church. Then there was a young college student, who saw the video and wanted to help.

He didn't even know us, but he was so compassionate that he set up a *GoFundMe* online—a group funding account—for our family. He collected about $12,000; which we combined with other money people had given, and donated it to Africa New Life Ministries, a mission in Rwanda. They used it to take fifty boys off the street who were living on a landfill! They fed and clothed them, taught them about God and the value of their lives, and also provided them with a skill to go back to their village or stay and mentor other kids. That young man had one idea; look what it turned into! After seeing Ben's video, people from everywhere wanted to help, be more benevolent, be better parents—it was so incredible to hold people's hands and walk through this together, as they made big changes in their lives for the good.

Everything that was happening kept Ben's spirit alive; it extended his being and gave his life purpose. My soul was so thankful that his message was making that kind of difference . . . it was like having a front row seat to seeing what God's love really is. There was just this much bigger, all-encompassing loving presence coming from different places, like a giant circle of caring from all around the world.

I began to realize how Ben had invested his life and work in giving advice, love and compassion to other teens. At the same time, I became kind of introspective; I realized that none of us know how long we are going to be here, and I wanted to live my life helping others too. I wondered what I could do. I didn't complete my college degree, but I am comfortable being a mom. I realized I could help other parents of children with health conditions, and could advocate for parents with kids in the hospital. About nine months after Ben passed away, I joined the Family Advisory Council at Dell Children's

Medical Center. When you have a sick child, you need every ounce of your energy. We make sure families are comfortable, know their rights and have access to everything they need. I typically go every Thursday for several hours and for a monthly meeting. I am about to spend more time working in the bereavement area with families who have lost children, because the parents are so lost themselves.

Every time I go to the hospital, I take the same path that we took during that last horrible ambulance ride on Christmas day when Ben passed away. It is a difficult journey, and I relive the experience of losing Ben every single time. But then I remember that there are other families going through something similar to what we went through, and I want to give them some sense of peace . . . so I keep going. I *so* love doing this work. There are times I help with grieving and loss, sometimes all I do is sit and listen; regardless, I know that I can use our suffering to make a difference for someone else.

I am constantly blessed to give back in this way, and the families are so grateful to have any kind of support. When these two things happen together, the whole thing snowballs, and it is way more powerful than anything you can do on your own. It also keeps me from being stagnant—being quiet has its own place, but you have to keep moving and growing somehow. If I were to just dwell on Ben not being here, I would be depressed. I still grieve, but it gives me purpose to help another mother of a child who is challenged. I also sense that God has helped me become a better me through all of this.

Watching all of this unfold has allowed me to see the fulfillment of Ben's purpose—knowing that who he was has been honored and appreciated, and that his legacy will help so many others. It is a bittersweet experience to lose your child, causing inexpressible sadness, but to have the blessing of seeing his life's purpose completely fulfilled, brings an amazing amount of joy. Ben showed me, through how he lived his life, that we have the gift of this *one* life on earth, and the best way to use it is to tap into our giftedness, and use it to give back to the world in positive ways.

When Ben left this world, he left us a gift of hope and peace for what comes next. And when he prayed to God to give us the peace that he already had, just one short week before his last breath, his prayers were answered. I feel like Ben is still with me and that he is not really "away"—I know we will be together again in heaven.

—*Deanne Breedlove*

Part Two:
"Transforming Pain to Purpose"

"This life is not our life. Our life is eternal, and that is God's gift to us. And this life is our gift to God. I don't know why God brought you back, and we may never know. But what you have to know is that if God chose to bring you back, he must have a very important purpose for you here."

—Ally to Ben, December 10, 2011

SOUL MODEL: Ally Breedlove

CHALLENGE: Supporting her brother Ben in living as normal a life as possible, being strong for the rest of her family.

CHANGE: Shepherding Ben's message to the entire world.

SOULUTION: Actively seek the good in life . . . instead of dwelling on adversity, look at it as an opportunity for growth and perspective, using the talents and gifts you have to enhance the world—that is purpose!

I shared those words with Ben the very last night we would ever sit out on the dock behind our house together, two weeks before he passed away. He was so sad to have "come back" this last time, and the stillness of the lake gave him a tiny bit of the peace he'd experienced when he'd been gone. He agreed with me, adding, "I think God let me have that vision so I wouldn't be afraid of dying . . . and, so I would know that heaven is worth it." We cried and held one another. I knew he had one foot in heaven, but I didn't want him to go.

Ben and I were best friends and spent a lot of time together. He was always smiling from ear to ear, and always entertaining me. Even though he was younger, our personalities complemented each other, and I looked up to him in some ways. I'm the analytical one, and Ben was always helping me lighten up and be less stressed out—he knew what really mattered and what didn't. He was so compassionate and accepting; he had a way of making everyone feel like they were the most important people in the world. He was a great big brother to

Jake, and I think he had a lot to do with building Jake's character with all those qualities.

Even with scary health issues happening all the time, Ben was always joyful and thankful. He never complained or wanted to dwell on his problems; he wanted to brush them off and get back to living his life. We never acknowledged something was wrong unless we had to in that moment. Deep down inside, I never wanted to make him feel afraid or like he was dying . . . I tried to overlook that part and just help him live in the moment. The semester before Ben passed away, I came home from school every weekend; I think deep down there was a realization that he wasn't going to be with us much longer. If I hadn't done that, we would never have had that poignant conversation out on the dock.

When there was a crisis to deal with, I knew there was nothing I could do to help Ben, so I tried to look out for my mom, grabbing her shoes or bag or whatever she needed, hugging her or trying to be supportive in some way. Our parents gave us the gift of encouragement, helping us believe that our natural gifts could grow into our life's purpose. They always supported me in acting and writing, and, with Ben, they encouraged his filmmaking. When he decided to create "Breedlove TV" on YouTube, my dad wanted him to approach doing it as a summer job with a set daily schedule, and Ben took that on.

Because I am the oldest, I've always been afraid to pursue things that weren't secure. That's why I decided to pursue a degree before a career in film or writing. Still, there was always part of me that felt empty—school wasn't enough; I didn't feel like I was producing something of value. Writing was always a passion, but I never really figured out what to do with it. Through Ben's passing, I was given the chance to write a book about his life, and once I started, everything just "clicked." Every day when I woke up, I knew it wasn't about me, and that I was doing something to better the world. It's been a miracle to unite my passion in this purpose. Not only has it been an incredible learning process, but I feel so blessed because I never realized how therapeutic the writing would be. It has been a huge release for the tension, anxiety and sadness. At the same time, it has helped me relive all the good memories.

The biggest lesson I have learned through Ben is that when you commit yourself to your passions and what you believe, you will be taken care of. I never imagined I would leave school to write about Ben—it is incredibly liberating to let go of the expectations others have of you and go after your dreams. Even if this means going off the "normal" path, you are so much happier and full of purpose. Other people's opinions don't matter, because you are confident that what you are doing is right in a much bigger sense. And, when you use your passion to bring truth or light to society, the satisfaction is a million times bigger than if you were only doing this for yourself.

I have also discovered that adversity makes you so much stronger. It gives you a deeper sense of empathy and insight into people that you wouldn't have had before. Hardship is an opportunity to find positive things that bring hope to others. If Ben hadn't had heart problems, he never would have created "This is My Story," and touched millions of lives, and I wouldn't have been graced with the outlet to use my gifts to carry on his message.

I am so proud of Ben for being incredibly brave and for exposing some of the deepest and most intimate parts of his life. He could have gotten any reaction; it could have been all negative, but he didn't care, because he knew it was important. Ben was totally himself: he said what he wanted to say without trying to convince anyone that it was real, or that his way was the right way. He wasn't afraid to show his flaws to people—he proved that you can step out of your comfort zone, be 100 percent authentic, and have a huge impact on the world. Everyone can be exactly who they are and make a difference.

When Ben passed away, my family received an outpouring of love and support from people everywhere, and it still continues. I don't think people realize how much their one tiny act of service added up and helped so much with our grieving. This understanding of using your gifts to serve others can give all of us the same peace that Ben felt.

Ben's video has inspired two consistent messages from around the world—one is from people with physical conditions who are no longer afraid of dying, and the other is from people who had no faith and are now discovering that connection. Even if you don't believe, I encourage you to ask questions, keep an open mind, and always seek the truth. And, if you have any inclination, just ask, and God will show up for you in some way.

Ally Breedlove's *When Will the Heaven Begin?* was released by Penguin in September 2013, and was an instant bestseller. When Ally isn't home with her family, she travels the country speaking and sharing Ben's story.

Leap and the Net Will Appear!

SOUL MODEL: Kim Barnouin

CHALLENGE: Lifelong battle with severe depression and learning difficulties; never completed high school.

CHANGE: Hell-bent on happiness; discovers clean diet as one component. Compelled to write sassy, irreverently-styled book in order to help and educate others: *Skinny Bitch* becomes mega bestseller.

SOULUTION: We are born with everything we need to accomplish great things, regardless of our circumstances. You need to take on that responsibility by taking care of yourself first. Doing that will put you in a place where you can say, "Ok, I'm ready, I'm feeling great; now I can go after my dreams—that is power!"

It may come as a shock to many people due to my holistic approach to eating that I am on medication for depression. I was diagnosed with Bipolar Disorder 2—a very treatable disorder. I am admitting this because I want women to be okay with taking medicine if they really need it and getting help by any means necessary. I have tried going the natural way for a long time, but it just doesn't work well enough for me. I have a chemical imbalance, and am probably starting perimenopause on top of that. I combine many treatments for my symptoms, because I know how much having a well-balanced life helps my healing.

My mom and dad divorced when I was three, and my mom remarried. My real father was in and out of my life only for a few more years, and then I never heard from him again. Even though my stepfather was great, I was really sad being left, and that caused a lot of abandonment issues for me.

I have two half-sisters, and my parents were very disciplined—you didn't talk back, ever! I'd be so God-awful scared to really say what I was thinking or feeling right at that time, and that made me extremely repressed. I ended up being painfully shy, which still is one of my ultimate struggles. I am also a true Pisces dreamer, which made me sort of the black sheep to my parents. I was always searching, living in my own world a lot of time.

From the time I was little, my mom watched lot of old black-and-white movies with me, which was my first taste of Hollywood. This was one of the biggest escapes of my life, because for two hours I went someplace magical. I envied actresses like Lauren Bacall and Audrey Hepburn, and got really obsessed with reading their biographies, because it was like stepping into their lives. I wanted to fit into any world other than the one I was in. Ultimately, they inspired me to think, *One day I can be strong enough to be like this person!*

School was such torture . . . I was always the quiet one in back of class that just didn't want to be noticed. I had a tough time concentrating and couldn't learn like everyone else. So I was scared just being there, because I was seriously afraid to be called on. At around fourteen, I started having episodes of depression that made everything even worse. It was like all of a sudden a fog was creeping in, and everything would get really heavy and dark. I felt like I was falling into a hole, and I couldn't stop it from happening. It would last anywhere from a few weeks to a few months, and the feelings were so intense, I just didn't know what to do with them. I was really afraid to tell anyone—I had crazy thoughts, like what if my parents wanted to put me in an institution? So I just kept it all down, suffering by myself, feeling so alone and isolated. At seventeen, my gynecologist put me on the pill to try and balance my hormones, but no matter how many different pills we tried, one just made me crazier than the next.

My parents didn't understand what I was going through, and I had no one else to talk to. Looking back, I can see how completely overwhelming it all was, and why I ended up dropping out of high school. I felt sad, ashamed, and embarrassed, almost all the time. And I didn't want to share it with anyone, because I felt like there was something so wrong with me, and I couldn't control it.

When I left school, there was never any preparation at home like, "Here are your strengths, try this." Instead it was, "Bye, see ya, have a nice life!" I had no clue what to do, so I decided to try being an actress. Everyone told me that was ridiculous, but it was my way of wanting to express myself. I signed up for acting classes three times, but as soon as that monologue came along I just couldn't let go enough to do it. So I just drifted from one job to the next for a while, and managed to go on with my life.

When I was twenty-six, I moved to Florida and got a job waitressing. From the beginning I was struggling there, and I finally fell into one of the worst depressive episodes ever. After about a year, it got so bad I had to go back to my parents' house for a few months to get some help. I said to them, "Okay, you are going to have to put me in a clinic or something, because this isn't good. I need to be medicated, monitored, therapy, the works." I did get some therapy and tried some antidepressants, but nothing helped. I remember sitting in the bathtub and literally making my mom sit next to me on the toilet seat because I couldn't bear to be alone—it was a dark place for me. And that went on for almost a whole year.

Finally, I remember thinking, "This can't continue. I can't physically kill myself, that's out of the question—but I can't feel like this anymore either. So I don't know how, but I'm done feeling this way." At that point I wasn't even remotely religious, but I just chose life, and started praying . . . *a lot*. In that instant, I was on the floor sobbing, and I threw my hands up, begging for help from anyone. I just said, "I want to be happy!"

From that moment, something happened and everything clicked. I was *done*, at least for then. I moved back to Florida, got a great roommate who became my best friend, and I literally turned into a different person. I was fun and light-hearted and just had a really great time. I started dating the guy who became my husband. I was a waitress at night and went to the beach during the day. I had so little responsibility . . . I was a beach bum, and that was a wonderful time!

I started thinking about my father a lot. After hating him for so many years just because my mom did, I felt like I needed to let that go. I didn't want to judge him anymore, because I didn't know what his life was like, so I started looking for him. I didn't have much to go on, and it took me about ten years to find him. It turned out he lived half an hour away from me in Florida—by some miracle we were living thirty minutes apart.

We set up a meeting in a restaurant. He had some friends with him, and I brought my best friend with me. We talked for about two hours, and said everything we needed to say . . . like him saying he's sorry, and telling me how difficult his life had been. His real mother had died, his father had remarried and his step-mother was awful. She'd made his dad put him and his brother and sister into foster care. When he was with my mom, he kept gambling away their rent and food money. He never remarried or had other kids, and he never could hold down a good job. He was alone a lot, and it was really sad.

We held each other and I said, "It's okay. I forgive you. I'm okay." We left the restaurant, and three months later he died. It was really hard, but at least we'd had a chance to say everything we needed to. It's not like he needed me to forgive him, but his life was so tough, and I feel like he's finally at peace.

By then, I felt like it was time for a change. Living in California had been a lifelong dream. I still thought that magic happened there and I wanted to be a part of it. So my husband and I packed up, rented a moving van and took off. Things always happen for some bigger reason, and right there, stuck in between the back seats of the van was this book—Deepak Chopra's *The Seven Spiritual Laws of Success*.

I will never know how it got there, but I began reading it as we were driving. Right then, the first door of possibility opened for me.

When we got to L.A., I started waitressing again, and one of the girls I was working with gave me *Real Magic* by Wayne Dyer. That book changed everything for me, because Wayne was the first person I had ever come across who said the exact words I needed to hear: *You can create your own life.* And I really didn't know I could, I'd always thought, "Who am I to think I can do this or that?" And he's saying, "You can do anything, anything is possible!" That book made me realize I could completely change my attitude toward everything. So I also started reading self-help books by Louise Hay and Tony Robbins too, who were all saying the same thing—that you can change your life by changing the way you think by doing "affirmations." Meaning that if you get rid of the negative thoughts that make you doubt and replace them with positive, affirming thoughts that help you believe in your dreams, you can manifest *anything*.

All of this started something really powerful for me. In the spiritual world, I felt much more in control, and realized I could attract a lot of things. I still had no idea what I wanted to do with my life, but I started affirming some basics—that I wanted to work for myself, so when I had kids I could be with them. I wanted an outlet to express my creativity, and I knew I wanted to help people because there *had* to be a reason I'd gone through so much. I was so excited I wrote to Wayne's publishing company, and said, "I have no money, I am so broke . . . but I need a couple of my friends to read this book who are broke too, because it is so inspirational. Is there any way you could donate a few?" They sent me six copies, which was absolutely amazing.

I kept affirming and being open to whatever the universe had in store for me. But then the depression hit again, and I just couldn't control it. I had no energy; I was a total mess, and for the first time I started to get awful panic attacks. I was determined to figure it out, so I started researching my symptoms. Everything I came across on the web was food-related, and I thought, "Well that's nuts, I'm going to keep digging." In a bookstore one day I picked up *Potatoes Not Prozac* by Kathleen Des Maisons, and it was like the light bulb went off in my head. I thought, "Holy shit—someone like . . . *gets* me. This is how I feel all the time!" She explained how you can be sugar sensitive, and it can turn you into a "Jekyll and Hyde." For the first time in my life, I knew I wasn't crazy—and I could possibly help control what I was going through. I knew right then that I was going to heal myself—and, if I could get to the other side, it was going to be my life's mission to talk about it.

I was a major junk food addict, so I had to completely overhaul my entire life—I was on the pill, smoking and eating tons of sugar and white flour products. I wasn't eating enough fruits or vegetables and I wasn't exercising. Your body can only handle so much shit on a daily basis, and it was all so obvious! It took three or four months before I got the hang of it, and finally, the diet changes took me out of my misery. I started reading more about health and nutrition and learning that there are so many diseases that are preventable, if we just eat better and get the crap out of our diet. It disgusted me that there was so much we didn't know, and it angered me into taking action. I wanted *everyone* to know that the way we eat is bad for humans, bad for animals, bad for the environment. I was like a kid in school learning things for the first time; that was such a high for me. I was totally on fire!

I had been friends with my co-author Rory for a long time. She'd been a vegetarian forever and had always wanted to convert me. I told her about the diet changes I'd made, and she gave me brochures from PETA that horrified me. That took me to a whole other health level, so I finally became a vegetarian. I kept telling Rory, "I don't know what we're supposed to do, but we need to do something . . . because I just changed my life by eating differently!" It took months to convince her, but finally, I wore her down, and the book was born.

I was in such a zone and so filled with purpose, every minute of the day—during that whole time I had no depression and no anxiety. None! It was like, "There is no focus on me at all right now. I am just so obsessed with being a part of this solution!" Looking back, it's pretty amazing that I felt so great and had no stress because I was waitressing, taking a class, and my husband and I were pretty broke. But for the first time, I wasn't in limbo anymore with my life. There was finally this huge reason for all the years of fighting the darkness, and all I cared about was spreading the word.

It was crazy! Rory and I had no writing background. I had dropped out of high school in eleventh grade, although I did have my GED. Rory had paid people in college to write her papers. I decided to enroll in school, but I was broke. I couldn't afford to go to a traditional university and study nutrition, and I wanted to learn alternative, holistic methods, so I enrolled online in the Clayton College of Natural Health. I wondered if people would take me seriously, but at the time that was my only choice, and everything I learned from that program helped me do all the research for *Skinny Bitch*. I remember how many people laughed when we told them we were writing a book. But it was so meant to be! We got an agent very quickly with only a few chapters and a proposal—and, after getting turned down a bunch of times, we got a publisher.

We wanted the book to be conversational, like you were talking to your girlfriend. And of course every woman secretly wants to be skinny, so we intentionally marketed to that. We also wanted to be hard-core, because people need a wake-up call in America. Our health is failing badly, our children are obese, and we are doing them no justice at all with the food we give them in school. People still aren't getting the message . . . it's not time to hold someone's hand.

In the very beginning we got a lot of shit because people thought it was false advertising; they thought they were getting something completely different, and we were okay with that. All we wanted to do was get the book into people's hands because once you read it, it's so compelling. The research was really important, because we had to be credible. That part was mine, and the more I learned, the more empowered I got. I was no longer naïve and trusting of every label. I was so compelled to share all this information. It was wild! I had been repressed my whole life, and here I was not able to shut up!

One day I was driving home from a waitressing job in my crappy little car, and I walked into a bookstore and handed my book to one of the salespeople to see if they would carry it—a few months later they did. It was exactly the time Victoria Beckham was shooting her reality show, and they'd been calling her the "Skinny Bitch" in England. She saw the book in the store and thought it was funny. She didn't even buy it, she just held it up. The cameras got it and that was all that needed to happen; that photo circulated everywhere in the world almost instantly. I remember Rory calling to tell me that line from Jerry McGuire, "Our little project, our company, just had a big night, a very, very big night!"

We both started crying and yelling, "Oh my God!" I knew then my life was about to change, and it was a feeling of such joy. I had a six-month-old baby, and until that moment I had no idea if the book was going to sell enough to make a living from it. Thanks to Victoria, I was able to.

Skinny Bitch is dedicated to Wayne Dyer and Tony Robbins, and about five years after it got huge, my husband and I were in Florida for the winter. Well, Wayne has a whole slew of daughters, all so gorgeous and sweet, and one of them e-mails me and says, "My dad is not computer literate, so I wanted to contact you for him, to tell you that someone gave him your book because of the dedication." The girls all loved the book and thought it was hysterical.

Next, his wife calls my cell phone and says, "We live nearby, come for lunch, and hold on . . . here's Wayne," and she puts Wayne on the phone! I'm in tears, because he is solely responsible for saving my life. Within two weeks he got us on *Ellen*; six months after that he was in Los Angeles, and I got to meet him. He was really warm and gracious, and his family is beautiful . . . that was an incredible full circle. My other hero, Tony Robbins, invited me to one of his seminars, and I am so grateful to have met him too.

I finally was having that Hollywood moment I dreamed about, and I felt so blessed. I had imagined it for so many years there I was, doing it—on a much smaller scale, but doing it, nonetheless! Truthfully, I am torn on the whole red carpet thing. I hate getting dressed up, and after thirty minutes I'm ready to leave and get back to my little family. But that little girl in me who never got the validation that I was worthy enough really enjoys that bit of attention.

My biggest lesson in all this has been learning to take care of myself first. When you do that, you can give back in the simplest ways, just by being a better friend, partner or mother. I always wanted to be a mom, and I'm so grateful that I am! My son Jack is my biggest motivator. I want him to see me as a strong, compassionate, inspiring role model so he can expect that from his future wife. I really want to tell other women who look at my life from the outside that sometimes it's a struggle just to get through the day, take care of my son and get any sort of work done, *but I am hell bent on wellness.* I am finding the exact right formula for my healing that will enable me to keep the peace and joy around.

As I grow along this journey, I see how I am being channeled into new ways of helping women overcome challenges, and embracing this is also a huge part of my healing. *Skinny Bitch* has been incredible, but it was just the start for me. I know that it is my job to experience and work through my issues so I can really help other people. I may not be able to cure someone who is depressed, but I am so proud to be part of the solution. I can say, "Oh my God, I've been there—I *really* know how you feel." And for someone who is depressed, that's huge—it gives them hope. And knowing I can do that for someone gives *me* hope.

Half the battle for anyone who is depressed is admitting it to one close friend or family member. Just being able to say, "It's here, and it's bad," relieves so much of the burden. And there are options— free clinics and support groups where you can get help. Also, asking yourself: "What do I have control over? What am I putting in my mouth, am I nourishing my body?" I am not saying that diet alone is the cure. But I know for a fact that it is a key component to healing, and the day-to-day maintenance of living with depression, even if it's just PMS. Trying to eat as cleanly as possible and getting some kind of exercise is easy enough to do, and just getting rid of sugar, caffeine and white flour might make a huge difference. Thinking outside of yourself is also a huge part of the answer. And you can't go, "I'll wait to feel a hundred percent perfect and thin and secure, then I'll try to fix everything else or find my path—you'll be waiting forever! Affirming who and what you want to be *today* is what counts.

I want to motivate all the women and girls out there who feel lost, and like they can't do what they want in life. I want to let them know that there I was, a high school dropout. I hadn't even gone to a real four-year university, and I ended up finding this path and doing something amazing with it! You have to hang in there—believe in yourself and your dreams! I also think you are happiest in life when you start to embrace the shit you've gone through and you say, "Okay, that's another one of my battle wounds, but look what I learned. Look what came after." It's all about growing. Whether we live a million lives or this is it, this is all we remember, so we have to make it count. All it takes is just that spark in your soul and some trust. Everything is possible!

Kim Barnouin is returning to school to study psychology and food science. Her goal is to have the best possible understanding of the physical and emotional reactions we have to food, and to help us understand how to take the most control of our lives.

Every Mother Counts

Christy Turlington Burns is one of the world's most famous supermodels, having appeared on over 500 magazine covers. She has established a diverse career as a model, author, entrepreneur, spokesperson, advocate, and filmmaker. After almost thirty years in an industry that is thought to be consumed with what's new, she continues to represent brands like Calvin Klein in 2013, a relationship that began in 1987. For much of her career and life, Christy has been a dedicated advocate for preventative health and well-being. Christy presented the 2011 CNN Hero of the Year Award to fellow Soul Model, Robin Lim.

SOUL MODEL: Christy Turlington Burns

CHALLENGE: In 2003, after her own post-delivery complication, postpartum hemorrhage (PPH), Christy learned that more than half a million women were dying each year from childbirth-related complications like the one she endured and survived.

CHANGE: Became a global maternal health advocate, made the documentary *No Woman, No Cry*, sharing heartfelt stories and disturbing facts about preventable maternal mortality rates in order to inspire others to take action. Founded non-profit Every

Mother Counts to create a place where people could learn more about the problem (barriers to accessing care and services), and solutions (programs that improve maternal health and address access to reaching and receiving critical care), with the aim to invite others to contribute in meaningful ways.

SOULUTION: We are each born with unlimited potential. Difficulties in life can provide valuable opportunities for us to use this potential to confront, overcome, and ultimately benefit others. Challenges can be gifts, too. In my mind, the purpose of life is to serve others. By facing challenges we learn about ourselves and the human condition.

I always knew I wanted to have an unmedicated vaginal birth. Yet I was fearful of having this type of birth experience in a hospital because I knew that it was now harder than ever. There were hard rules about when and how they'd intervene, and I didn't want unnecessary interventions in what I view as a normal physiological process. I also thought of hospitals as places where sick people go. For our first child, my husband was supportive of the birth I wanted, but still not comfortable with a home birth, so we compromised and decided that I would deliver our daughter in a birthing center located within a hospital in New York City.

That first labor was intense, but it went pretty much the way I imagined. I labored at home, in the tub, out of the tub, walking, rocking, and riding the wave of each contraction until my midwife agreed it was time for me to go to the birth center. My husband was with me the whole time, but I was grateful I had my doula, because when I needed assurance and the strength of her hands she was the one that I trusted most. She was the one who had led us to the midwife's practice that was affiliated with the birthing center. Labor was so intense and so different than I'd anticipated, but I got through each contraction, one at a time, with a lot of focus on my breath, warm water, and guidance from my support team. I never got to "the wall" they talk about reaching when you just want to go home and give up, but there were definitely times when I wondered just how long this would go on. Then it all speeded up suddenly and I was ready to push. I pushed a few times and then there she was; our daughter was in my arms.

It was the most incredible, empowering experience of my life, equal parts amazement of what my body could do and magic of meeting the little girl who had been kicking inside me, and who didn't seem like she was ever going to be ready to come out and meet us face to face. The relief and the joy and the surprise of it all completely enraptured us. A girl? Really? I had no idea she was a girl. Thank you, she is a girl. She is our gift. Her name is Grace.

Thanks to my filmmaker husband, almost every moment was captured on camera. We spent the first hour of Grace's life cuddling, breastfeeding for the first time, and waiting for the fourth stage of labor, when the placenta detaches from the uterus and is delivered. We waited for about an hour, which I found out later is an unusually long time. That's when the obstetrician was called in. I didn't know it at the time, but a retained placenta is often difficult to remove and can lead to infection. In some cases it can create enough blood loss to require a blood transfusion or hysterectomy. The doctor had to literally reach inside my uterus with his hand and manually tear the placenta off my uterine wall, and I began to bleed heavily. The pain was excruciating—delivering my baby without drugs was nothing compared to this. Everything went from exhilarating and empowering to deflating and slightly terrifying.

I had seen birth before, witnessing my sister's deliveries, and it did strike me as odd that this wasn't just happening easily for me after all the effort that went into getting the baby out safely. This bit didn't match the rest of the story. We were enjoying our happy ending and then there was the threat that that might not be.

The most wonderful day of my life had just become the scariest.

Fortunately, I got through it. We had an amazing team of providers that I had chosen and had come to trust and love. They worked together to manage the situation and that gave us confidence that everything would be okay. I would soon learn that too many women around the world don't have access to that kind of care and reassurance.

As I was recovering from the birth I wanted to understand why this happened to me. Did I do something wrong? Did we let the baby stay in too long? She was born two weeks after our "due" date. There are no explanations. It was completely random. But I did learn through researching retained placentas that PPH is the leading cause of maternal deaths related to childbirth. In 2003, when I became a mom, it was estimated that more than half a million girls and women died every year from complications of pregnancy during childbirth—that is one woman every ninety seconds, or 1,000 women every single day. Since then and because of the dedication of a lot of people working on this issue for decades, statistics have changed a lot and currently, the global estimate is closer to 300,000. That's still an unacceptably high number and the real tragedy is that 90 percent of these deaths are completely preventable.

Over the years as I've watched my daughter grow, I have been haunted by these shocking facts—and compelled to do something about them.

* * *

"Where, after all, do universal human rights begin? In small places, close to home—so close and so small that they cannot be seen on any maps of the world."

—Eleanor Roosevelt

I grew up in Danville, California, the second of three sisters. We were born very close to one another, within the span of three years, and we have managed to stay close throughout our lives. My father was American, of British and German descent. He was a pilot and Flight Training Captain for Pan American Airlines for most of my life. My mom was born in El Salvador, raised in Southern California, and a flight attendant turned homemaker once she became a mother. Because both my parents worked for the airlines, travel and seeing the world was always an important part of our lives; I definitely inherited my sense of adventure from them.

When my sisters and I were young, we traveled to Central America periodically to visit family until the war started. That early exposure made me see my connection to people outside my little world and ignited my interest in health and equity. Back home in California there were many immigrants from Latin America and it was sometimes difficult to know where we fit in.

I grew up Catholic but was always interested in all spiritual paths. My family on my mom's side is Roman Catholic, and my father and his family were Protestants. My dad was more of a naturalist who found his connection to spirit outside of a church. My sisters and I were baptized Catholic, went to catechism classes and to church fairly regularly until I was about eleven or twelve years old.

As a child, the conversations that I liked to have with my friends—or with anyone, for that matter—were always about religion. The big questions always fascinated me, like other people's interpretations of where they would go after they died, what their real values were, or the principles that they believed in.

When I was ten, our family moved across the country from California to Miami for my dad's job. Many of my friends there were either Jewish or Baptist, and I would often accompany them to temple or to church. The more I saw and learned about other faiths, the more fascinated I became. I always looked for the common threads among belief systems, rather than to the things that separated them.

I never thought about modeling; modeling found me. I used to compete in horse shows and trained after school daily during the school week. When I was fourteen, a photographer approached my sister and me at the stable where we rode and asked to take some photographs. I don't recall ever being told that I was beautiful before then; I was five foot eight, had braces, and was at that "awkward stage." I had very little confidence in my physical being. Fortunately, most of my friends were feeling the same way, so I wasn't alone.

The photographer sent the pictures to a local agency, where the agent told my mother that my sister was too short, but I would be able to find some work. At that moment, I wanted nothing more than to trade legs with my sister so she could find work as a model—not me! At fourteen, I was thrust into the "world of beauty" before I had any sense of what that meant. I went from cleaning stalls at the barn for five dollars an hour to making sixty dollars an hour, having my hair and makeup done for me, and being photographed wearing nice clothes.

I began to model pretty regularly after school and during summer break to make extra money, and at fifteen, after we'd moved back to California, I went to Paris for a month over the summer with my mom. We stopped through New York on the way home and that's when I decided that I wanted to live there. I returned to New York City for the summer the following year. I stayed with my agents Eileen and Gerry Ford of the Ford Modeling Agency, with them as my guardians in their town house on the Upper East Side. Other teenage girls from around the world would come in and out all the time. It felt more like a boarding school than a town house—there was no competition and we all supported and commiserated with each other when we lost a job or missed our families. I quickly started to get more regular work with magazines like *Vogue*, learning through my experiences and from the people who were surrounding me. It became harder and harder to return to school after spending time in NYC for longer and longer stretches, so I transferred to Professional Children's School back home in California in my junior year.

My modeling career flourished. It was an exciting world of chauffeurs picking me up in limousines and constantly being booked on jobs—some that would last for weeks. I was hanging out with all the famous photographers, designers, hairstylists and makeup artists in the industry. We had so much fun going out in New York! My older friends picked me up at my agent's house and everyone knew I'd get into trouble if I got home past curfew. They'd drop me off on time, then honk the horn to terrorize me.

It was interesting to be at that awkward age and getting all kinds of attention, when most girls hate the way they look. Occasionally, I would hear photographers talking loudly about what was or wasn't quite right about the way I looked, and I just didn't give it that much power over me. Somehow I knew enough to take everything with a grain of salt. I developed a thick skin and also some self-confidence in the abilities that I did have some control over.

I started to enjoy the recognition I sometimes received, but at the same time I became more observant and quiet. Many people around me seemed to have character flaws that I desperately wanted to avoid—there were those who thought too highly of themselves, and those who didn't give themselves enough credit. I never felt totally comfortable, although no one seemed to care or notice.

Traveling was always the biggest draw to modeling, and my mom would accompany me on the international jobs in the beginning, which was such a nice opportunity to have her to myself. All the work and travel definitely disrupted my education, but my mother kept on me about finishing high school, even when it was the furthest thing from my mind and I couldn't see the value in it. She had emigrated from El Salvador as a young girl and she understood the value of education, especially for girls. When I finally received my high school diploma in the mail, I didn't even open it—I mailed it to her and said, "This is what you wanted? Here you go!" In the end, I am so grateful she pushed me to finish school. That would have been a huge mistake and I would have regretted it forever.

At eighteen, I began living on my own in New York City and working full time as a model. I met my first serious boyfriend, who introduced me to yoga. He practiced and meditated all the time and was incredibly disciplined about it. I found it really intriguing. I think his dedication to a spiritual practice is what attracted me to him in the first place. I was moved by the discipline, quietude and commitment.

It was at that time that I began to practice yoga regularly. I also meditated daily and started going to retreats. Because I was traveling and working a lot as a model at that time, I relied on many of the tools I learned through meditation and yoga to help me stay calm and grounded throughout my career. I didn't always have an asana practice (physical postures), but I continued to use meditation, mantra repetition, and breathing exercises to stay balanced and centered.

The word yoga means "union" and refers to the unity of our mind, body and spirit, and our unity with all things. It was through these practices that I first began to seriously consider my human potential. Before that, when my looks and career were dictating that was *all* I was—modeling felt very limiting. It had gotten to the point where I wondered what I was going to do with my life. Yoga gave me insight into myself and showed me who I really wanted to be.

At nineteen, I signed with Calvin Klein as the face of "Eternity." This was a huge turning point in my career. It was 1989 and the industry was about to change. The "supermodel" era was about to begin. In the 1980's, the Ford Agency had a televised competition called "Supermodel of the World." It was like Miss America for models. I was never a contender, but that's where I first heard that term. A few years later, I ended up on the cover of *British Vogue* with a few others who were each individually successful at the same time. Because of that photograph and what transpired afterward with the group of us models and the designers and photographers of that time, I will go down in history as one of the originals.

It was a fun time but it was also a crazy time, too, and that's when I decided it was time to finally move on. The constant travel took its toll on me physically and it was too hard to create a stable home life that I was starting to crave. Through it all, yoga had become much more than a physical practice—it became my spiritual lifestyle as well, a way of living that "connected" me to myself, strengthening my own sense of purpose, and keeping me balanced in the whirlwind of my life at that time.

There is also a part of yoga philosophy called "*seva,*" which means service. By 1994, my practice was prompting me to do something more fulfilling.

Throughout my early career as a model I had been a smoker, having had my first cigarette in my early teens as a kind of "rite of passage." By sixteen, I was smoking a pack a day and pretending I was older than I was. I tried everything to quit once I realized I was addicted—the patch, hypnosis, acupuncture, and a variety of other methods, but nothing seemed to work. Finally, almost ten years later, I made up my mind to just stop. I recommitted myself to an even stronger yoga practice, and to changing my lifestyle. I stopped drinking coffee and alcohol, since those things increased my desire to smoke. When I finally stopped for good, I knew it was one of the biggest accomplishments of my life.

After a decade in a career that I had never planned for, I decided to go to New York University to pursue a liberal arts degree, with a concentration in philosophy and religion. I applied to NYU that spring and began taking classes in the fall.

Shortly after Christmas, about a year or so later, my dad, who was a lifelong smoker, became ill with lung cancer. He finally quit but it was too late for my dad—he died of lung cancer just six months later.

My father's death had an enormous impact on every aspect of my life. When you lose someone close to you, you lose a part of yourself too. I realized it was time to begin reevaluating other relationships in my life that were holding me back; I was ready to move forward.

With my renewed commitment to yoga and current direction of my studies, I couldn't help but feel compelled to do something more with my grief for my father. I wanted to create something from his absence that would honor his life and memory.

I decided to go out and tell my story—not just my own struggles with addiction and the process of quitting, but what I learned about lung cancer and smoking-related diseases during my father's illness. I thought I could find a way to share my experience and loss to make a difference, hopefully helping people who were struggling with similar issues. I reached out to the American Cancer Society and the Centers for Disease Control and Prevention and offered my services.

I began campaigning against smoking along with Vice President Al Gore and others, and co-created a series of award-winning anti-smoking campaigns. They were very emotional and very much about my personal story. As a result, many people over the years have come up to me and said, "I quit smoking because of you." It makes me feel so proud when I hear that.

This anti-smoking activism got people to see me differently and that motivated me to continue advocating for preventative health and wellness. I realized that my yoga practice and dedication to living a whole and authentic life that included service was part of that.

When I made the decision to go to college I had the security of a few long-term professional relationships, such as my contracts with Calvin Klein and Maybelline, which supported my decision to continue my studies. I continued to work sporadically as a model but only with those who would honor my full-time status as a student and agree to work around my school schedule. After I graduated in 1999, I started two businesses that were very much related to yoga and well-being.

I met my husband in 2000, during one of the most professionally and emotionally challenging times of my life. I was writing a book and running two successful businesses. We got engaged right away and were married three years later. We are both middle children who come from middle-class backgrounds. We were raised Catholic and have a strong work ethic and a love of family and tradition. By the time we met, we both knew what we wanted in life.

We were married in 2003 and I became a mom later that same year. In the months that followed my daughter's birth, I began to really think about the importance of advocacy for natural birth and also what my complication meant for women without access to prenatal and postnatal care. I learned that it can, and often does, mean death for thousands of girls and women around the world, even here in the U.S. I became obsessed with the social justice aspect of birth and the human right to maternal health care.

Once I learned about all these senseless deaths related to pregnancy and childbirth, I needed to know *why*. If almost all of these deaths are preventable, why are we allowing so many girls and women to die?

In 2005, when I was seven months pregnant with my son, I travelled with the global humanitarian organization CARE to rural villages in El Salvador, the country where my mother was born. During that trip, I spent time with other women who were doing extremely strenuous work to support their families with very little help. As a mother, I felt my connection with these other women in such a profound way. My being pregnant alongside of them allowed me to feel that "sisterhood of motherhood."

In these villages, there was no electricity, no paved roads, and no clean water. I couldn't help thinking, "What if I had my birth complication with Grace in these surroundings?" I realized that had I delivered my first child there, I would have died. That awareness made me realize that we could do a much better job helping these women. It also made me wonder, *"Why* aren't *we?*

I returned from that trip with the women I had met in El Salvador on my mind. A couple of months later, after a relatively easy delivery with my son, I still couldn't stop thinking of those other moms. How had they fared? Had they survived? Had their newborns survived? The maternal mortality rates in their area were staggering and weighed heavily on my conscience. I knew I had to do something; I just didn't know yet what it was.

In 2007, I traveled to Peru with CARE to visit the FEMME Project, a highly successful partnership in the highlands where maternal mortality rates had decreased by 50 percent in less than five years. For the first time, I felt a sense of hope—I knew that if I could figure out how to share the personal stories I experienced there, and the amazing progress being made, people would be as equally inspired as I was to take action. That's when the idea to make a documentary film was born.

No Woman, No Cry explores the barriers and challenges women face in accessing critical life-saving maternity care in Bangladesh, Tanzania, Guatemala, and the United States. Filming took two years and was a life-transforming experience. The issues are complex, especially since 15 percent of all pregnancies will result in some complication that requires extra medical attention, and we can't always know who is at the greatest risk. Most complications can be addressed and managed if mothers seek care in time, and if providers are trained well enough to manage the case.

In rural Tanzania, or any rural community in sub-Saharan Africa, a pregnant woman might have to walk at least five kilometers (approximately three miles) in the blazing sun to receive basic care. She may have to walk an entire day in heavy labor, without food or water. If she or her baby needs serious medical attention, she could be dozens of miles or hours from the nearest medical facility. And that can be the difference between life and death.

In Bangladesh, 91 percent of births occur outside a hospital—the barriers there are often hidden underneath the surface. The women pray to never be taken outside of the home to give birth, because of the stories they've heard that babies are taken away and sold in the hospital or the treatment they are subjected to when they arrive there. If there is a complication, it is considered the woman's "fault." Dying as the result of childbirth is culturally "accepted" and even considered heroic in many countries.

Guatemala is second in the region for maternal mortality largely because of the indigenous population that is at disproportionate risk for maternal deaths and because a high number of unsafe abortions occur there, even though abortion is illegal, including in cases of rape and incest. As a result, women frequently die from unsafe abortions. The stigma of abortion is so great that women will refuse to admit they had one, even when they are on the verge of death.

The United States ranks fiftieth in the world in maternal mortality —an astonishing statistic. Currently, in this country, one in five women of childbearing years has no health insurance (a barrier we are currently on the verge of changing with the Affordable Care Act), which can be a disaster for someone who is pregnant. It is ironic that while women in some of the poorest countries have trouble getting the care they need, when they do get it, it may be free. Here in the U.S., where providers and services are abundant, health care is anything *but* free. In fact, it's so expensive, that many women avoid getting prenatal care because they can't afford it. As a result, women run to emergency rooms for help when problems arise or they go into labor because they have nowhere else to go. Ironically, these same women, who have no means to access a health-care provider during pregnancy, are often judged harshly by the health-care community for not having gotten proper prenatal care.

There were countless stories to tell and it was a real challenge to pick among them for the final cut of the film. We did our best to include the ones that were most representational of many others.

I have returned to each country to premiere the film and continue to follow up with many of the women featured. I wanted to see them and their children again. When you invest in people's stories and share their most personal and sacred moments, you want to stay connected and follow their progress. Since we first visited Bangladesh in 2009, there has been a 40 percent reduction in their maternal mortality rate. This proves that it *is* possible to change social norms and improve health systems so they can better attract and serve mothers and families.

No Woman, No Cry premiered at the Tribeca Film Festival in 2010 and aired on the Oprah Winfrey Network the following year. The amazing response it received validated the fact that the message was meaningful to many—and that it could also move them to action.

After the film was edited, it felt like a disservice to present the information without providing some kind of call to arms to audiences. That's when I launched Every Mother Counts (EMC), with the goal of reducing preventable deaths associated with pregnancy and birth. We started as an advocacy campaign but have evolved into a 501(c)(3) charitable organization. We now raise funds to support programs in five countries that focus on access to skilled providers and services that will improve maternal health outcomes long term. Every dollar raised by the public that is donated to EMC goes straight to these programs.

I've learned a lot in the years since founding EMC about what it takes to prevent maternal deaths. For example, I know now that it begins by supporting the mid-level health-care providers on the ground, such as midwives, nurses, and community health workers. If we can continue to link vulnerable moms to the providers and services that can save their lives at birth, we will be here for as long as it takes.

It starts with education. For girls ages fifteen to nineteen, pregnancy is the leading cause of death in the world. We have to teach them about how their bodies work and about reproductive health. They have to learn the signs that a complication is occurring and help them understand that they can't go through childbirth alone. We need to make sure they are linked to health-care systems, and ensure that they have transportation to more advanced facilities if something goes wrong. Making these connections is critical so women feel 100 percent supported during their pregnancies and births.

In Uganda, we've created a voucher system for transportation. Now, when a woman goes into labor, she has a way to get to the health-care facility. In Haiti, we are supporting a class of seventeen midwives who will each go on to deliver 200 babies per year. In Florida, we're funding a grant to increase access to prenatal care and prenatal education for underserved women. In Malawi, we'll be working with WeCare Solar to provide portable lighting solutions in areas where for lack of electricity and a light, women die having babies. We're working in Indonesia with Robin Lim to fund ongoing projects at Bumi Sehat Birth Center, including building a laboratory so that every mother who delivers there is tested for HIV/AIDS. The lab will also include voluntary counseling, prevention of mother-to-child transmission programs, education on prevention, cervical cancer screening and treatment, nutrition counseling and testing, and treatment of tropical diseases in pregnant women.

I met Robin Lim in the fall of 2011. Robin is the incredible midwife who founded Bumi Sehat in Bali, Indonesia, an organization of clinics that ensures that mothers and newborns receive the highest quality of care possible. I had just run my first New York City Marathon, to raise awareness and funds for Every Mother Counts, and people thought I was crazy to hop on a plane to Indonesia a day later. CNN had invited me to fly to Bali to meet Robin Lim and interview her on camera to learn more about her work as she was nominated for their CNN Hero Awards, which awards unsung every day heroes who dedicate their lives to improving the lives and well-being of others—I jumped at the chance, as I really wanted to meet Robin and see her working in her environment at Bumi Sehat. When I arrived at Robin's home that first morning, she stuck her head out of a second floor opening and invited me up to chat as she got dressed for the day, like we were sisters who had known one another for a lifetime.

I believed that Robin deserved this recognition because of the extraordinary compassionate care she provides to women in her community and others who travel from all around the region to have her deliver their babies. Bumi Sehat is an energetic, bustling hub of the community just down the road from Robin's home, but it is bursting at the seams. Robin was nominated for this award by the people who have been touched by her personally. She told me what her dream was for the prize money if she were to win. She had plans to build a bigger, better-equipped Bumi Sehat up the road. We walked the property with dozens of neighborhood children; most of whom she'd delivered and knew by name. I was honored to be there the night Robin won this award several weeks later. We shared her story with the Every Mother Counts community. They helped to raise additional funds after she won, and continue to stay in close contact with Robin.

Every Mother Counts raises funds for the programs we support through public engagement, such as races like the New York City Marathon as well as through partnerships. These races have become symbolic journeys of the distance that millions of moms-to-be face around the world. Most maternal deaths occur because of what are known as the three delays. The first is a delay in seeking appropriate care. The second is a delay reaching the appropriate facility for the care that is needed, and the third is a delay receiving adequate care when a facility is reached. So many women don't seek care because they have no means to reach care. I like to say, "We run so they don't have to."

Over the last ten years, we've seen the number of maternal deaths worldwide drop by almost half, from half a million a year to 287,000 and we have played a vital role in raising global awareness about this issue by supporting proven efforts to improve maternal health. I envision a world where pregnancy and childbirth are safe for all moms.

This advocacy work has become so much more than I could ever have imagined. I became an advocate for other mothers when I became one myself and that connection to the mothers of the world is what inspires me every day. I continually challenge myself to do meaningful work, and make sure the time I spend with my children and family is of the highest quality it can be. I know that I am a better mom because of it.

When I look at my own children I feel grateful for my health and theirs. I am also grateful that I had an experience that would connect me to so many other women. I believe that every experience is an opportunity to learn and grow. My children teach me that every day. When they were younger they preferred that I didn't travel, and didn't understand why I was so compelled to. But as they got older I would share stories with them about all the people I meet. I let them know that there are millions of children in the world who don't have mothers. They used to have a map on their wall and depending on where I was traveling, we would look together and talk about that place and measure the distance. Tanzania was one of those places and when I was finally able to take them there last year they were well prepared. I hope one day my children recognize their own connection to the world and are inspired to make a difference.

This work has been the most gratifying work I've done and also the most satisfying. I'm inspired by the women I meet, and I'm motived to be working with so many others towards a shared goal to improve the health and well-being of girls and women everywhere. This is my *seva* practice—service in action.

I'm at a point in my life where I recognize that I'm able to do this valuable work because of the experiences I've had. My career as a model has given me so much access to the world and I am proud of the endurance of some of the relationships it has allowed me to have, like Calvin Klein who is now partnered with Every Mother Counts and a sponsor of our marathon team this year. I am grateful every day for so many things, but mainly because I have found a way to live a life of meaning and it is incredibly satisfying. That has been a long-term goal and now I am living it daily.

I have always had a pretty healthy attitude about aging. I believe that experience brings wisdom and compassion and those things go hand-in-hand with getting older. I welcome everything that comes with these gifts.

I would offer the same advice to a young model as I would to any young woman: take advantage of the opportunity to get an education or continue your education because that will give you more confidence no matter what you think you look like. Be kind. Be compassionate. Be fair. If you respect yourself, others will respect you too.

The way I try to live is this: Be here now. Be gentle, kind and loving with yourself, and be your best self today. This might mean working through a challenge, facing a fear, or following your passion. For me, it means being the best mom and citizen of the world that I can, and connecting mothers around the world so that we aren't alone. Each of the hundreds of thousands of women who die every year is a mother, sister, friend; she's a cousin or a wife. If everyone thinks of it that way and imagines the impact a senseless tragedy would have in their own lives, we may begin to understand and find a way to do something about it. Those of us who have a voice have an advantage many others don't have. If you have one, you must learn to *use* your voice. Together, we can make pregnancy and childbirth safe for all moms.

Christy Turlington Burns is the founder of Every Mother Counts, a campaign to end preventable deaths caused by pregnancy and childbirth around the world. Every Mother Counts informs, engages, and mobilizes new audiences to take action to improve the health and well-being of girls and women worldwide. In 2010, Christy directed and produced *No Woman, No Cry*, a documentary film about the global state of maternal health. Christy is also an avid yogi and merged her love of the practice and writing to author her first book, *Living Yoga: Creating a Life Practice* (Hyperion 2002). She also founded two successful lifestyle brands; SundAri, an Ayurvedic skin care line, and Nuala, a yoga inspired apparel and accessories line. Christy is an advisor to the Harvard Medical School Global Health Council and the Harvard School of Public Health Board of Dean's Advisors. Christy has a BA from New York University's Gallatin School of Individualized Studies and is currently pursuing a MPH at Columbia University's Mailman School of Public Health in New York City, where she lives with her husband, filmmaker Edward Burns, and their two children.

Living for Love

"I imagine a world in which all humans are born with an intact capacity to love, and I am willing to devote my life to making it happen."

—Robin Lim

SOUL MODEL: Ibu (Mother) Robin Lim

CHALLENGE: Losing sister, niece, midwife, and best friend all in one year; learning that 981 mothers die each day after childbirth because they can't afford proper care.

CHANGE: Became a midwife and has delivered approximately 5,000 babies; founded Bumi Sehat health clinics, offering free prenatal care, birthing services, and medical aid to impoverished women in Indonesia. Authored many books on childbirth and women's issues. Travels extensively as a speaker and advocate for Gentle Midwife to Mother Care.

SOULUTION: When life is hard, cry . . . it waters the garden of your heart. Be sad, worry, and stomp your foot in anger. But then, get on with it. Take the next step, whatever that step may be. We are not expected to perfect our lives, only to take baby steps—they will take you very far, indeed.

If you google Ina May Gaskin's "Safe Motherhood Quilt, Christine Jehle Kim," you will see the quilt piece I made to memorialize my sister. Through this quilt, she is honored, along with my never-born niece.

It happened on a dark rainy morning. My children were sitting down to breakfast. I was in the garden, having just milked Lizziebell, our goat, when my dear friend Margo appeared. The look on her face was all I needed to see. Someone had asked her to come—come to tell me something so painful it would shatter my world.

"It's Christine."

I don't know how I ended up on my knees in the mud. I'm pretty sure that I tore Margo's blouse. The scene certainly frightened my children.

"Not my baby sister. No, No, NO!"

Not the baby sister whom my mother had placed into my fifteen-month-old arms with this mandate, "You must protect her. She came down to Earth to be with you."

So, why was I living in Hawaii and she, all grown up, living in Alabama? Like twins conjoined at the heart, hadn't we slept together nearly every night of our childhood? In middle school, we had pushed our beds together and used my father's old army belts to lash our legs one to the other so that we would not drift apart at night.

Two days earlier, my sister told me over the long distance phone, "I don't feel well; this pregnancy is different from my first two." I encouraged her to share her concerns with her physician, which she did. Tragically, even though she had health insurance, her OB-GYN did not have time to address my sister's pregnancy-induced hyper-tension. He promised to handle it at their next appointment, in two weeks. Two weeks never arrived for my sister—Christine was thirty-two years old when she died.

Christine's death began long before that rainy morning. In the winter of 1961, she was struck down by pneumonia. Her military doctors prescribed large doses of cortisone to strengthen her so that she would "pull through." Christine returned home so bloated that, to my four-and-a-half-year-old eyes, she appeared lost inside of herself.

"Where are you Chrissy? Are you in there?"

Chrissy was in there, but now she was twice as large as I remembered her from when they had taken her away just three weeks before. From that time on, for the rest of her short life, she would struggle with a weight problem diagnosed by doctors as a hormone imbalance. She was poked and prodded, tested and put on crash diets. A balloon was put in her stomach, and at some tragic juncture, doctors stitched up part of her digestive tract, all to no avail. At any given meal, Christine, though more than double my weight, ate less than half of what I did.

While I grew up healthy, strong and slim, Christine grew out and was chastised and called "Fatso." Already marginalized by cruel classmates for being mixed-race kids, it became routine for me to fight off Christine's persecutors at the school bus stop.

When Christine grew up, she married a Korean man. Her English was perfect, but her husband was still learning the language. They were a struggling young family and had to tighten their belts just to afford the cost of minimum health-care insurance.

In that last conversation we ever had, my sister told me she couldn't find a midwife to do her birth, since they all considered her a risk because of her weight. She said, "I keep changing doctors, because none of them really cares about me."

Christine's pregnancy-induced hypertension caused a stroke that killed her in her sleep at twenty-eight weeks gestation. Had her doctor paid attention to her climbing blood pressure, she would never have died.

My baby sister's death is a shameful statistic. Fast forward twenty years . . . we can still read the same shameful statistics in Amnesty International's report, *Deadly Delivery: The Maternal Health Crisis in the USA*. Unfortunately, I *can* imagine the suffering that families experience in the United States caused by the loss of the two to three women, mothers, who die every day in pregnancy and childbirth.

The total amount spent on health care in the United States is greater than in any other country in the world.[1] According to a report in the *Huffington Post* in 2012, hospitalization related to pregnancy and childbirth costs some $98 billion a year in the United States, the highest hospitalization costs of any area of medicine.[2]

Despite this, women in the United States have a greater lifetime risk of dying of pregnancy-related complications than women in forty-nine other countries. In fact, the maternal mortality rate in the United States has doubled in the last twenty-five years. If you are a woman of color, your risk of dying due to pregnancy/childbirth related causes is 3.2 times more likely than that of a Caucasian woman.

If we compare maternal health care in the United States with George Orwell's *Animal Farm,* Napoleon the pig would say, "All pregnant women are equal—but some are more equal than others."

When my sister Christine and the daughter she was carrying died, I was shattered, but I did not get angry—she wasn't an angry person, and she had taught me to always choose peace. In her honor, I chose to live my life for love, with the intention of preventing the deaths of other mothers. The day she left this earth, I was reborn as a birth-keeper. It was a painful labor and birth, but here we are, Christine and I, saving lives together—that is the miracle of healing.

There have been times when I am completely alone and have felt Christine "tap" me on the shoulder, telling me to pay attention. Usually, when on speaking tours overseas, I check my cell phone messages before going to bed, just in case one of the moms in Indonesia needs some help. Then, I turn it off. One night in Italy, each time I was going to turn off my phone, I felt Christine "tap" me on the shoulder and tell me, "No!" So I left it on.

At three AM, a text message came in from a woman who was thirty-six weeks pregnant and bleeding a lot. I immediately called her; from what I could deduce on the phone, thousands of miles away, she was suffering a placental abruption, which means that the placenta is detaching from the uterine wall, an emergency for both baby and mother. Quickly, I had her lie on the floor and call for her husband, whom I instructed to immediately take her to the hospital. I called the surgeon and arranged to have them met at the door with a surgical team. The mother was saved. The baby spent one night on a respirator and pulled through with zeal, all because my sister Christine would not "allow" me to turn off my cell phone. At the time that happened, Christine had been dead for twenty years.

As for the 800-plus mothers who die every day on Earth from complications of pregnancy and childbirth, *each one is my sister, and your sister, too.* These sisters are not elderly, they are not ill; they are in the prime of their lives, doing the most human possible thing, having a baby. Their numbers are underreported. They die, usually from hemorrhage following childbirth, or malnutrition driven by poverty. Their deaths are, for the most part, preventable. Many of these young mothers could be saved, if only they had access to skilled midwifery care. This is why I am passionate about teaching gentle childbirth skills to midwives and birth-keepers all over the world. Imagine . . . the number of women dying from complications of pregnancy and childbirth per day is equal to about two 747 jet planes crashing every day! If two airplanes fell from the sky every single day, would you fly?

* * * *

My childhood was very interesting. My mother is Filipino-Chinese, and my father was German-Irish-Native American. In the 1950s, when the world was not yet accepting mixed marriages, my parents built a bridge of peace across many cultures. I was the eldest of five siblings, and we took some heat in school in America for having a non-white mother. As Asian-American children, we were taught to respect our parents, and for that I am still grateful.

I gave my parents plenty of worry, but compared to most, I was quite okay, as were my siblings. I was a good student and extremely independent, but very shy. Although I had wonderful friends, we were not the "popular" girls. I wrote speeches, thinking I would someday be the first Asian-American woman President of the United States.

I saw the world as a place of many injustices. As a very young child I remember the footage of the Vietnam War on television: the body count; the faces of children burned with Napalm; the women running with babies in their arms, gunned down as their rice harvest was burned. How were they different from me?

I dreamed of world peace, and vowed I would find a way to contribute to that goal. My sister Christine was always there for me. She was smarter than I was, and had a beautiful singing voice. We shared dreams, staying up nights whispering. Once, my younger brother, Carl, was choking on something. Our neighbor, an African-American nurse, ran to our house. She was able to dislodge a piece of metal in Carl's windpipe. She did CPR and saved his life. In that moment, I felt a seed of commitment was planted in my heart. I thought, *I will grow to be someone who can help people.*

My hero was my Filipino grandmother, my Lola. She was a "Hilot"—a traditional baby-catcher and healer in the mountains of Luzon, Philippine Islands. When I was in grade five, I was sick with a life-threatening kidney infection, and my Lola massaged me, healing me with corn silk tea. When the military doctors wished to medevac me to Manila, she did not let them take me. Because of her special brand of love, I recovered. It was then that I learned I had sprung from a long line of strong women.

We moved to California when I was twelve, and, at fourteen, I took family life education for the first time. I was also taking a class in Reproductive Health. It was so exciting, learning how babies are made. Somehow, this subject stood out as my favorite, and just the fact that this knowledge existed made other problems go away. After all, we lived in a world full of miracles!

As a student leader in high school I was considered a "nerd," enjoying Women's Coalition Club rather than cheerleading. I met and married my first husband, Ed, in high school, and by the time I was nineteen years old, we were living in France and expecting a baby. We returned to Santa Barbara and Déjà was born at home. Just days after giving birth, we moved to Iowa, where my husband pursued his education, while I breastfed my little "Guru" and made handicrafts to support our little family.

After becoming a teen mother, my love for Christine had deepened. When my daughter Déjà was but eight months old, she looked at my sister and shouted gleefully, "Auntie Mama!" It was her first time to put two words together. Déjà and her Auntie Mama became inseparable.

Four years later, I gave birth to Noel. He was just a baby when Ed left the marriage. At twenty-four, I was a single mother with two children and a broken heart. I moved with my children to Hawaii, to reinvent my life. I found I could be a stay-at-home mom by making crystal jewelry at night when they slept and selling my crafts to tourists.

I was a fledgling writer, with big dreams and no skill, looking for my own voice. I met a man named Ching and became pregnant with my third baby. I researched an article on postpartum care and found nearly nothing about it, so I decided to write a book on the topic. I began reaching out to every midwife I could find an address for, asking them what was needed in a book on this topic. They were super-helpful and encouraging. I was not yet a midwife, but I was becoming a birth-keeper: someone with a calling to guard and protect mothers, babies and families.

Between April 1985 and August 1987, I wrote my first book and had two more children, Amanda Zhòu Lee, and Zion Pao Shun Lee. The marriage ended badly; it is not a chapter with good memories, and I don't want to be negative about someone I once loved. However, I am grateful for the children that came through that relationship. I found myself a single mother with four children in a very support-ive community in Maui. I was the soul support of my family, still making and selling crystal jewelry, while dreaming of becoming a published writer.

I worked passionately on my first book, *After the Baby's Birth*. Because the world is full of wonder and serendipity, Suzanne Arms, a birth activist and author I admired so very much, came to Maui on a short vacation. She stayed right up the road from my house. It was hard to muster the courage to knock on her cabin door and introduce myself, but I did.

My manuscript was tucked under my arm, and my baby Zion was nursing at my breast. Suzanne sat down and started reading. An hour passed as I was sweating and breastfeeding. Suzanne looked up at me and said, "I'd like to take this to David Hinds at Celestial Arts/Ten Speed Press in Berkeley. He'll publish it." She was so matter-of-fact about the miracle that my book would get published!

Christine was pregnant then, and *After the Baby's Birth* would be released just after she was to give birth. I was determined that she would be the first postpartum mom to benefit from my book, but she never had that chance.

There I was, a single mom, with four children, a published book, and a broken heart, still grieving my sister. Before the year was up, my own midwife, Sunny, and my dear friend, Brenda, both died in automobile accidents. I became afraid to answer the phone, worrying that bad news would arrive, and someone else I loved would be dead.

Brenda's husband, Wil, brought their children from New Jersey, back to Maui, to fulfill Brenda's dream of raising them in a wonderful way. I was already living on a farm, milking goats, drying bananas, herding ducks and home-schooling children. Wil rented a cottage on the same farm. Having Brenda's children together with my own was just wonderful. Brenda's daughter Lakota moved her toothbrush to my house declaring, "Little girls need mothers." Her son, Thor, and my son, Zion, were both just three and inseparable. One night Wil stood below my window and sang me a love song of his own invention. It was beautiful, and I did what I thought was impossible—I opened up and trusted enough to fall in love one more time.

We took a huge leap and moved everyone to Bali, fulfilling a life-long fantasy I had had: immersing my family in a culture that worshipped children and respected elders. We were welcomed in the village of Nyuh Kuning. In 1993, our youngest son, Hanoman was born at home, into Wil's arms.

During my own pregnancy in Bali, I became aware of the unmet needs of mothers. It was an island where hemorrhage after childbirth was a leading cause of death. One thing led to another, and soon Yayasan Bumi Sehat (Healthy Mother Earth Foundation) was founded in 1995. It is an Indonesian not-for-profit organization. We advocate for marginalized, displaced, low-income people from all islands, faiths and cultures.

We believe that access to quality health care, especially reproductive health care, is a human right. We advocate for mothers, families and for the smallest citizens of Indonesia, babies at birth. We are building peace, one mother, one child, one family at a time.

Currently, we operate two family health and childbirth clinics, both open twenty-four hours a day, serving the poorest people in the villages, and anyone who comes in for help.

Our midwives are skilled at prenatal care and culturally appropriate gentle birthing techniques intended to ease pain, reduce Cesarean rates, and improve the health of our moms and babies. At Bumi Sehat, beggars and prostitutes can feel like cherished queens. Babies are the smallest, most vulnerable citizens of this world—when you take care of the mother she is healthier, and that is better for the baby.

I am blessed to be a midwife and have a family who supports my work. I am continually motivated, inspired and astonished by my husband Wil and our eight children. My family gives me safe harbor in the windstorms of this midwife's life, which can get dramatic. When I have to resuscitate a baby born dead, because his mother has AIDS, it is my family that holds me tenderly. Sometimes I need to talk about it, and sometimes silence is more healing—they allow me all of that.

I am never alone in my work, because the Bumi Sehat Team and our community are extraordinary. Sometimes I feel lonely when it comes to fundraising; then something miraculous happens. We midwives, nurses, and doctors are the hands in the field. The donors are the heart, keeping us pumped with nourishment, so we can do the humanitarian service that we so love.

In early 2011 the phone rang in the wee hours. I answered on the first ring, assuming it was an emergency call from the clinic. "I'm from Turner Broadcasting, you have been chosen a hero."

"Are you pregnant?" I asked.

"Why no."

"Is this an emergency?"

"No."

"Okay, please call back in the morning," I said, and hung up.

The phone rang again, and this time I answered and listened; it seems I was nominated by a friend, Liz Sinclair, and others, to be a CNN Hero. "Can we send a film crew out to Bali in a few days?" In October I learned I was chosen a Top 10 CNN Hero, which made me very happy, as we desperately needed the prize money to keep the clinics operational.

CNN sent another film crew, and Christy Turlington Burns arrived. She had just run a marathon for her non-profit, "Every Mother Counts," gotten on the plane and showed up in Bali tired, but excited to meet the Bumi Sehat mothers and team. Over the next few days Christy and I became life-long friends.

Christy is someone who answers every e-mail I send her. She has raised funds for us, and Every Mother Counts is supporting the Bumi Sehat HIV and sexually transmitted infection (STI) testing lab, where we save lives in partnership. Christy came back from the brink of death in the process of having her own first child, committed to mothers and children, all over the world. We share a vision and a bond of love between us.

I have been called a "hero" but I don't feel I actually "help" others. I simply *believe* in them. They really do the work themselves. Each mother in childbirth—*she* is the real hero. For example, one can reduce the risks of motherhood, but on labor day, it is the woman herself who must go the distance. We can rub her back; if she hemorrhages, we can control the bleed, but she must *live*. So, looking after others is really just enriching one's own life. I don't feel "generous," because it all comes home to my family and me. In a way, living life as I do is selfish.

I remember having intense back and sciatic pain for about three years. While women were in labor I found myself thinking: "She is so blessed—once she pushes out her baby, her pain will stop, but my pain will continue." Then, a woman came to me carrying a baby who was no longer alive, but not yet born. Her pain will never stop. She taught me something I cannot articulate in words. My issues were *many*, but somehow I have outgrown them. It's easy to forgive and not "sweat the small stuff" when one works in the doorway between life and death.

I am most proud of becoming a mom and catching my own grandchildren with my hands. My children inspire me. Some of them did body recovery after the tsunami in Aceh. Their generation is so ready to heal this world—they all glow with love and inspire me to keep making this world a little nicer, a little more beautiful, a little more peaceful, every day.

Love is a boomerang. Sharing it is like setting a dove free; it comes home to roost in your own heart, every time.

Robin Lim is a poet and author of *After the Baby's Birth, Wisdom for Mothers, Eating for Two . . . Recipes for Pregnant and Breastfeeding Women, Placenta the Forgotten Chakra, Eat Pray Doula, The Geometry of Splitting Souls,* and many more books in Bahasa, Indonesia, that are available online. Her novel, *Butterfly People,* is available via Anvil Press in the Philippines.

To help Bumi Sehat, contact Robin at: www.bumisehatfoundation.org

---

1. *Deadly Delivery The Maternal Health Care Crisis in the USA,* Amnesty International Publications 2010.

2. *www.huffingtonpost.com/2012/08/24/maternal-mortality-rate-infographic_n_1827427.html*

The "Mother of Movements"

SOUL MODEL: Candace Lightner

CHALLENGE: Thirteen-year-old daughter was killed by drunk driver who was out on bail for DUI and had three prior DUI convictions.

CHANGE: Founded Mothers Against Drunk Driving, which is estimated to have saved approximately 600,000 lives by putting a face to the victims and changing the nation's attitudes. Recently founded We Save Lives, a non-profit with a mission of encouraging and promoting safe driving focusing on the 3D's: Drunk, Drugged, and Distracted driving.

SOULUTION: Never take no for an answer if you really believe you are right about an issue. Passion is critical if you want to succeed and right a wrong. Courage is just as important—it takes courage to challenge the status quo and it takes courage to overcome whatever obstacles are thrown your way. There are many examples of one person making a difference—you could be that one person, whether it is in the halls of Congress, in your community or within your family.

It was the day after Cari's funeral that I drove by the spot where it had happened. I was still completely in shock and exhausted from crying and the incredible pain. I had a houseful of people who were staying with me, and no food, so we decided to go out to eat. We had to drive by the spot where she was killed, and I happened to see the police cordoning off the spot with yellow tape. They had no idea who I was, and I asked them if they were investigating the death of Cari Lightner.

Police: "Are you her mother?"

Me: "Yes."

Police: "Were you called?"

Me: I said, "Yes,"(I was called and told they had arrested the man who killed Cari but nothing else).

Police: "Then we guess you know the man who did it was arrested. Did they tell you the circumstances, that he was out on bail from another hit and run?"

Me: I said, "Yes," even though they hadn't.

Police: "Then you know he was drunk when he killed your daughter, right?"

Me: I said, "Yes," even though I didn't.

Police: "Then you know he had a number of priors. . . ."

Me: I said, "Yes," even though I had no idea. My immediate thought and next question was "How much time will he spend in prison?"

Police: "Lady, you'll be lucky if he sees any jail time, because that's how the system works."

I got back into the car with my friends. My anger and rage were unbelievable. *How could it be that someone would be convicted three times for drunk driving, kill my child, and go scot-free?*

When we got to the restaurant, they didn't have a table ready, so we had to wait at the bar inside the restaurant until one became available. I shared what I'd found out with my friends—I was so angry and made up my mind that this acceptance of drunk driving could not continue. This man should be penalized for killing my child and the system that allowed this to happen needed to change.

My sister said, "I know you; you will do something about this!" I said, "Yes, I will. I am going to start an organization." My best friend Leslie jumped in: "And you will call it MADD—Mothers Against Drunk Drivers." (The name was later changed to Mothers Against Drunk Driving.) In that moment, I knew what I was about to do was meant to be.

* * * *

I grew up in the military, and my family moved around a lot. It was amazing—I lived in several other countries and islands, like Guam, France, and Germany, and travelled to numerous other countries such as Italy, what was then Yugoslavia, Sweden, Norway, Denmark, and more. Due to my travel and our military lifestyle I was able to have a very different life than most people. Both of my parents worked, so my sister and I learned to take care of ourselves at an early age. My mother was the first woman truck driver in the military during the war where she met and married my dad who was also in the military. My father was a real renaissance man in those days. He cooked and cleaned, and it was very much a 50/50 household.

From an early age, I was rebellious, and could never accept status quo. When I was twelve years old and in Catholic school, I decided to be a nun. When I was told I was too young, I started my own order.

I rallied five of my best girlfriends and let the nuns know what we were doing. I called it the Junior Order of the St. Vincent Pallottine nuns. We wore rosaries on our uniforms, washed out the nuns' laundry and went to mass everyday before school. We were really devout. The nuns thought it was great, and let us help out in church every morning. When I got my first kiss at thirteen in the church tower, I decided being a nun wasn't for me.

When I graduated high school, my dad got orders for Germany, and I chose to go with him. We had already been stationed in France and I loved Europe and couldn't wait to go back. I fell in "love," became pregnant, and the father refused to marry me or help in any way but I was keeping the baby, so I returned to the states. My girlfriend Mary told me about a resort in Sausalito where she had gone to have her child. She invited me to go live there with her, and off I went. When I arrived in San Francisco, a guy with long hair and robes picked me up at the airport. His name was Brother John—we got to the "resort" on the beach, and it was basically three shacks. I thought he was the clergy.

I was greeted by "Buddha," who immediately informed me that he was stoned, though it was two o'clock in the afternoon. I couldn't understand why people were getting drunk at two in the afternoon. Little did I know. Mary asked me if I had ever smoked grass—I didn't even know what drugs were, and I had no idea what was going on. I thought she meant grass from the ground and when she asked me if I dropped acid, I asked her if it burned going down your throat. The "resort" turned out to be one big commune where everyone slept together on the floor. In the end I got my own room, because they were afraid that, in my innocence, I would slip up and tell someone on the outside what was really going on.

I was really uncomfortable being there, and when I found out I was having twins, I decided to move into San Francisco to be closer to the hospital. At that time, I was receiving military care because I was still considered a dependent upon my father. Mary left with me, and we hitchhiked into San Francisco and found an apartment. I found out from the hospital there were other women in my position, "unwed mothers." This was long before it was socially acceptable to have a baby out of wedlock, and we were all called "Mrs. So and So." When I learned there were others in the same predicament, I started a support group for us with the hospital's permission. I was living on welfare, and Mary couldn't deal with the idea of my keeping the twins, so, in the middle of a day, while I was at the doctor's she took off, leaving me completely alone.

My family was in Germany, and I had no idea how I would even pay the rent. A few days after Mary left, her friend Dee Dee called, and I told her what happened. She asked me to hold on and when she came back on the line she said, "I talked to my mom—you are coming to live with us." They came and got me that night. I will always be eternally grateful to that family for taking me into their lives.

I named the twins Carime (Cari for short) and Serena, and stayed with Dee Dee's mom Dory, for about a week. Because I developed toxemia and was hospitalized for about a month before the twins were born, my father had come back to the states on emergency leave to be with me during their birth. He helped me get an apartment in Fairfield, California. When my mom returned from Germany, we moved in with her, I started junior college, worked and took care of the twins. My goal was to be on my own as quickly as possible. I managed to do that within a few months of her return.

When the twins were three, I met my ex-husband who was an officer in the Air Force. We married and he adopted them, and about a year later we had my son, Travis. In April of 1975, when Travis was four, he left a toy at a neighbor's house, and Cari took him across the street to get it. On the way back, she was holding the toy in one hand, and Travis's hand in the other, so they could safely cross. He wanted his toy; she wanted him to wait, and he broke away from her to come tell me.

Travis ran down the driveway and was hit by an unlicensed driver who was on prescription Valium. I was on the phone when it happened—all of a sudden a neighborhood boy was banging on my door, shrieking, "Travis is dead, Travis is dead—you have to come out!"

I went running outside, screaming for an ambulance. There was a doctor (psychiatrist) who was driving behind the woman who ran over Travis, and he grabbed onto me. I said, "Is he dead?" He said, "No, he's not but he is seriously hurt." The car was literally pinning Travis down by his head, with his tiny leg somehow wrapped around it.

Together, with some neighborhood kids we picked the car up off Travis's head, and Dr. Warren tended to him until the ambulance came. He'd suffered terrible head trauma, along with numerous broken bones and other injuries. The doctors told me they didn't think he would survive the surgery. I didn't believe them and I kept saying, "I know you can fix it." It was devastating, and Steve was gone on temporary duty—we were still trying to reach him so he could come home. We barely made it through each day. First, it was waiting to see if Travis would survive. Next, it was hoping he would regain consciousness. Then, it was hoping he wasn't severely brain damaged and would walk again. He had multiple surgeries, and the whole back of his skull was removed, requiring him to wear a helmet in place of the missing skull. We were really fortunate that an acrylic skull that would grow with you had just been developed, so within a year that was ultimately fused with what was left of Travis's skull. For an entire year, there was just one medical issue after another, hoping for the best, anticipating the worst and being prepared for the next crisis. I never found out why the driver who hit Travis didn't have a license.

Just six weeks after Travis was run over, my fifty-nine-year-old mother went to the hospital to have surgery for diverticulitis, and I went to see her right afterwards. She was feeling better and really looking forward to coming home. A week or so later, she had a sudden heart attack and died. I was grief-stricken. Travis was still in the hospital—I was overwhelmed with worry about him—and now about my father, who had his own heart issues, and was all alone.

Needless to say, my entire focus was my family. Cari had the hardest time, because she blamed herself for what happened to Travis. The entire neighborhood pulled together and did everything they could, including donating blood. We sued the driver and she got a ticket, but I am not sure what happened criminally because I was too involved with Travis's care to pay attention. Thankfully, Travis survived, although he had learning disabilities and ongoing health issues.

I had been unhappy in my marriage for several years, and had debated leaving my husband, Steve. Unfortunately, that was about the same time that Travis was hit and my mom died, so I decided to wait. Then, Travis had some complications during his recovery and required several more operations. It was after his last surgery when I told Steve I wanted to separate. We did try marriage counseling, but

I realized I didn't love him the way I should. It was no one's fault; I just wasn't happy. I had gone from being a child to having children, and had a strong desire to be on my own. I was already working as a Realtor, which had been put on hold for the year Travis was recovering, and I decided to continue working and raising my children. Steve moved out and I was back where I started, raising children on my own. During this time, Steve continued seeing the children and helping out, although that changed after he remarried. However, I enjoyed being single and I loved real estate. I was successful and could work around my children's activities to some degree. I honestly didn't picture myself marrying again, but continuing with my career and investing in real estate. My life was planned—raise my children, work in real estate, invest in houses, and retire at an early age, thanks to my investments. I had good friends, and although I didn't have a fabulous love life, I was frankly too busy working and raising kids to notice. I was content. Travis had survived and although he was in special classes in school due to his learning disabilities resulting from his injuries, he was doing better than the doctors had expected. The girls and I went through the normal mother-daughter issues, but they were also at the age where they argued over who was going to do my make-up and hair when I went out on a date. Life was good. We had survived a horrible trauma and the children were adjusting to the divorce.

All that changed on May 3, 1980. Cari was walking to a church carnival and was killed by a multiple repeat-offender drunk driver. You can't imagine the shock—I couldn't believe this could happen to me twice! I remember thinking, "Not again, God, how could you do this to me *again*?" It was beyond devastating, and so unbearably painful.

In order to survive, I had to take action—there was no time for grieving. I promised myself that I would fight to make Cari's senseless death count for something positive in the years ahead.

Within days of losing my child, I set out to learn about drunk driving, meeting with anyone who would see me. I was incredibly naïve. When my girlfriend, Sue, who became our biggest volunteer, asked me if I wanted to meet the attorney general, I asked her how many stars he had. I put ads in the major newspapers asking if anyone who had been the victim of a drunk driver would contact me. No response. I had no idea what I was doing, but my mission kept me going.

The pain of losing Cari was so excruciating; there were times I was completely suicidal and couldn't get out of bed. I would think about what it would be like to die and end the pain. But, because I had gone public with MADD, I had to keep going. I remember a close friend calling at one of my worst moments and saying, "When I get depressed, I clean the house and I turn on music." I got up, started vacuuming and kept going.

My naïveté turned out to be a great advantage when I started MADD—if someone said "No," it didn't even register. It was 1980—there was no Internet, so I called the National Highway Traffic Safety Administration (NHTSA) and got information about what other states were doing. NHTSA became my "google"—they put me in touch with Cindy Lamb, whose daughter Laura had been critically injured by a drunk driver. Cindy wasn't ready to start a MADD chapter, but she gave me the idea for the governor's task force on drunk driving.

That August, we held a press conference and picketed on the steps of the capital in Sacramento, calling on California Governor Jerry Brown to create a task force on the issue of drunk driving. We had

Cari's twin, Serena, all of her friends, students, and people from the attorney general's office there, all signing petitions. Hence, SADD was born. At that time, we called it Students Against Drunk Drivers, and it was launched by my daughter Serena. It was eventually picked up by other schools and MADD chapters, and it really had a life of its own.

An article with Serena and I from that press conference went out across the country, but other than that, there was literally no press. I was starting chapters with people who had children or family killed by drunk drivers, and there was no way I was giving up. I finally realized why it was such a huge challenge getting the media to take the cause seriously. Everyone drank and drove, including the media.

At that time, drinking and driving was the only socially acceptable form of homicide in our country. It was the topic of nightclub jokes and TV shows, and was promoted by movies. People literally only got slapped on the wrist when they went to court for drunk driving. And there I was, telling all these people who drank and drove that they needed to toughen up and tighten laws. I had to really learn how to strategize and be innovative to get their attention. Whenever we had a committee hearing, we had mothers come in from all over California, until eventually, the media became very supportive. Once that happened, when the legislatures played games, we would threaten them with negative media.

Supporting my family while I was doing all this was a huge challenge. I had minimal child support, and for the first eighteen months, all of the insurance money, every last dime, went into MADD. My father chipped in to help and I tried getting back into real estate—but the first time I showed a house to someone with three children who wanted three bedrooms, I broke out in tears and had to leave.

I was also starting to meet people in high places and have big meetings, and I needed to be available. I thought, "What is most important, selling houses or saving lives?" I gave up my career, and, with my dad's help we managed until the board of MADD finally agreed to give me a salary.

I surrounded myself with people who knew what they were doing, and after a while the legislature couldn't ignore us. It was a totally grassroots effort made up of a lot of angry, passionate people from every state who had no voice before MADD came along—that is eventually what turned the tide. We were changing attitudes at the same time we were changing laws. I began sitting in the courtroom when people would be tried for drunk driving—they would come in saying they couldn't pay their fine, but would be wearing expensive sneakers. We went to the judges in Sacramento, and one of them became my advocate—finally, a two-day, mandatory jail sentence was put into place for offenders. However, this came after my calling the press to complain that the judges were willing to enact a policy of mandatory two days in jail for prostitution, but not for drunk drivers. After that, we approached judges across the state to see if they if would do the same thing.

It was a matter of strategy—I was tackling California, but Governor Brown still wouldn't see me. He was very preoccupied, because tsetse flies were destroying the crops in California. I was on my way to a press conference in Washington, D.C., where Cindy Lamb and I picketed the White House. Jimmy Carter was in office, and we were calling on him to form a National Commission on drunk driving. At the press conference, a *Los Angeles Times* reporter asked me if I had met with Governor Brown. I said, "Governor Brown is more concerned with tsetse flies than he is with dying children."

Several days later, I had a meeting scheduled with appointees in Brown's office. I didn't want to go, I had come home from the Washington, D.C., picketing and press conference sick, so I decided I could just cut it short. During the meeting, one of the governor's aides suddenly came in and said, "Candy come with me—the governor wants to see you."

I went into a little room, and Jerry Brown was sitting right there. He said, "I understand you want a task force." I was going on and on about why it was so important, and he stopped me and said, "It's okay, Candy, you've got it." I started crying, and told him I took back all the nasty things I said about him.

This was only six months after Cari died, and it was a huge victory. The task force introduced bills in 1980 that were passed in 1981. Lives were being saved, and attitudes were finally changing—drinking and driving was no longer socially acceptable. Within four months of announcing MADD, we had chapters in about four states. In 1983, a movie about my life was released that brought us even more attention. By 1984, The National Minimum Drinking Age Act was passed, which introduced a federal penalty for states that didn't raise the legal drinking age to twenty-one. My daughter had not been killed in vain.

By October of 1985, I was burned out. MADD was becoming one big power struggle. The more powerful we became the more everyone wanted a piece of the pie. I was playing politics with the board more than with the politicians. Everybody wanted to get into the White House, and yet no one wanted to do the work involved, such as fundraising, etc. It was time for me to leave MADD. I found myself crying at odd times and missing Cari as much as if she had died the day before.

I came to realize that I had postponed grieving because of MADD, and, once I left, it all poured out. People who haven't experienced tragedy have no concept of the grief. Everybody thinks there are five stages to it, and that at a certain point you should be over it. I always say that there are three stages, the beginning, the middle, and the rest of your life. You can't give it a timeline because it never goes away—it is like a river; it ebbs and flows, but is always part of your life. In 1990, I co-wrote a book called *Giving Sorrow Words: How to Cope with Grief and Get On with Your Life* to share what I'd learned and dispel the myths.

Grieving is also a completely individual process—I needed to grieve on my own, but there are church groups, grief counselors and grief groups that may help someone else. There are non-profits like *CompassionateFriends.org,* and *Griefhaven.org,* where you can find help and support—the idea is to seek what is right for you by any and all means.

I try not to focus on how Cari died, and there are many times I think of her with absolute joy. She was an athletic, charming and very mature young girl. Everybody loved her, especially adults. There were over 300 people at her funeral, most of them kids. She was the one who gave advice to all her friends and she was also the biggest tattle-tale. She always told me things about her sister, such as Serena was smoking, etc. It is funny, but one of the first things I thought of as I was coming to grips with her death is, "Who will tell me what Serena is doing?" I remember once there was a boy who liked Serena, but she didn't have the heart to tell him she wasn't interested, so Cari pretended she was Serena and let him down gently. She had a wonderful sense of humor and was also a great imitator. She would imitate her teachers and others, and we would laugh and applaud her. Cari had real courage and heart. Around holidays and anniversaries, I still sometimes cry when I think about her, but more often than not, I don't, and that's a good thing. I still miss her, and I treasure the few times I still dream about her.

The press dubbed me "The Mother of Movements." I am most proud that what I achieved set an example for other people, and that numerous other causes were started because of MADD. People come to me all the time who want to make a difference. I see myself as showing them they *will* survive it and they *will* become semi-whole. When they say, "I want to do what Candy Lightner did," I am proud that they believe they can do the same thing.

I'll never forget when I first started MADD, talking to Jim Nichols, who was the head of NHTSA. He said, "Candy, if you make a dent before ten years, I will eat my hat." Three years later at a conference, I handed him a hat.

Candace Lightner is a recipient of the President's Volunteer Action Award, and she has three honorary doctorates. She has co-authored *Giving Sorrow Words: How to Cope with Grief and Get On with Your Life* and she was the subject of an Emmy-nominated television movie, entitled *Mothers Against Drunk Drivers: the Candy Lightner Story. Time* honored Ms. Lightner as one of "Seven Who Succeeded;" *Esquire* picked her as one of "America's New Leadership Class;" and *Ladies Home Journal* listed her as one of the "Top 100 Women in America." Her many other honors include: The Jefferson Award for Public Service, the President's Volunteer Action Award, the YWCA Woman of the Year Award, The Patricia Neal Courage Award from the Women's International Center, and the Film Advisory Board Award for Excellence and the Women's Center Annual Leadership Award.

Operation Beautiful

"Beauty is not in the face; beauty is a light in the heart."
—Kahil Gibran

SOUL MODEL: Caitlin Boyle

CHALLENGE: Born and raised in a city that values appearance and money above all else.

CHANGE: Start the viral Operation Beautiful Post-it note movement and wrote bestselling books; helps girls and women everywhere feel good about themselves.

SOULUTION: Everything you already need is already inside of you! Never be afraid or ashamed to reach out to someone for help, and *keep* reaching out until you get the help you need.

I grew up in Miami and lived there until I was eighteen. This had a huge influence of how I think about beauty and what it all means, because appearance is the entire focus there in a very stereotypical way. When it's hot out people don't wear a lot of clothes, and your body is completely on display.

I was always taught to do well in school. At home, there was thankfully never an emphasis on physical appearances, so being "smart" became my identity. Still, from the age of twelve or thirteen, I really struggled with depression. I went through a very dark period where I engaged in self-harming behavior, even cutting. Despite my loving parents and good grades, I still had all these feelings of "not good enough." I think I felt this way because there is so much pressure in our society to be perfect and great—especially when it comes to appearance. The media completely perpetuates that whole thing and it really stuck with me. I wasn't popular; I was average—but I wanted to be *special*.

Of course money and status were also a part of the whole self-image thing. My family didn't have that, and I couldn't magically change it. I'd meet other kids, and be reminded of this all the time when they asked what my parents did for a living. I am an only child, and my parents divorced when I was seven. They are both wonderful people—my mom always worked so hard, and she loved me unconditionally. She always saw something great in me even if I didn't see in myself. My dad had been a cyclist, but was hit by a car and suffered a head trauma, so he was out of work for most of my childhood. But in a way it was a good thing, because they were both very involved in my life.

Still, my life was just so different from the other kids I knew. They all had really successful parents and were driving Audis to high school—that was just not my world. And I think especially when you are young; it's natural to be materialistic. It's really hard when you look around and everyone has a ton of things you don't—you feel like you will never measure up. I don't want to generalize an entire city, but my experience was that status, money, and appearance were highly valuable. My perception of what was important got really messed up.

I remember being on the phone with my best guy friend at the time, telling him that my greatest fear was being mediocre. (Maybe it still *is* my greatest fear). He said, "Caitlin, you are good enough exactly the way you are!" Something about the way he said it really stuck, because he saw me for who I really was, even when I couldn't see that myself. Then he said, "You know, why not think positively for a change? It was like, *Wow, I could do that?* The idea that I controlled the way I saw the world was a foreign and interesting thought to me! Just that one phone conversation really shaped me into having a much more positive outlook about things.

It was around this same time when I figured out I was really good at writing, and this also helped my self-esteem. In Florida, you are required to take writing exams in middle school that are scored between one and six. I scored a perfect six, and that was one of the first times, I thought, *Whoa, maybe I am a good writer!* So I did all of these things you'd do if you were young and thought you were going to be a writer. I loved reading as well, especially other people's real stories, and advice columns like *Dear Abby* and *Ann Landers*. We had a converted garage, and my dad was into electronics, so we had the Internet and a computer and printer before any of my friends. I would spend a Sunday afternoon making up fake magazines, writing articles and printing them, and my dad was so encouraging. It was like the blog post of yesteryear, and I can see how I ended up doing what I do now.

I went to a great public high school that really encouraged students to push themselves and excel. I had one English teacher who got me thinking about writing as a career, and I actually earned twenty-two college credits. Slowly, I was gaining confidence in myself, and about what I could share with the world.

I spent most of high school counting the days until I could leave Miami, and, when I finally graduated, I got a scholarship to the University of Pittsburgh. This was a great boost, because of my parents' financial situation. Pittsburgh was so different from Miami—there was snow and history; people seemed so much nicer—it was a different world. I was so excited to get away from the negativity of Miami and do my own thing.

After college, I got a technical writing gig, but really began to hate my job. The market was tanking, and people were being laid off right and left. I'd walk in every Monday wondering if it would be my week to be fired, and it was so incredibly stressful. Three years into it, I decided to make a career change. I had an English writing degree, which made it hard to get a job in such a bad market; so I decided to go back to graduate school and become a physical therapist. Because I had never taken science, I had to take biology and chemistry as prerequisites. I was doing this on top of working forty hours a week and blogging on my personal blog, which was its own part-time job.

I was feeling so overwhelmed and miserable—I am not a science kind of woman and was doing really poorly at chemistry. I was taking a mid-term, and went into the bathroom with all these negative thoughts rushing in my head—like, *You are so stupid, you are going to fail. All these eighteen-year-olds at community college can figure this out, why can't you? You'll never pass Chem 1 or 2.* I was just freaking out! Finally, I just told myself, *STOP!* To this day, I don't know what made me do it, but I reached into my bag and pulled out a sheet a paper and wrote, "You are beautiful!" on it. I stuck it to the bathroom mirror, photographed it, went home, and blogged about it. I put twenty seconds of thought into the name, and asked my readers to jump in and participate—within three days I had seventy-five notes in my inbox. I didn't know what do with them, and my mom suggested I start the "Operation Beautiful" site. I didn't want to spend $10 on registering the domain name, so she offered to pay, and I launched it three days later.

I was completely unprepared for the response. I was enjoying a moderate level of success with my blog, and was very active in the blog genre. Other bloggers just kind of picked up the idea, started blogging and telling their readers about it, linking to it on Facebook and Twitter—that was the initial push. Then a friend of mine e-mailed the *Orlando Sentinel*, and they did a great article. It was so exciting! Once that story came out, the AP started republishing it in other papers across the country.

While most of the notes said, "You are beautiful," the messages were so varied and creative. One said, "Scales measure weight, not worth." Another read, "Be the change you wish to see in the world." My favorite message is, "Change the way you see, not the way you look." People post notes anywhere and everywhere you can think—on vending machines, in library books, and on treadmills, although the bathroom mirror is still the most popular.

I honestly struggled with self-doubt the entire first year the site was up. I kept thinking one day people would stop coming and sending me notes. But they didn't, and it was so amazing to see it continue, because for the first time in my life, I loved my job! Realizing that you don't have to wake up every day and hate your job was a huge turning point for me and my overall happiness. My mom had always worked so hard; her job was not ideal and she was always unhappy with the hours. I had hated my job for three full years. Now, every morning I rush to my computer; I can't get there fast enough. It is such an awesome feeling; I have definitely found my purpose and passion. I shelved the idea of going back to school because, soon enough, I realized that running Operation Beautiful was exactly what I needed to do with my life.

And Operation Beautiful was what a lot of other people needed, too. I received an e-mail from a woman who, while in treatment for an eating disorder, felt so broke and alone. Finding an Operation Beautiful note felt "like a message from God" to work to get healthier. I followed up with her six months later and was shocked to hear her describe finding the note as her turning point. I received an e-mail from a man who confessed he had stepped into the elevator to get onto the roof of the building—he was planning to jump off! The only thing that stopped him, he relayed, was a cheerful note stuck to the inside of the elevator door. "I felt like someone, somewhere, cared," he wrote. A woman found a note in a courthouse bathroom, and she described it as "the only reason" she pressed charges against her abusive husband. The notes kept coming. The stories kept coming. Lives were being changed—all because of simple Post-it notes.

With stories like this, I don't think of Operation Beautiful as "my" book or "my" site. It is a much bigger, community effort. What's amazing is how great it's been for me, because I have become so much nicer to myself—whenever I have negative thoughts the "OB mentality" kicks right in. It has been incredible to hear stories from people who have found or posted notes and how it has affected them.

My favorite story is from a teenager in Canada who was in a treatment center for severe anorexia. Her doctors were concerned it was going to eventually kill her. She slipped into the bathroom to throw up her lunch and found an Operation Beautiful note on the stall. The simple message—"You are good enough the way you are"—made her pause and reconsider her destructive behavior. She followed up with me a few months later and said she was out of the hospital and healthier than ever. She knew a stranger posted the note, but she felt like the timing was a message from God.

Operation Beautiful has restored my faith in humanity. So many people think others don't care and people are mean; that high school girls are catty and middle school girls are bitchy—but that's just a stereotype. Running the site and hearing from so many people has restored my faith that people are kind—they *want* to help themselves and help others. The idea that someone would do this for a stranger is the biggest eye-opener about how good people are, and is so uplifting. People purposely place these notes in locations where negative self-talk often occurs, like the bathroom mirror, the scale, or the changing room at the gym. The problem is that there is so much of negative messaging in our society, and the issues start young—the average girl goes on her first diet when she's eight years old! The biggest mistake we make is beating ourselves up for not looking like models or celebrities. It's time we stop emulating or striving for a type of perfection that doesn't even exist in the real world, and not take in this negative messaging from the media. It's okay to look like a human!

It's also important to remember that the goal for our bodies is *health*, not size or weight, and that is different for different people.

Eat healthy foods and enjoy treats in moderation. Find something active that *you* like to do and regularly incorporate it into your life for pleasure, not because you feel like you 'have' to do it. And remember: You are beautiful, exactly the way you are!

Caitlin Boyle is the author of *Operation Beautiful: Transforming the Way You See Yourself One Post-it Note at a Time* and *Operation Beautiful: Changing the World One Post-it Note at a Time*. She has been featured in *Glamour, Fitness, Women's Day*, FIRST, and on the *Today* show. The book includes 125 incredible notes and stories, as well as tips on how to lead a happier and healthier life. She lives in North Carolina with her husband, son Henry, and two dogs. Her blog, *HealthyTippingPoint.com* documents her life as she strives to maintain health and balance while inspiring others to do the same.

Play It Forward

"Over the years I've learned that some of the best poems don't rhyme, and many great stories don't have a clear beginning, middle, or end. Life is about embracing change. It's about taking a moment and making the best of it without knowing what's going to happen next."

—Unknown

SOUL MODEL: Marcus Mitchell

CHALLENGE: Made a promise to his dying wife to "pay it forward" on her behalf for the rest of his life.

CHANGE: Has given away half of his winnings from the craps tables, amounting to tens of thousands of dollars since 2009. Uses the other half of earnings to support his son and the foundation he created in honor of his wife.

SOULUTION: Show the world all the good you can do *while* enduring your own grief. No matter what is going on in your life, no matter how bad it is, do good in the world, and it will come back in some amazing way shape and form.

In 2007, I was married to the love of my life, and we were thrilled to be expecting a son. When Noah was eighteen months old, my wife passed away from stomach cancer. Sometimes, things don't work out like you expected. Still, I have been truly blessed by the love and support I received while she was alive and after she passed. Now, in her honor, I want others to feel the kindness and joy I experienced.

All I ever wanted was a "real" family. I grew up in Maryland and was very close to my mother and older sister, but I never knew my father. I was lucky to get a ton of male love and attention from my mother's two brothers, Uncle Junior and Uncle Charles, who lived in another state, but I always knew if I had my own kids I wanted to be around for them all the time.

I have great childhood memories. My mom worked for the CIA, so there was always a steady income. She and my grandmother were heavily into prayer, and they took me to church on a regular basis. Sometimes they would spend the whole day going through Bible verses, and I would sit down and listen—it fascinated me, and I wanted to learn more. As I got older, I developed my own relationship with God and didn't think I had to go to church every Sunday to connect. I thought that as long as I lived the right way, I could still have that connection. I always dreamed of being a dad, having a house, a bunch of kids, and those "sit down dinners," which I'd seen on television and at friends' houses. I remember thinking, "If I could have that, I would be totally happy."

I was always doing different creative things, like inventing board games that I would draw on the inside tops of shoe boxes. In fifth grade, my friend brought dice to school, and we'd play craps at recess. We'd play for things like toy cars or other small toys, and the fun we had always stuck with me.

Uncle Junior was a doctor in California, and every summer I would visit him. He taught me responsibility—by the time I turned fifteen, I was shadowing him at work, pulling charts, taking temperatures and blood pressures for his patients. His trust meant so much to me. On our drives home, he would explain that some of his patients couldn't afford treatment and he didn't charge them—that really inspired compassion in me.

As I got older, I noticed that a lot of the patients felt sad. I would try to cheer them up, telling them about my life, what I was learning, how I enjoyed being there, and how I wished they would get well. Because they were so used to not having anyone really talk and listen to them, they loved that I gave them my time. When I returned to Maryland, I always checked in with my uncle and asked about everyone. Even when they passed away, I was happy to know that I had brightened their days.

After high school, I started training with the CIA while going to junior college for basic studies. I went on to attend a technical school to become a computer specialist, because that knowledge supported my work at the agency. I always remembered how much I loved playing craps. Since Maryland is less than a three hour drive from Atlantic City, I headed there when I was twenty-one and was re-introduced to playing. I would go on my time off, and really listen to older players about how to play. Before long, I started winning $100 here and there. I remember thinking, "This is something I can do part time and pay little bills." I was always fortunate enough to win more than I lost, and to know when to walk away.

After about five years working for the CIA as a trainer for agents, I married a woman I had known only for a few months. We had a daughter, and after just two and a half years, it all fell apart. Maybe it was too fast or too much too soon; we were both very naïve and had a lot of outside interference in the relationship from friends, which I think was a big part of why we couldn't make it.

When I was twenty-seven, the CIA wanted to send me overseas. That wasn't really in line with raising a family, and I felt like my time there was done. I decided to move to Las Vegas and be with my mother. There were difficulties with my ex, and I resigned myself to thinking I'd have vacations and summer visits with my daughter and at least be able to talk to her on the phone, but that didn't happen. I did everything I possibly could to stay connected, sending support, clothes and money. But for years, my ex kept moving around and disappearing. When there was no forwarding address, there was nothing I could do. I documented everything and saved all the receipts so someday I could show my daughter. It was killing me not to see her—I prayed on it for a long time, and eventually I had to let go and give it to God.

I found a short-term job in a warehouse in Vegas as a material handler, scanning in returns from big stores. Then I met Yanira, a beautiful woman who was working there in quality assurance. She was from El Savador and one of the most amazing women I had ever laid eyes on. She was kind and beautiful in a million ways, especially with people of all races and cultures. She was bilingual, and everyone loved her because she was always courteous and took the time to listen. Because of her, I couldn't leave the job at the warehouse. It took me seven months to get up the nerve to introduce myself. We started dating, and it wasn't long before we decided to live together. From the beginning, I told her the whole story about my daughter—it made her so sad, and she was 100 percent supportive.

Whenever we wanted something extra, or I wanted to spoil Yanira, I would play craps. I always won comps to shows, beautiful rooms or some spare cash that helped on top of our salaries at the warehouse. We wanted a family, and after about five years, Yanira finally got pregnant. We were so excited—when we found out the baby was a boy, we settled on "Noah."

Throughout her pregnancy, Yanira complained of stomach pain and a feeling of "fullness," but the doctors blamed it on being pregnant. It wasn't until after Noah was born and the symptoms remained that Yanira's doctor paid attention. When Noah was three months old, the doctor ordered an endoscopy. During the procedure, he saw internal bleeding and did a biopsy, letting us know that the results would take two weeks. He said he'd found "linitis plastica," but downplayed the whole thing, and never said the word "cancer." We left the appointment thinking it was an ulcer or something, and Yanira could take medicine and be better. We headed for my mom's house, and while she and Yanira were talking, I went into another room and googled "linitis plastica." I found out it was stomach cancer and was terrified—but because I didn't want to scare Yanira and my mom, I told them what I'd read, but didn't elaborate. They got very quiet, and tried to make light of it, saying, "You can't believe everything you read online." But the statistics were there, and I knew our lives would be changing drastically.

We tried to keep our spirits high while we waited for the biopsy results. When we went to the doctor he confirmed our fears. His words, "You've got stomach cancer," still ring in my ears. He told us it was very aggressive and they would "do the best they could." We tried to hold it together while we were in his office, but once we got into the parking lot, we both broke down. We still didn't understand how serious it was, and would have to wait another few weeks to have a CAT scan, which would show how much the cancer had spread.

Noah was just a few months old, and my mother was helping take care of him. We had to continue working so we could keep our benefits, but Yanira was losing blood through her stools, which had been happening since her pregnancy. She was a strong woman, but getting weaker and weaker. One day as she was walking up the stairs at the warehouse, she said she felt like her heart was about to jump out of her chest. She insisted on staying at work to get the overtime, but the next morning I took her to the emergency room. After examining her, they said her hemoglobin was only 2.5 and that she should have been dead. The doctors immediately started a blood transfusion and authorized a CAT scan, which confirmed that she was at the end of Stage 4 stomach cancer. They told us that Yanira had about six months to live. There was nothing more they could do, and simply said, "It's too late."

We cried and cried. I told my mother, and she got on the phone with Uncle Junior. He found a doctor in California who had some success removing the stomach of cancer patients. We felt like there could be some hope, but we had to get to California. Our co-workers heard what was happening and came to see us in the hospital. They brought a card and a large jar filled with money. The jar was filled with almost $1,000—we couldn't believe it! We had health insurance through our jobs, but were forced to take out cash advances on credit cards to cover the rest of the costs. Because we still had all of our other bills to pay, the cash advances didn't get us very far.

Once we got to California, the goal was to shrink Yanira's tumor so it was safe to operate. After about two months, the tumor had shrunk down to where they felt comfortable removing it. During her first chemo treatment, I kept praying, asking God, "What do you want me to do, what good can we make out of this?" I "felt" the answer—it was helping others with stomach cancer. I shared the idea with Yanira, and we were excited for her to be well enough so we could start making a difference.

It was August 2007, and I was traveling back and forth between California and Vegas every week. I needed to keep my benefits, so I switched to three twelve-hour weekend shifts so I could spend weekdays in California with Yanira. We were completely broke, and started falling behind on our car payments and credit card bills. It was devastating, and I didn't have the time or an ounce of strength to go shoot craps. Thankfully, our co-workers continued their kindness. They would host raffles, and when I would show up to work they would give me anywhere between one hundred and three hundred dollars, apologizing that it wasn't more. One hundred dollars was the world to us at that point, and somehow, we always made it through.

So many people showed us kindness. Between traveling, working, caring for Yanira and trying to spend time with Noah, I wasn't getting much sleep. My supervisor allowed me to go into the office and get rest. He knew I needed the pay and ensured I was able to keep my job. This was remarkable, because he and his wife had a daughter who had been born blind and was autistic, but he still kept helping us.

Then there was a man at the airport parking lot in Los Angeles. Because I was there every week, he remembered me. One time I didn't even have the seven dollars to get my car out of the lot, and I just broke down. He said, "It's okay, I know you come through here all the time and you always look like you have something on your mind. Go ahead and pay me next time—if you don't, that's okay too."

All of those acts of kindness helped us keep the faith. I would pray to God before bed, saying, "I'm lost, I need your guidance," and wake up with the answers. Sometimes it was a decision we needed to make or a medical question about something I'd never heard of. I'd get up in the morning and know exactly what to ask the doctors, where to look for the information—all things I had no clue about the night before. It was like the knowledge was put in my head when I slept. I always felt that God heard my prayers, and I kept believing.

After two months in the hospital, the doctors removed Yanira's stomach and spleen in a ten-hour long surgery. They told us they removed every visible sign of cancer. They said if she could stay cancer-free for five years, her chances of survival would be good. It was October, and we had real hope—we were so grateful, and kept talking about the organization we would start to help others with stomach cancer, once she was better.

Yanira stayed in the hospital until December, and we went back home to Vegas right before Christmas. In February, we returned to California for follow-up scans, which showed that everything looked good—that felt like a miracle. In March, Yanira returned to work. No one could believe it! Then, just two months later she began having sharp pains in her back and side. We went back to California, and the doctor operated to see what was going on. The cancer had returned with a vengeance—even with no stomach, it was everywhere. The doctor told me that Yanira had about two months to live.

Yanira took it better than I thought, like it was no big deal. She said, "I know you did everything you could, we always knew this was a possibility, and you just need to start preparing. It's all in your hands, and I trust you." She wanted me to move forward, be happy and not let this end my quest for a family. She said, "That is why I wanted to give you Noah—you will always have a piece of me; he is my gift to you." She still wanted me to start the foundation. "It doesn't have to be big, Marcus. Promise me you will remember our struggles and, despite what happens to me, you will help whoever you can." I didn't respond to her then, I just listened.

Three months later, we went back to Las Vegas. Everything was going downhill quickly, and Yanira's organs began shutting down one by one. On August 18th, she woke up and nothing was relieving her pain. I knew if we went to the hospital, she wasn't coming out. We had always wanted a big wedding, and now there was no time to do anything but get married in the courthouse. Every second mattered—I filled out the paperwork ahead of time so we wouldn't have to wait in line, and when we got there, we jumped ahead of about forty people. We got married, and went straight to Sunrise Hospital for our "honeymoon." It was that night in the hospital that I promised Yanira I would dedicate my life to helping other people.

On September 6th, Yanira died. Of all the men God could have put in her life, he chose me, because he knew I would be there until the end and help her.

****

I took Yanira's death very hard. I was fading away, and resigned from my job after the funeral. I couldn't be at the warehouse—everywhere I turned, all I could think about was Yanira. Noah was eighteen months old, the housing market crashed, and the two of us moved in with my mother. I went to a doctor who put me on anti-depressants and anxiety medication. I hated the feeling of the medicine, because it made me numb to the world. I started sleeping twenty-three hours a day, only leaving my bed to eat and drink water.

One day when I got up for food and was walking down the stairs, I "saw" Yanira, sitting on a step with my grandmother. I sat down next to them, and could feel a beautiful warmth and energy, like nothing else mattered in the world. Yanira asked me, "What are you doing? This is not what I wanted you to be. You need to bond with your son. Go do all those things you promised you would do!" I told her I missed and loved her, that I wanted to go with her. Something told me if I kept saying that, she would fade away. A few minutes later, she was gone, and I knew what I had to do.

It had been about four months since she died, and I weaned myself off all the medication. After a few weeks, I started to feel a little like myself. It was time to start reconnecting with Noah, time for him to see me every day and be in his life. My sadness was still there, but I was able to handle it. I was alert and grateful; somehow I knew everything would be ok.

* * * *

December 4th was my birthday, and I forced myself to go out. I had some old casino comps from before Yanira got sick. One of them was being able to see the first *Twilight* movie in a private VIP booth, so I went. I was looking through the one-way glass thinking, *I could bring people in here with me, but instead I am sitting here all alone.* That's when I started thinking of this whole "pay it forward" idea.

I knew I wanted to start giving away the rest of the old comps I had before they expired. I thought if I started a Twitter account, I could let people know about all the stuff I had to give away. In April 2009, @GuyNSinCity was born. Everyone thought I was crazy. My first "pay it forward" idea was to buy pizzas for everyone in the hotel casinos. I worked it out with Villa Pizza in Santa Fe Station Hotel to keep the pizzas hot while I gave them away. I tweeted out that I was going to give away twenty pizzas and all you had to do was come by—no one showed up! I began offering them to total strangers in the casino. I told them all to enjoy the pizzas and "pay it forward" in their own way. It took a while for the online world to realize I was the "real deal," but as those who received my "pay it forward" acts tweeted what I was doing, my following began to grow.

I starting playing craps again, building up new comps. I only played with what I could afford to lose, which wasn't much, and always gave away half of my winnings. At that point, I was really just doing it to clear my head. Slowly, I began to pay off some doctor bills and debt. In less than a year, I had 2,000 followers on my Twitter account. The dollar amounts I gave away varied, but it was always half of what I won. If it was $1,000, I would keep $500 and use the other half to buy gift cards, show tickets and hotel rooms to give away.

Even with the "pay it forward" acts I knew I had not upheld my promise to Yanira. It was November 2010, and I had terrible chest pains the entire day. At one point, I lay down on the floor, trying to relax. I can't explain it, but I felt like I was dead. The pain disappeared, and I only felt peace. I saw Yanira again, but she wasn't happy. She told me she was going to take me before God. She led me into a white room with nothing in it, except a guy from my childhood who

I had barely known. Growing up, I had always been amazed by him because he could do the coolest tricks on his bicycle. He was older now and somehow, the "image" of God. I was shocked—I thought, *YOU? You aren't what God is supposed to look like!* As weird as it was, I was comforted. He asked, "Marcus, did you do everything you wanted to do?" I started crying and dropped to my knees.

I told him I wanted to do more for stomach cancer and had run into financial problems. I was taking care of Noah, and trying to keep it up with the "pay it forward" stuff, but it wasn't working. He nodded, and said he understood. I was still crying, saying that now it was too late because I was dead. He walked passed me, touched me on the shoulder and said, "You are going back."

Suddenly, I was awake on the floor, coughing and gasping for air. My heart was racing and my face was covered in tears. God had lit a fire under me. Within days, I was online figuring out how to form an LLC on Legal Zoom using express service. Within two weeks, I incorporated the Stomach Cancer Relief Network, and a week later, I set up an office to provide one-time grants to people suffering from stomach cancer and their caregivers. I started doing school fundraisers, finding sponsors to donate pizzas to the classes who raised the most money. I was printing flyers so kids could take home the information and share it with their parents—I was finally keeping my promise. More and more help started showing up, and somehow I was always able to keep up with the expenses.

By January of 2010, I had my first event, which brought in about fifty people. I would play craps and win enough to pay for the venue, food, and prizes so people would come, get to know me and learn about my cause. Somehow, the money would always come back to me. I didn't believe it at first, I really had to pray—I kept asking God, "Am I supposed to really give back *half* of everything?" He told me if I did exactly what he said, I would be continually taken care of, and I have been.

I know it sounds crazy to say I feel guided by God to play craps, but that's how it is. Some days I wake up and just know it's a going to be a good day; other times I even know which casino I should play in. If I need a few thousand dollars to put on a good event because I don't have sponsors, I think, "If I get this money, I can help people." Usually, it only takes one or two trips to the casino.

Since 2009, I have given away about $10,000 a year from my winnings at the craps tables and thousands more in casino comps. I've never really kept track but I do know that our foundation has probably helped 100 people with stomach cancer. Sometimes I make donations for research. I still love doing my "pay it forward" acts, because I get so much more out of it than the people I give to. The expression on their faces is therapy for my soul! They just light up, especially the ones who are really down and out. I always ask God to have me cross paths with those who need the most help, and it never fails. I will be out, and literally "feel" the energy that a specific person deserves a little more kindness. They come from all walks of life. Even if they seem like they "have everything," I know that God wants me to help them. I know that if I do, I've just changed their view of humanity and now they might "pay it forward" to someone else. You just never know the ripple effect you are creating.

I still communicate with God through prayer, either before bed when everything is quiet or through meditation. I just ask questions, and his voice comes to me in my head. I am in awe that what I hear is coming from a higher source, that someone is really listening and answering my prayers.

Finally, my life feels complete. My sixteen-year-old daughter reached out to me recently because she felt something was missing from her life. I told her everything I could about what happened in her childhood. I know Yanira is at peace and very proud that I am doing what we both envisioned. She is with me in my heart, proud that I am raising our son the right way, teaching him to be kind to everyone, that we are all equal, and here to help each other.

Everybody goes through different kinds of stress and grief in their lives. My "soulution" is to show the world all the good you can do *while* enduring your own grief, because you can still have a positive impact. No matter what's going on, no matter how bad you have it, if you do good out there in whatever way is right for you, it will come back. You can still be who you were before the bad times—that makes you the special person you are.

If I can inspire people and give them hope through my story, that is another "win." If I can get one more person to pray, I've just brought someone closer to God. Even if you secretly don't believe in any of it, what is there to lose in trying?

> **Marcus Mitchell** has been spreading kindness through Las Vegas trips, show tickets, and gift cards to strangers around the world since 2009. He brings Noah on his "pay it forward" adventures and has no intention of stopping.

Everyone Needs Magic

"I try to help people realize their dreams by using magic to tell stories that educate, move and inspire."

—David Copperfield

SOUL MODEL: David Copperfield

CHALLENGE: Realizing his dream of being a magician despite hardships and parental pressure to pursue a career outside of entertainment.

CHANGE: Became World's Greatest Illusionist; founded Project Magic, where teams of magicians and occupational therapists work together to teach sleight of hand magic to physically challenged patients to aid in their rehabilitation. Project Magic is currently used in 1,000 hospitals in thirty countries worldwide.

SOULUTION: Go beyond your own personal capabilities and use these three words: passion, preparation and persistence. Be passionate for something, be really prepared for it, and then be persistent about achieving it—and never give up!

My grandfather taught me my first magic when I was five. It was a simple card trick that I still include in my shows today, and I was instantly hooked.

Like every kid, I was searching for something special, and went through the same things all kids do, like playing on the soccer or baseball team. As the only child of a family growing up in New Jersey, I was continually looking for ways to be accepted and interact with people.

When I discovered magic, it was something that came easily to me and made me feel good about myself. I was shy, and magic was something to share—it was my way of communicating with people.

Because there weren't many other kids around our apartment complex, I watched a lot of television. I was inspired by Paul Winchell, who was a brilliant ventriloquist at the time. Watching his television show made me want to do ventriloquism. I put together a little act and spent time entertaining the adults in the community with my ventriloquist dummy.

At one point, I went looking for a better puppet, so I went to Macy's magic counter. A demonstrator was there who made a masterpiece out of the effect where the coin vanishes on a little wooden board, as well as other classics, like "Cups & Balls" and "Professor's Nightmare." He made his living pitching magic, and he was really skilled.

That little wooden board at Macy's was probably the first magic I bought. On a trip into New York City, I remember looking through the New York phone book for a magic store, and I found Louis Tannen Magic. I went there, the elevator door opened, and I knew my life was changing. Everyone knows that feeling, like you've walked into heaven. I walked in and just went, "This is it!"

Tannen's was a landmark institution for professional magicians, and it became the center of my world. Each week I could offer the adults and kids around me a new reason to look at my performance in wonder. I remember one trip when the store manager tried to discourage me from buying the magic cane because he thought it was beyond my skill level. I bought it anyway, and went home and practiced it until it was perfect. I returned the next week and showed him the act. Negative reinforcement was always a motivator for me to spend extra time preparing and mastering a skill.

When I was in fifth grade, my music teacher asked me to host the talent show. That was a really huge thing, because I wasn't doing magic, I was doing ventriloquism. I was very nervous, but got through it. When I returned to the classroom, all the kids who had never paid any attention to me were cheering and applauding. It was a new revelation for me—I felt important. That was the beginning of all of it, and what motivated me to keep dreaming. My parents were totally for it at the time; it was a good hobby and kept me off the streets.

Eventually, the store manager at Tannen's had business cards printed with my new stage name . . . "Davino, Boy Magician." I was just twelve, but I began booking small parties, local events, charities and performing in old folks homes. I just wanted to share the magic, and would go any place where people would watch. That same year, I was the youngest person to gain admission into the Society of American Magicians.

It was about that time that I had my first illusion involving one of the old Flair pens published in the Tarbell Magic book, which was called Mento-pen. By then, I was truly embracing my passion. Both my parents were supportive, but they still had hopes I would move on from it as I grew older. My mother wanted me to have the stability of a non-entertainment career, like my dad, who ran a clothing shop. He'd been accepted to the American Academy of Dramatic Arts before my parents were married, and my mother did not want to live a life of uncertainty. In many ways, she was projecting the same thing on me, really out of love.

That negative reinforcement for my type of personality really helped; I used it to work harder and tell myself I could do it—I'm really thankful she was that way; it was a totally positive thing. My father supported me 100 percent. When I announced I wasn't going to college, they were both a little disappointed, but I had to follow my dream.

I really loved the theater and Broadway. I modeled myself after the film directors I admired, and developed my own form of storytelling through magic. Magic had not been approached that way before, and I dreamt of a career with magic where I could do something that had never been done. When I was seventeen, I ran an ad in *Variety* as a magician/actor. A producer saw the ad and told me he wanted me to audition for a show in Chicago called *The Magic Man*. I had taken very few acting classes, so I knew I needed to practice. I went over to Juilliard in New York City. I knew no one, and walked the halls until I found someone practicing the piano. I said, "I'm about to audition in an hour for a musical comedy and I have to sing—would you practice with me for a half hour?" She said, "Yes!" She practiced singing with me, and an hour later I was in the Schubert Theatre in New York. I got on stage, did my first audition for a show, and got the job. Whoever she was, she had a lot of compassion for me, and helped me in a moment when I really needed help.

The part in *Magic Man* made me a local celebrity in Chicago. The show ran eight months and became the longest running show in Chicago. I thought I had "made it," but when I returned to New York I didn't get more parts in shows, and my father had to help pay my bills.

A few months later, Tannen's Magic Shop had an annual show. A man named Tony Spina suggested I headline, but Mr. Tannen, the founder, was worried I would not be able to carry the show. Fifteen hundred magicians would be watching my every move to discredit me if I made one mistake. I practiced hard, and after the show, everyone jumped to their feet in a standing ovation. I felt that same sense of accomplishment and warmth I felt back in the fifth grade.

That show opened the door for television. I pitched the show as taking magic as an art form and combining it with storytelling and the inspiration that I got from the movies. The producers loved it, and *The Magic of ABC* came to life. I was just twenty years old, but the network was open to my ideas of incorporating theater and continuous camera shots, proving to viewers that the illusions were real. We unified magic with themes from classical dramas and musicals. I was able to bring together the two things I love ... theater and magic.

I spent the next twenty-three years touring around the world performing illusions like making the Statue of Liberty disappear, walking through the Great Wall of China and floating across the Grand Canyon, while perfecting other illusions before landing in Las Vegas in 2000 for my show at the MGM Grand Hotel & Casino.

To this day I have three or four techniques for each illusion to ensure if someone gets close to figuring out the technique I can keep the illusion in the act. Having three or four techniques gives me the chance to change the illusion if something goes wrong, or if someone figures it out.

Years ago, when I was visiting Turkey, a man figured out one technique, and it was all over the Turkish media. I still had more shows to do, and I knew everyone would be watching, waiting to be disappointed. I kept the illusion and changed the technique. You could see the skepticism in the audience until I performed the magic—they could see it was not done the way they thought it would be, and they were in complete awe—there was thunderous applause. They got to keep the magic and wonder that night.

I have always enjoyed performing in hospitals or for people with special needs, but as my career grew I wanted to do something more. I thought about my Uncle Morty, who used to drive me to my magic shows when I was a kid. He was very positive and never had a mean thing to say about anyone. Later in life, he developed multiple sclerosis and was wheelchair bound. His illness really made me appreciate all the blessings I had been given and inspired me to do even more for people in need.

In 1982, I founded Project Magic to help children, as well as adults, overcome disabilities. I remember how magic helped me in my own childhood. I wasn't physically challenged, but I used magic to learn to communicate. It was therapeutic for me, and I wanted to share that.

When I first presented the possibilities of using magic as therapy to a group of therapists and doctors, they were entertained, but unconvinced that it would work. Julie DeJean, who heads up Project Magic, was my first contact in the rehab world twenty years ago—she saw the possibilities.

The program builds confidence and self-esteem by using sleight of hand (techniques used in performing magic) to help children and adults regain their manual dexterity. Physical rehab is very hard work, but as people learn magic, they can get through tasks that may otherwise seem painful, intimidating or in which they've simply lost interest.

Magic can engage and motivate continually. With most therapies, there is a limited number of times you can get people to continue practicing a routine task, like zipping a zipper or getting a button through a buttonhole. But with magic, it takes repetition to master the skill, and it is entertaining, which is another draw. Kids get to entertain their friends and family, and older adults like to show their grandkids something special. Many of the patients practice endlessly, and that translates to better and faster results.

Project Magic also improves every disability—it works for kids, adults, drug rehab, memory, planning, fine and gross motor skills—all of it. Even many of the most severely disabled can learn magic. "Mind reading" magic is popular with extreme physical challenges—it's something they can do that astounds their fully mobile friends.

I am in the "creating wonder business." I dreamed of doing something with magic that had not been done before. The most important part of doing anything is to have the passion and to believe in it. Each illusion can easily take two years to perfect, but the joy it brings to the audience, and the joy my staff has in watching the audience, makes it all worthwhile. People need to be amazed and transported. I can walk through the Great Wall of China, or make the Statue of Liberty disappear, but the real magic is in the people's faces. When I watch people feel that every night on stage, I know the hard work is worthwhile. For me, the best part is when people come to the show, and are inspired to do important things in their lives. Motivating them even in a small way is more rewarding then any standing ovation or award. Giving back in this way is especially life-affirming.

As my career has grown, so has my passion for my work. It is not just about entertaining—it is about showing audiences the possibilities that exist. I call my show "Live the Impossible." That whole message is important—helping people realize that what's impossible today will be possible tomorrow. No matter how successful or unsuccessful you are, everyone has issues. You struggle through them, and they resolve themselves with time. Every day there are obstacles and challenges no matter what you have or who you know . . . it's just a fact. My best advice is to just . . . get out of bed and keep moving forward.

We need to encourage people with dreams, mentor them and make sure they continue. My secret is these three words—passion, preparation and persistence—not just for magic, for everything. Be passionate about something, be really prepared for it, and then be persistent. Start small, take baby steps—little actions mean a lot. You can change the world, one person at a time.

David Copperfield has made the Statue of Liberty vanish, walked through the Great Wall of China, and flown through the air. He has set eleven Guinness World Records, received twenty-one Emmy Awards, holds the record for the most Broadway tickets sold in a week and is the highest grossing solo entertainer of all time. He is the first living magician ever to receive a star on the Hollywood Walk of Fame.

Love Means Making Something Grow

"I wouldn't trade my autism for anything in the world."

—Temple Grandin

SOUL MODEL: Temple Grandin

CHALLENGE: Born with autism in the 1950s; teased relentlessly all through childhood, passionate about an industry that was highly prejudiced against women.

CHANGE: Became an activist, Ph.D., professor, and noted lecturer on behalf of both autism and animal behavior. Pioneered a system for cattle slaughtering that helps over five million cattle per year die humanely.

SOULUTION: If the things that you do, no matter how big or small, make the world a better place, that's enough. Like someone that works in a convenience store, just being nice to the customers when they come in—that's purpose!

I grew up in the '50s and '60s. In those days they didn't tell you anything was wrong, so I didn't know I was different than other kids. I was at the higher end of the autism spectrum, but I was more severe than what you'd now call a mild Asperger's type, because I didn't speak until I was four, and I had a whole lot of other symptoms like tantrums, spinning, and rocking. The doctors wanted to put me in an institution, but my mother wouldn't have it. She insisted on keeping me in normal schools all through my childhood, to make sure I was socialized in the real world. I was good at doing projects, and other kids really liked doing those with me. I remember making things that were fun, like caveman tools or building a tree house. Autistic children need to be shown interesting stuff all the time, and I was lucky because I had that.

Back then, kids were also taught much more responsibility. They had paper routes, they shoveled snow, they worked on a farm, or in their dad's store. Mother was always pushing me; it was her idea when I was thirteen to get a job hemming clothes for a woman who did sewing out of her house. I was very good at this because it was quiet, and there was not a lot of stimulation. By the time I was fifteen, I was taking care of nine horses. I had to be responsible—if I didn't feed them, that would have been a huge thing because they would have been hungry, and I knew that.

Puberty and my teenage years were absolutely the worst part of my life. Boys, teenage girls—I didn't understand them at all. They were like people from another planet; they teased me all the time, laughing and calling me names—it was just terrible, and I was constantly having awful anxiety and panic attacks. In the ninth grade, I got kicked out from the all-girls' school I was in, because I threw a book at a girl who was making fun of me. At that point, mother sent me away to a special school for gifted children with emotional problems. I got in a fistfight there over teasing too, but something happened and after that, and I switched from hitting to crying.

The summer I was sixteen, mother sent me to my aunt's cattle ranch in Arizona. I was absolutely terrified to go, but she didn't give me a choice other than to "go for two weeks or the whole summer." This ended up being the best thing that ever happened to me. By the second day I was there I was making horse bridles. I was so happy because I knew I was doing something real that other people appreciated. I saw lots of things around the ranch that needed to be fixed and my aunt encouraged me to do all of them. For example, every time we went to town for supplies, I thought it was so stupid that we had to get out of the car and open and close the gate. So I made it my mission to figure out a lever system that if you pulled on it from the car, the gate would open and you'd have exactly forty-seven seconds to drive through. We called that the "magic gate."

The ranch was also where I got the idea for what I called "the hug or squeeze machine." A lot of autistic people don't like being touched, and I was one of them. I wanted the nice feeling of being hugged but the stimulation was too overwhelming. One day I was watching the cattle get vaccinated in a squeeze chute that immobilized them by applying pressure to both sides of their bodies. I saw how this made them relax, and I made a connection: maybe something like that would help me. So one day I talked my aunt into letting me try it, and when I climbed in, it completely calmed me down and really helped my anxiety. I was a different person when I came out of that machine, and I was able to be more social. So my aunt let me make one for myself, and I used it for a good part of my life.

When I got into high school, I didn't want to study; I wanted to hang around and take care of horses. My professor, Mr. Carlock changed my attitude. He was a huge mentor because he understood that I think creatively, and he was willing to work with that. I think in pictures—words on a page don't mean anything to me until I convert them to pictures. Not every autistic person is like this; some think in patterns or mathematically. My brain is like an Internet search engine, and my thoughts are like a series of Google images. As I load more and more information into the database, I can look up the images and read the pages and find the information I need. I can also see things I am engineering in my head from all different angles. I can walk through something, walk around it, or fly over it like an airplane.

I didn't know everyone didn't think this way until many years later, but Mr. Carlock understood way back then that my thinking had great potential. He knew I had the goal of becoming a scientist, so he gave me projects that stimulated my brain, turned me on academically and challenged me. I was fixated on finding the answers, which made the other kids tease me even more because I was so obsessed about it. I would get terribly frustrated, but I just refused to give up until I had solved something.

When I got to college, I did my master's thesis on cattle handling, including feed lots and the behavior of cattle in different types of squeeze chutes. A lot of my professors thought this was ridiculous, which just made me push harder to prove that I wasn't stupid. The work I did back then ended up being very important and impressive! Having autism made it easy for me to figure out how cattle think, because they reacted to a lot of the same things I did, like bright lights and loud noises. So I just observed them all the time to do my research. I would get down on the ground like them and spot something that I knew would scare them, like a hanging chain, or a piece of clothing someone left over the fence, and I would get rid of it. People thought I was just crazy, but I didn't see any reason the cattle should be scared and poked and prodded all the time when you could get them to just walk calmly.

It was also very sexist in the feed yards back then, and they didn't want women hanging around. One time when I got in my vehicle to leave, the men at the feed yard had completely covered the whole thing in bull testicles because they didn't want me to come back. They thought that would get rid of me, but it didn't work. Instead, I headed over to a cattle auction and chased after the owner of the *Arizona Farmer Ranchman* magazine so I could convince him to let me write for them. I knew if they hired me, I would get a press pass and the feed yard would have to let me back in. I got my revenge because it worked! Once my research was published, I earned everyone's respect, which really helped my confidence. The ranchmen all knew that if Temple Grandin wrote the article, it was accurate, and I never had a problem again.

People always ask me if there was any single turning point in my life where I knew I was going to make a big difference, and there really wasn't. There were many events that were super important, especially understanding how my thinking was different. When I saw cattle being slaughtered, it made me think about the relationship we have with animals, and everything they do for us—we depend on them for so much, and they deserve to be treated humanely. It also made me look at my own mortality, and that motivated me even more to make sure my life had a real purpose. All the teasing, the people who thought my ideas were crazy—none of it really mattered—what mattered was doing the right thing.

In the 1980s when my first book, *Emergence* was published, I realized that part of my life's work should be helping other people with autism. I wanted to learn about other autistic people to give me context, and there were very few accounts or other books about it. Mine was the first writing to come out of anyone on the spectrum.

I went to an annual meeting for the Autism Society to talk about my book. It started out as a small thing, but once I started talking, everyone else stopped what they were saying and wanted to listen to me. From that point on, the speaking engagements just came. Having people respond to what I said made me really pleased. I got to talk to so many other people on the spectrum. Until then, I had felt like I was all by myself, alone. I finally had some context for who I was.

I'm going into my sixties now, and I want to keep passing on my knowledge. I take everything I learn and download it into my books or onto my website and keep updating it. I divide my time among my animal welfare auditor training courses, the things I work on for the slaughter clients, and lecturing. My most important speaking engagements are for students in high schools, colleges and animal behavior departments. I feel very strongly about getting students turned on, especially the kind of quirky, nerdy ones that kind of get lost today, now that the hands-on things like wood shop and art aren't available anymore. These kids think differently. They might be labeled Asperger's and they don't believe they can do anything, so I'm someone who motivates them to succeed. A lot of students have written me and said, "I became a veterinarian or a special ed teacher because of you." That's purpose to me, because I made a real difference. I think that's what gives meaning to life.

Everyone is absolutely capable of doing things that have meaning and make change, and I think we need a lot more of this in our society. There are so many problems we can solve if we just stop talking about abstract things and just get out there and *do* stuff. According to what you are good at, there are lots and lots of *real things* that make a difference. You can volunteer in your community, you can tutor kids or deliver meals to people who are hungry. You can just be supportive to a friend. You can help someone by just recommending their work to someone else. Lots of people have helped me, and I always try to return the favor.

As I get older, I've had some medical challenges, and I approach these just like any problem that needs to be solved. I go straight to what I call "Dr. Google," but you have to know how to separate the garbage from the good stuff. The way I look at it; I'm scanning for diamonds out there in the rubble. Six years ago I started going deaf from an autoimmune problem and it was very, very scary. I was going crazy from the tinnitus and ringing in my ears. The first doctor I went to was just going to let me go deaf, so he could sell me all his hearing aids. I thought, *Well I have to solve this before I lose my hearing,* so I started what I called the "Mean Science Project," and got into the research literature really deep.

I was on the Internet looking for solutions, reading research articles and people's posts on message boards. Those helped me the most, because anyone who writes on those is just really trying to help. They have no other motives. One lady wrote that nature sounds for sleeping really worked, so I bought a ton of new age CDs. I found one that helped me tune out the tinnitus—it had two types of sound on it, it had water and birds chirping, which is why it worked, because the brain can't listen to two things at once.

I was still terrified I'd lose my hearing if I didn't get to the bottom of the whole thing, so I just kept sifting through literature. I just approached it like a job; I was on the computer day and night. One article said prednisone worked; another said it didn't. So, I went to another doctor, and he was finally able to knock the problem back with one big dose. The damage couldn't be fixed, but at least the inflammation and progression were stopped. If I hadn't done my own research and gone to a few different doctors, I wouldn't have figured that out. Doctors can be too quick to do procedures you don't really need. It's really important if you are thinking about doing something invasive to get different opinions.

Anyone can go online to find information that they can bring to their doctor, even if they don't have a research background. I always give more weight to the websites that are from what I call the "official" medical ones. If a website is trying to sell me something, that goes straight to the bottom of the pile, because they have a conflict of interest. You have to look at the source, and don't discount it if it's just a blog post or a message board. Message boards can also be scary, because people can have the same thing as you, but be affected much worse. It's important to remember that everyone is different, so the same things might not happen to you. The main principles for "Dr. Google" are to look for very simple solutions, ones that are not expensive and not dangerous.

People often ask me if I think I am missing out on things other people experience, like emotional love, but I also have talents that other people don't have. I would never give up visual thinking because this gives me very clear thinking in scientific and technical things that help me solve problems. Having autism has given me insight into how animals think and feel that I don't believe I would have had otherwise. My emotions may not be as complex as everyone else's, but I definitely understand caring. My mother wrote one time that "love was making something grow." That's sort of the way I look at it, in an intellectual kind of way.

One thing I always tell the parents of autistic children is that there is a continuum of solutions for a continuum of behaviors. Autism is so variable; everyone thinks differently and has different sensory experiences. You have to watch your children closely to see the signs, and deal with each one individually. Observe what your child likes to do, and use those activities to teach them.

It's especially important to get these kids to be responsible from an early age. You've got to expose them to lots of interesting things, even if they are afraid. You have to be very careful not to give them sensory overload, and absolutely no multi-tasking, but you have to engage them in things that stimulate their brain. If you constantly work one-on-one with a child on the severe end of the spectrum you might be able to teach him language and simple tasks. If you don't, he will never learn.

I'm proud that my work has given people insight into the autism spectrum and helped them to achieve. I've really cleaned up slaughterhouses all across the U.S. and Canada, and the impact has been around the world. What I've done helps millions of cattle experience a humane death every year. When my time comes to die, I want to know that I have contributed something of great value in the world.

Real change on the ground—that's what I'm about. And we need a lot more of that!

> **Temple Grandin** was recently voted one of *Time* magazine's "100 Most Influential People." McDonald's, Burger King and Wendy's have hired Temple to train their food safety teams and implement her work, ensuring that the hamburgers eaten daily by millions of Americans come from cattle that died without suffering. The HBO story of her life, *Temple Grandin*, starring Clare Danes, received seven Emmy Awards.

Love Does Not Draw a Line in the Sand

"When you know better, you do better."

—Maya Angelou

SOUL MODEL: Mary Griffith

CHALLENGE: Twenty-year-old son Bobby committed suicide as a result of his family's intolerance of his homosexuality.

CHANGE: Relentlessly crusaded to help save the lives of other gay and lesbian children, becoming one of the greatest gay advocates and activists of our time.

SOULUTION: Listen to your children, be open and trust that what they are telling you is the truth. Put aside your own feelings and hear what they are saying, whatever it is.

I grew up as the fourth of seven children, and my father was in the Navy. For the most part, my childhood was very lonely. I had a very domineering and controlling mother; you couldn't raise your will to her. We were never allowed to socialize outside of school, and she used God as a control factor to frighten us and keep us in line. Of course I was terrified, and I grew up feeling like I wanted to speak up but couldn't, out of fear.

My mother kept me completely away from other people who might have helped give me confidence in my own judgment, instead of my believing everything I might do would be a sin.

As a teenager, I started to strike out and began to sneak to parties where I didn't really belong. But in the end, I just wanted to be home, because it was familiar and safe. When I was in high school, my parents were always arguing because there were so many money problems, which were hard on everyone, and I almost didn't finish school. After barely graduating, I decided to be a nurse. I called up the nursing school in Oakland, and asked, "Do you have to know a second language to be a nurse?" Well, the girl on the other end laughed so hard, like I had said the most ridiculous thing. I felt so embarrassed and self-conscious that I just hung up. That was it, I never called again!

I also always thought I wanted to write, but I put that idea away because I never thought I could do it. When I was nineteen, I met my husband Bob and got married. I thought I would try being a phone operator, and when Bob said, "No, you don't need to do that," I didn't challenge him. I didn't know how to speak up, and anyway, that's the way it was in the 1950s. Before our first child was born, I had a miscarriage. I also lost a baby girl at just two days old, which left me thinking that God was punishing me for sneaking around so much before I was married. That threw me even more deeply into religion.

We went on to have four children: Joy, Ed, Bobby and Nancy. I taught Sunday school, and we went to church every week. My husband wasn't much into it, but I took the Bible very seriously, and the kids did too. I ran my house with the idea that we were all born sinners, and we needed to accept Jesus in order to have salvation, because that's all I knew. In my mind that's one of the biggest problems with the church. They tell us that we need to "take" something they have to give us for God to love us, not that it's all inside of us already.

When I look back to when Bobby was little, I always knew he was different. I remember having this dream where Bobby was a baby, and the focus was on his head. Not that there was anything wrong with his head. It just felt like a message to me that something was "different," but I didn't know what to make of it. He always wanted to play with dolls, and he would get into his sisters' drawers and dress up in their clothes. When Bobby was sixteen, and I first found out he was gay, I was terrified. To me, this meant our family wouldn't be united in heaven, and that Bobby would surely go to hell as a sinner, because that was what the Bible said.

I loved Bobby with all my heart, and I believed with total conviction that God could "cure" him. So I was constantly reading the Bible and praying for him. Poor Bobby, the whole thing really frightened him. He was so young, and I brought him to a Christian counselor. He asked me why we were going, and in my ignorance I said, "Well, you want to be the kind of person God wants you to be." Ridiculous now, as I look back. There he was, already perfect. Bobby even left a book for me on his bed one day, called "Loving Someone Gay." I just picked it up and threw it back on the bed because I was not going to go there. I was so sure of myself, and of the church because of how I was raised. I was also so embarrassed and afraid about the whole thing. I remember how nerve-wracking it always was, thinking friends would look at him and be able to "tell" Bobby was gay. It was terrifying! And, as much as I loved him, I was also so angry at him. I thought being gay was something he could change, and he just wasn't trying hard enough. On occasion, I would get so frustrated we would have fights, and I'd ask him, "Has anything changed?" Looking back, I'm embarrassed with myself!

My husband Bob didn't really understand any of it. He tried to help and spend time with Bobby. My son Ed was worried for him, like we all were. Joy and Nancy didn't really think Bobby was sinning. They actually went along with who he was, and enjoyed his company, but they were all pretty sure I'd never change.

There were a few times I felt, "It's okay, Mary, let's just forget this whole thing and just love Bobby." In those moments I just wanted to love and accept him for who he was, but I didn't trust my conscience. I thought Satan was trying to convince me of something evil. You should always trust yourself, but religion doesn't let you, because the Bible is supposed to have all the answers. I was absolutely positive Bobby would be cured.

As time went on and he wasn't "cured," my biggest frustration was with God, wondering why he wasn't "healing" Bobby—I just couldn't understand it.

Bobby was living in Portland, Oregon, when he took his own life at the age of twenty by free falling off a freeway bridge. I was at work when I got the call, and just went completely numb from disbelief. When the pain came, it was so unbearable that it was hard to function, and the tears never seemed to stop. Christians teach you all about the glory of heaven, but they don't teach you anything about grief. I couldn't fathom what had gone wrong. Being gay wasn't allowed by the church, and yet God hadn't saved Bobby—that really threw me! I started questioning everything, and I went through the Bible, almost page by page looking for an answer. And with those old tapes playing in my head, I was really afraid—but I kept going because I needed to understand what had happened, and where Bobby's soul was. According to the Bible, he was in hell for not repenting, and I was never going to see him again. It just didn't make sense. Why would God allow my son to go hell if it was in his power to cure him?

The pain of losing Bobby felt like it would never end, but I forced myself to keep going for my other kids. We all sat down a lot and talked about how we felt, but it really didn't solve anything. It was such a shock. Everyone had to go through their own kind of coming to terms with it. For me, thinking about Bobby was just a daily thing—wondering where his spirit was, and where God was in all this. I was very, very angry and confused. We found Bobby's journals, and reading about how he had suffered made it so much worse. He had written about how he hated himself, how badly he hurt, and how I'd never quit preaching and trying to "fix" him, trying to "steer him on the path of righteousness." How he had given up on love.

I'd been deaf to my own child's agony, and understanding my role in it was almost worse than all the grief. I couldn't go on without figuring out what had gone wrong. My family was very supportive, and since my kids were older I didn't have to be involved so much with school anymore, but I still cooked dinner and made sure everyone was doing okay. We were very close, and they were there for me all the time. I don't think it would have mattered if they hadn't understood. For the first time in my entire life, I went with my heart and just did what I needed to do without giving it a second thought. But we were all on the same page, because we had come to the conclusion that we'd been misled by the people we trusted the most.

I started visiting the gay church Bobby had gone to, which back then was a tiny house in Concord. I felt better because the pastor there, Reverend Larry Whitsell, had been married and had a daughter. He'd seen Bobby a few times. I have to say that the moment I walked into that church, I felt a love there that I had never experienced in any other church in my life. I told the Reverend that I really felt God's presence there like I never had before. They were teaching that God is *within* you, not something you needed to be "given." In my entire life of churchgoing I had never felt this kind of real camaraderie and love. I remember thinking that this was remarkable.

Reverend Whitsell started teaching me about gays and what they'd achieved through history. I learned that gay people had openly contributed to the world throughout history, but somehow politics and society had changed all that, and then held back the information. He showed me the book *Gay Men and Women Who Have Enriched the World*. He helped me understand his interpretation of the Bible, which made so much more sense to me than how I was raised. He explained that the Bible was written by regular men, as a reflection of those times. He pointed out all the other verses that Christians didn't live by anymore because they didn't make sense in today's world, and that the church's interpretations were completely selective to fit their agenda. Why did the church still say gay people would go to hell, but they didn't believe in stoning a child to death for being disrespectful to his parents? For the first time I could see that the meaning of the verses was really ambiguous. I remember feeling so angry and cheated, thinking, "What else is out there, and why was this kept from us?"

Learning all this was a double-edged sword, because the more educated I got, the worse I felt. I could see more and more how my ignorance had contributed to Bobby's death. There was no comfort because I knew the truth—that I had been wrong. I did everything out of love for Bobby; I had no idea that what I was doing was pushing him away. Being born gay was just like being born with blue eyes or brown hair. It was genetic, and part of me had always known. *God hadn't cured Bobby, because there was nothing to cure.*

The grief and the guilt seemed endless. I couldn't find any comfort or any way to forgive myself. Reverend Whitsell told me, "Mary, you can't go back and erase what happened. But you've got a story to tell, one of ultimate truth. Maybe you can touch a life early on, before another tragedy happens." What he said made sense, but I didn't know where to start, and I didn't feel like I was smart or strong enough to go do anything like that. He said it didn't matter; I should try schools, churches, and the community—anywhere.

It was so painful to go speak to anyone. But I realized that every parent needed to listen so another child might be saved, and I started doing it as often as I could. I had to tell parents, "Don't make the mistake I did. Cherish your children exactly the way they are." In some ways, knowing I was doing something good balanced the grieving too. It helped me put it on the back burner a little bit because I was thinking of someone else instead of myself. The hardest part was when I wasn't talking to other people because I was left with my own thoughts about Bobby, but I kept going. My purpose had become righting an injustice for him, and all the kids and parents out there too.

Reverend Whitsell introduced me to PFLAG (Parents, Families and Friends of Lesbians and Gays), and just knowing about them and letting them help me became my lifeline. I was amazed at what everyone there was learning about gay people. I remember the first PFLAG meeting I went to, and I put on that badge that said, "We love our gay and lesbian children." I looked down and was terrified that here I was, openly wearing this button, because the church was so against the gay community. But then I thought, *Mary, you are here to help; you cannot let people go on pushing each other around and dictating their lives like that,* and I wasn't afraid anymore. When I was speaking to different groups, I could tell that what I was saying was helping other people, and that helped me stay even truer to my convictions. I started wearing a button with Bobby's picture on it, everywhere I went. After that I always felt like he was with me.

There was so much activism beginning in our town right at that same time. The Reverend and the gay community in Concord were petitioning for "Gay Freedom Week." Many people wouldn't have any of it; there was going to be a city council meeting to decide. Reverend Whitsell wanted me to speak, and I was really terrified. I almost backed out until I heard a few conservative people in the town making terrible comments about gay people, speaking from ignorance, just the way I had. Their words took away all my fear. The more they said things, the angrier I got, and I just forgot about being afraid. The gay groups were so happy that I was there, and I knew I was making a difference. When I got home that day, I was so exhausted, and I was sitting in the kitchen, meditating quietly. I could feel Bobby with me, and I felt like we were talking. I told him, "I hope I helped a lot of people, giving that speech." I heard as clear as day. He said, "You didn't have to do that, Mom, but I'm glad you did." I knew I had to keep going.

In 1986, I went to my first Gay Pride Parade with my friend from PFLAG, Betty Lambert. It ended up being such a wonderful experience, even though it didn't start out that way. I got there feeling so ashamed that everyone would know how ignorant I had been. It was also quite a rude awakening for our whole family; to realize that there were so many lies out there and that's what had killed Bobby. But the way the people in the parade responded to me was so healing. There I was, feeling kind of embarrassed because I had been so ignorant; then I realized that kids don't hold things against you. They were so pleased I was there for them, and I started to feel like I was there for all the Bobbys who were still alive. It wasn't long after that I felt in my heart that Bobby's soul was at peace.

My family advocated when they could too. The more I could see how my words had an effect on people, the more courage I got. Every parent I helped understand was easing my own grief, a little at a time. After a few years, I started holding the PFLAG meetings in my house. I'm so proud of each time I helped a parent come around because it gave meaning to Bobby's life. I started meeting more people who were involved in gay activism and we started going all around the country, speaking at schools, in communities and even to the Board of Education. We were trying to get anti-discrimination laws passed that would stop gays and lesbians from being harassed so much in schools. Eventually we succeeded in getting the first legal acknowledgement of sexual minorities in schools, so there were some grounds for protection.

All this activism led up to the articles in the *San Francisco Examiner* in 1989, which is how Leroy Aarons, the writer, found me. In 1990, we started the Bobby Griffith Memorial Scholarship Fund, and in

1991 his book *Prayers for Bobby* was published. Leroy and I traveled all around to get it into as many schools as we could. A lot of them rejected it, or it would even disappear out of the libraries, but we did not let that stop us.

The main thing I was learning is that it is never too late to right an injustice. We had all been so wrong, and that's really where I went with it. It was such a huge betrayal to find out everything we had learned from the church and done as a result of that had been a lie. I just had to make that right. I knew there were other kids out there like Bobby, and I had to keep going. The more I did, the more strength and confidence I got, and eventually I wasn't fearful anymore. I realized I had much more to offer than I was led to believe when I was growing up. We all come here with what we need in this life. Whoever raises you may take it away from you in different ways. From my own experience in grammar school, if I didn't catch onto something quick my mother called me "lame brain." I didn't know what that was, but I knew it wasn't something good. That really does something to a child. Kids need to know that they are intelligent and bright, and have everything it takes to succeed and make a difference. It doesn't have to be anything big. You can give of yourself and your time—just listening to someone who needs to talk or giving a big hug. One size fits all!

When someone suffers a loss, the main thing is to know that acceptance comes in time. The pain never goes away, but it becomes easier to live with it. You need to be willing to do something that gives back in some way to help you through it. If it's the loss of someone, and you can somehow be involved in a support group for people going through a loss, that is a way to find something good. After Bobby died,

I was so busy with what I was doing and seeing the fruits in it. I think that is a big part of healing because it helps you to go on. And, there is always someone in a worse situation—people go through things a hundred times harder than what I went through. When I find myself complaining, I get annoyed with myself and I say, "Gee Mary, you have nothing to complain about—we're just human." Everyone has their own world of bad things that happen, and it might look like nothing good can come out of it. But in time, if you have the right attitude, you'll find it.

Over the years I've been to so many places telling my story, and I've answered hundreds of letters from kids and adults, some who are still trying to accept. I tell gay kids all the time, "You have a history! Just like blacks or whites or Jews or anyone else, there are gay heroes, all throughout time. We're all the same, and we're all in this together." They can't hear it enough. Kids are still taking their own lives because there is still so much bullying in schools. There should be laws against this, and there have to be some consequences. I believe it is the responsibility of teachers and parents to stand up for their children. Some kids can come home and tell their parents they are gay, and some still can't. Regardless, kids should be able to feel safe at school. If they can't tell their parents, they have to tell someone. Who else is there, if the school doesn't help? Where are they going to turn? Hopefully they have friends who will help them stand up. We can't ever do enough to help kids accept and love themselves.

I'm humbled that our story has been heard all over the world and has helped so many people. I think it's why I was eventually able to forgive myself. I can't say I would have chosen it, but I realize that all this was possibly what Bobby's life was about—the timing of it all and the work we're still doing. I feel Bobby's presence with me all the time, and I have no doubt that his soul is at peace. And while nothing can compare with the loss of losing him, in a way, his death liberated me, because I'm not afraid of life anymore. I've learned to speak up; that we all have a responsibility to be educated and make the world a better place, and that one person can make such a huge difference. If Bobby hadn't died, I'm sure I would still be begging God to cure him. I feel like I've walked through the fire, and I survived. I don't think anything could destroy me now. I never would have thought I'd be on this quest in a million years.

The number one message I want to share with parents is to listen to your children, be open and trust that what they are telling you is the truth. If they are hurting and you don't listen, they are going to do anything they can to stop the pain, and you could lose them. Put aside your own feelings and hear what they are saying, whatever it is—love does not draw a line in the sand.

The Lifetime movie *Prayers for Bobby* starring Sigourney Weaver premiered in February 2009, earning two Emmy nominations and one Golden Globe. Thanks to Mary, over 8 million people around the world know Bobby's story. Thanks to Mary, courage can truly be defined by accepting accountability, no matter how agonizing, and using it to help others. Thanks to Mary, gay and lesbian children all over the world can understand that they have their own place in history and are worthy of love. And, thanks to Mary, we can learn by example and look into our own hearts, ensuring it is the one place where intolerance for anyone will never find a home.

Taking in the Good

> *"We must look at ourselves over and over again in order to learn to love, to discover what has kept our hearts closed, and what it means to allow our hearts to open."*
>
> —Jack Kornfield

SOUL MODEL: Rick Hanson, Ph.D.

CHALLENGE: Observed unhappiness in the world, felt awkward and socially inadequate, was often unhappy as a child and young adult.

CHANGE: Dove into various practices and studies in order to heal personal pain; found and cultivated method to accelerate his growth process; committed to helping others do the same.

SOULUTION: Get on your own side. Honor your pain by treating yourself like it matters, and don't downplay it. Tell the truth in all ways, about what you saw and experienced as a child, about what you see today, and about how life is actually treating you. Be a good friend to yourself, like you would be to someone else.

I grew up in a loving and stable family living in the suburbs of Los Angeles. My dad was a professor of zoology, and my mom stayed at home. In my earliest memories from about three or four years old, despite the love in our home, I had a strong sense of others around me being unnecessarily tense, anxious, critical, or unhappy. There was a wistful, clear observing of the world around me and watching the people in it, both the kids and the adults. They seemed to be "sucking happiness out of the air," getting caught up in needless wrangling, worrying, fault-finding, or just stressing and fussing. That was a very powerful experience for me as a child. Along with it came a longing for a better way to "do life" altogether—I was interested in, and dedicated to, solving this dilemma for myself.

Also, I was pretty much an outcast with most of my peers from about third grade onward. I skipped second grade, and since I have a very late birthday, I began third grade at age six. I felt lonely, awkward and inadequate in my everyday dealings with other kids. My parents were nice, decent people, but I kept my problems to myself, so they couldn't be very helpful to me in what I was grappling with.

What was going on for me was not terrible in any sense, and I think not uncommon for many kids or even adults. I was not attacked, traumatized, or severely bullied. Still, even though I was functioning fine on the outside, on the inside I felt empty. I was naturally affected by my environment and quite unhappy. I was pretty neurotic!

The years passed and I sank increasingly into my shell. Then, at the beginning of my junior year in high school, my family moved to Finland for a year since my dad had received a Fulbright fellowship to study black grouse and to be an exchange professor. That spring, when I was fifteen, I fell in love for the first time. So for several months, I experienced loving, and being loved, in a way I never had before. Unfortunately, at the end of the school year, I had to leave Finland with my family.

That experience with love helped me step into much more openness, honesty and "realness" with another person. So, in addition to getting the benefits specific to loving and feeling loved, there was also a breakthrough into a whole new way of being for me, that had a huge impact.

I think for a lot of people in their childhood, and even in adulthood, something happens that could be purely random and knocks you out of your familiar script, rituals and worldview. It pops open a new door that says, "Hey, a whole other way of being or relationship is possible; there are different kinds of people you can be with that you have never even imagined." Or, you realize that you have capabilities you never knew you had, that you can build on in your life—that was my experience with this first love.

As I approached college, I knew that I was unhappy and socially awkward. I knew I wanted to learn how to be with people and be more comfortable with my feelings.

Pain is a great motivator to learn. So, when I got to college, I deliberately put myself into certain situations that I felt could affect me for the better. It is like making an autonomous choice to put yourself in situations in which you no longer have autonomy. You put yourself in situations that will be challenging, but hopefully in a good way.

It was 1969, it was UCLA, and the human potential movement was jumping. The whole counterculture was really in full swing, so along with getting good grades and all the rest of that, I was exploring humanistic psychology. I read all kinds of books about psychology and joined an encounter group, even though the prospect terrified me.

Because I was in pain, I got really interested in "learning how to learn." I knew I had to get to a better place, and that growing, changing and learning would get me there psychologically.

It became really central and important to figure out how I could help that learning really "stick to my ribs," so I would learn and grow more rapidly. And, honestly, how could I get through the pain faster? For example, if I could really get the value in this incredibly intense and confrontational encounter group, I would never have to be in another encounter group for the rest of my life.

I wanted to help myself change quickly—from both the high impact things I was doing, like being in an encounter group, or much more importantly, the everyday back-and-forth experiences we all have with other people in daily life. For example, somebody makes a comment at breakfast, and you know internally, "Oh, that's a good way to look at things." But normally, we just let that thought pass without really taking it in. Maybe, about the twentieth time someone makes a comment about a useful way to see things, or we read something similar in a book, or we get a fortune cookie that says it, finally, "Ba-boom"—the seed has planted! Why not help that seed land the first time you hear the comment, or the first time you have that thought, or the first time you have a new kind of emotional experience in your body that feels good? A way of learning where you notice right away, "Oh yeah, this is inner strength, I like this!" Or, "This is confidence; this is feeling loved, I like this!" Why not *really* help that sink in, so you learn more from it?

That began my motivation around "helping good lessons land." My growth curve accelerated, as it would for anybody. Also, it took me very much into my focus and practice of "taking in the good," which is the idea that while there's a lot to learn from negative experiences, there's usually much more to learn from positive ones. These are the primary source of our inner strengths, including resilience and feeling loved and happy, plus positive experiences usually feel good, which motivates us to have them and gain their value.

In college, I had fun, I made mistakes, and I had a normal college experience. Since I wanted to help myself change and grow, I tried whatever worked and was very pragmatic. I looked at the mainstream psychology of the time, which at UCLA was behavioristic and focused on animal research—pigeons pecking levers, rats chasing cheese in mazes, and what-not. That didn't seem very fruitful for me; I got much more practical value from humanistic psychology.

In the very last quarter of my senior year, in the spring of 1974, I needed twelve units. I'd fulfilled all my requirements and was able to take independent study. I don't know why, maybe it was grace, but I ended up doing twelve units on Eastern philosophy and religion. I had two professors, read a lot of books and wrote a huge paper. For the first time in my life, as a guy from a very conventional American suburban/casually Methodist background, I was exposed to Eastern views, especially Hinduism and Buddhism.

When I read about Buddhism, it seemed immediately rational, empirical and psychological—it focused on our direct experience and the evidence of our senses, rather than taking anything on faith alone. The fundamental teachings of Buddhism are that everything is changing and connected to everything else. And, if you live in harmony with these truths, you're more able to be happy, and to benefit yourself and others. But if you don't live in harmony with these truths, if you cling to changing things, crave them, and take life personally, you're going to suffer and create harm for yourself and others. That seemed deeply true, and really set me on my way.

Over the course of the 1970s, I took workshops and taught them, and experienced other teachings about humanistic psychology, body work, emotional release, and other aspects of the human potential movement. Even though, obviously, there were some excesses in some of the things I did, there were mainly wonderful, powerful, learning experiences. I think there are some excesses in the so-called "straight world" too, as in the conventional button-down, buttoned up, narrow, ordinary way of living life. I also believe there's been a kind of widespread and unfortunate sneering in our culture about this time in our history—the 1960s and 1970s. As if the 1960s contained only a lot of crazy hippie madness, and the whole human potential movement in the 1970s was only a bunch of unbridled, ridiculous narcissism.

Actually, the sixties and seventies involved huge surges in the civil rights movement, environmentalism, and respect for gay rights, and feminism. As well, there were large positive shifts in American culture. Obviously these movements had their roots long before then, but during the sixties and seventies, they really flowered, taking on a critical mass that had huge beneficial impact. People sometimes dismiss things that came out of the sixties and seventies, but the truth is, it was a phenomenal twenty-year run in American history that brought to light many different ways of seeing things that now, forty years later, have become mainstream.

Looking back on my twenties—which happened mainly in the 1970's—I think that three things in particular helped me heal and grow. There were still some major ups and downs, including some depression. But I kept trying new things, putting myself in new situations, sometimes trying fresh starts. Second, like a lot of people, I just kept plugging away, with a certain stubbornness and determination. Third, I kept trying, at least once or twice a day, to reap the rewards of every day experiences, such as "taking in" the sense of companionship with friends at breakfast before I had to rush off to class or some other task.

I grew a lot during that time. And, like a lot of people in their twenties, I settled down into one relationship, got married at twenty-nine and had children with my wife, Jan, some years later. I founded a successful seminar company, worked for a mathematician doing probabilistic risk analyses for things like the odds of a nuclear power plant melting down, and did management consulting. After studying for a masters in developmental psychology at San Francisco State University, I decided to focus on becoming a psychotherapist instead of a professor, and eventually received a Ph.D. in clinical psychology from the Wright Institute in 1991.

Since 1974, I had been meditating off and on, but my deeper dive into Buddhism began soon after my wife and I had children. As I approached my fortieth birthday, we had begun participating in the family program at Spirit Rock Meditation Center in northern California. I dove into the fundamental teachings of the Buddha found in what's called the "Pali Canon"—Pali is the language of the original teachings in Buddhism, our best guess as to what the Buddha or those people close to him actually thought and taught. This branch of Buddhism is now found mainly in Southeast Asia (e.g., Thailand, Burma) and in the "Vipassana" movement now spreading around the world.

Buddhist perspectives and practices about non-harming, impermanence, interdependence, compassion and love, acceptance, calming and observing the mind, and relaxing a sense of "I," of ego, or self really helped me, as they have many others, including those who would not use the label "Buddhist" to describe themselves.

Becoming more aware of the vast web of life and existence, and gradually developing more sense of ease with whatever *this* moment holds, had a huge impact on me.

As our children grew older, I became increasingly interested in the historically unprecedented meeting of modern brain science and ancient contemplative practices. With Rick Mendius, M.D., I founded the Wellspring Institute for Neuroscience and Contemplative Wisdom, a non-profit with a mission to offer skillful means for changing the brain to benefit the whole person—and all beings—in a world too full of war. It draws on psychology, neurology, and the great contemplative traditions for tools that anyone can use in daily life for greater happiness, love, effectiveness, and wisdom.

Now looking back about forty-five years to when I began college, one of the biggest parts of my learning about the mind is what I stumbled onto during college on my journey to end my own pain. Years later as a neuropsychologist, I realized that I was actually changing my own brain. We know now that we can use the mind to change the brain for the better—that is the power of "self-directed neuroplasticity," which is currently a very significant area of study.

There is a saying, "Neurons that wire together, fire together." In other words, what we think about and focus on actually changes our neural structure. Connections are built, more active regions in the brain get more blood supplies, and connections that are inactive wither away in a process called "neural Darwinism."

One of my favorite studies illustrating this power comes from Sara Lazar at Harvard. It compared the brains of long-term meditators with non-mediators. Meditators had measurably thicker neural cortex (gray matter) in regions that support self-awareness and empathy, and regions that are involved in controlling attention—meaning that meditation could support understanding oneself and others, as well as support attention at work or home.

Another thing we know now is that the human brain has evolved what scientists call a "negativity bias" based on the rough-and-tumble survival needs of our ancestors. They had to: "*Eat* lunch today, don't *be* lunch today." The ones who survived passed on their genes to us. Consequently, our brains are continually scanning for bad news; when the brain finds that bad news, it hyper-focuses on it, usually over-reacts (fight! flight! freeze!), and stores it quickly in memory: "once burned, twice shy." In a sense, our brains are like Velcro for negative experiences, but Teflon for positive ones.

This negativity bias was great for keeping our ancient ancestors alive to see the sunrise and pass on their genes. But it is bad for everyday well-being and effectiveness, bad for psychological healing and growth, and bad for long-term health. Over the 6 million years of the evolution of the nervous system and the brain, these negative factors didn't matter much, since most animals—including our primate, hominid, and human ancestors—died young. But these days, the short- and long-term costs of the negativity bias are not worth their benefits. This bias causes all kinds of problems including stress, unhappiness, depression, and wear-and-tear on the body, gradually eroding health. Many of us feel like we are "running on empty." We've got a Stone Age brain in the twenty-first century. If we don't take charge of it, it will continue to take charge of us. We need to be strong enough to control, work with, and even transform the negativity bias. A great way to do this is by building inner strengths and other resources by "taking in the good."

The first part of taking in the good—*activating* a useful mental *state*—is having a positive experience in the first place, usually just noticing one you are already having or creating one. Maybe you simply notice that coffee tastes good or flowers are blooming, or perhaps you create a positive experience by thinking of someone who loves you. Because of the negativity bias, we have to help ourselves see the whole mosaic of life, including those tiles—those facts—that are good.

The second part of taking in the good is to *install* this passing mental state in your brain as a lasting neural *trait*. For example, really stay with the good experience for ten seconds or more, and sense and intend that it sinks into you as you sink into it. Hang out with the positive experience, give yourself over to it, enriching it and making it as intense as you can. This way you can have many neurons firing and wiring together, creating true positive changes in your brain. In real life, we take these steps very quickly. It's the law of little things —just a few seconds can make a huge difference.

It's also important to notice the good in other people, and sense *those* experiences sinking in. Recognize that *we* are fundamentally good—not perfect, but good. Noticing the good in the world is especially important these days, when there are so many messages of darkness and despair.

Taking in the good also helps others. Research has shown that we are more able to be patient and cooperative, and more likely to help and treat each other well, when our own "cup runneth over."

My number one nugget to share is this: Get on your own side. Honor your pain by treating yourself like it matters, and don't downplay it.

For every person I've ever known who overstated their suffering, I've known twenty or even 100 people who downplay how bad it actually was. This means telling the truth to yourself, the whole truth, including what you saw and experienced as a child or what you see today. Tell the truth about how life is actually really landing on you. Be a good friend to yourself, as you would be to someone else.

Getting on your own side also means giving yourself credit and acknowledging when you apply courage in your everyday life. I think there are many examples of courage that don't get any press, but really deserve it. Obviously, it takes courage to run into a burning building. But for me, probably the most courageous, scary thing I've ever done in my entire life was telling my girlfriend in Finland in 1968 that I loved her. I think it takes tremendous courage to open your heart and be open to new things. It takes courage to allow yourself to change for the better, based on what you're learning, including from taking in the good.

Weave the small but real jewels of everyday life into the fabric of your brain and your being by using small moments like drinking a glass of water, receiving the smile of another person, or noticing how beautiful the grass looks. Also, take in larger moments like finishing a tricky e-mail, getting an unexpected compliment from your boss, or how good it feels when your child crawls into your lap. Take the extra ten or twenty or thirty seconds to really notice those things and help them sink in—that will build new, positive neural structures that support your own inner strengths, such as resilience and a positive mood. This is one good way to address the fact that life is often difficult, and to prevent feeling like you're running on empty.

Actively seek the experiences that will really fill you up. These are the ones that are your special medicine or your personal Vitamin C. Do what you can to have these experiences and absorb them. Using your mind to change your brain to change your mind is the hidden power of "self-directed neuroplasticity." It is something we all can harness to make our own lives better, and also to improve the world.

Rick Hanson, Ph.D., is the founder of the Wellspring Institute for Neuroscience and Contemplative Wisdom, and on the advisory board of the Greater Good Science Center of University of California-Berkeley. He has been invited to speak at Oxford, Stanford, and Harvard, and has taught in meditation centers, worldwide. A *New York Times* bestselling author, his books include *Hardwiring Happiness, Just One Thing, Buddha's Brain,* and *Mother Nurture.*

It's Not What Happens—
It's How You Heal with It

Soul Model: Elizabeth Bryan

Challenge: Forgiveness.

Change: Co-authored *Chicken Soup for the Soul: Count Your Blessings,* and *Soul Models;* uses art and art therapy to heal self and humanity.

Soulution: Forgiveness of self and others is the single most liberating life experience. Like it or not, we are here to learn and grow. Letting go of anger and blame unleashes boundless spiritual, emotional, and psychic energy that can be used to propel our lives forward and create miracles. Don't waste another minute—your dreams are waiting!

I'm inviting you to join me on a journey of forgiveness . . . beginning with the kind we owe ourselves, and extending to anyone we believe has "wronged" us. Anger, guilt, blame, and shame are heavy, painful emotions that color all thoughts and actions, conscious and subconscious. They hold us back in life and in love. I've experienced and carried the weight of all these negative emotions as a result of my so-called mistakes, as have many of you. As mothers, daughters, sisters, friends, sons, husbands, and partners, we tend to beat ourselves up for everything we think we've done wrong, rarely remembering to stop and focus on what we do right. Owning the idea that we made a mistake that hurt anyone (including and mostly ourselves) can be excruciating. It's also extremely courageous.

In my efforts to forgive myself, I've done everything from taking anti-depressants (yes, I have) to meditating, hiking, painting, journaling, smudging with sage, lighting incense, smoking pot (yes, I did), taking SAM-E and reading massive amounts of self-help—all in one day. Some of those things took the edge off; others just made me really hungry. Bottom line, here's what I learned: *If you take just a few minutes each day to forgive yourself or anyone else for something, you will be set free.*

Forgiveness is the pinnacle of compassion, you are hardwired for it, and it is key to healing and happiness. There are a million ways to express it from smiling more to holding a door open for someone, but this story isn't about those things. It's about being compassionate with ourselves and others through forgiveness, beginning by sharing what we believe to be the biggest mistakes we've made. Doing this is a *huge* step on the forgiveness path, and, as painful and embarrassing as it feels, I promise it's worth it.

I'm going to lead the way with my own story, even though I'm admittedly queasy, embarking on this confessional. Will you think I was an idiot? Maybe, and I probably was. Will you think, "Really, what's the big deal about *that* one?" (Okay, maybe I blew it out of proportion, although law enforcement might disagree). But, will *some* of you think, "Thank God I'm not the *only* one who drove through the garage door without opening it first?"

I'm guessing so, which is why I'm sharing my story. If my truth prevents you from repeating my mistakes, or if you feel better because you know you aren't alone, then what I did really does transform into a huge gift, *and I forgive myself.* It's selfish, really. You tell me your mess-ups, my heart opens in compassion, and we probably fall down in fits of laughter, trying to one-up each other about who messed up more. Sharing so-called mistakes *connects* us as human beings. It also ends the comparisons, forever leveling the playing field of life.

The truth is that we learn far more from each other by sharing our truth instead of the B.S. we make up to feel better about ourselves.

My theory is that if we all got real, from the billionaires of the world to your neighbor down the block, we'd forgive ourselves a whole lot easier, and love ourselves a whole lot more. Instead of thinking, "How was I ever that stupid?" We'd be thinking, "Damn! Good thing I didn't do *that*!"

Before you jump on this particular path, it's important not to share with just *anyone* that you ruled the ancient city of Atlantis and were responsible for the tidal wave that buried it in 7000 B.C. The key is sharing with the people who you believe will most benefit, saving the most bizarre details only for those you can completely trust. In the end, it is also wise and wonderful to keep some things just for you.

I begin my confession by confessing I am not a forgiveness "expert," I haven't researched it for the last decade, written any white papers, or been on TED—yet. But I do know this: If even one of you benefits from my story, your heart will be lighter, and so will mine. . . . that is a wonderful gift.

Here's how I sum it up: "It's not what happens, it's how you *heal* with it."

* * * *

For as long as I can remember, I've been an artist. By age five, I was designing togas from my bedroom curtains; by six I was excavating clay from the sewer behind my home to sculpt ashtrays for my parents. I drew gargantuan chalk figures in the street, with heads that began at the top of my block at Faith Menken's house, and bodies that ended seven houses down the street at mine (I still enjoy working large). I was incredibly happy, with a vivid imagination and a picture-perfect, middle-class life in a New York suburb. My parents were wonderful and still are. I was the "little doll" to my big sister and the victim of teasing by my older brother, who was also my greatest protector. We had two schnauzers named Fritzie, (the first one died and was "replaced"), five hamsters, half a dozen turtles, and one rabbit, along with a whole lot of love.

I illustrated handmade books, made up my own language, and told anyone who would listen that I was "Elizabeth from another land." As the youngest, I was always encouraged creatively, but left to my own devices. This resulted in a strong sense of independence, along with a good dose of "rebellious/experimental." My mother was a teacher, and I always did well in school. Dad was always present, building things around the house and being "best friend" to everyone in our small community. From a very young age, I was entrepreneurial and loved earning my own money. I picked scallions and sold them on the corner, was babysitting by twelve, and always worked at least two jobs each summer, still finding plenty of time to do all the things I had no business doing.

Rebellion got the best of me at nineteen, when my biker boyfriend decided to go out without me. I decided to "one up" him, and head to the "Studio 54," which was the biggest nightclub of its day. Driving home at 5 AM, with two friends in the car, I fell asleep at the wheel. The car flipped over, smashing into a tree. Miraculously, my friends were fine, but I literally "caved in" the driver's side door with the force of my body, was flung out the passenger's side, and somehow ended up pinned by my hair under the back tire. Both femurs, my nose, and several ribs were broken, and it was amazing that I survived at all. Five days later in the hospital, I had a blood clot in my lung that almost did me in a second time, and, it was close to one full year before I would walk again.

Some people might see my accident as a catastrophe, but for me, *it was the single greatest blessing of my life, and continues to be, every single day.* My friends weren't hurt, my family was there every step of the way, and I was *alive*— at nineteen, I was graced with understanding the "Gift of Life." Every moment, I drew from a well of gratitude and purpose, and still do, to this day. I had no idea why I had survived, but I knew there was some much bigger reason. I had fallen asleep driving, but "woken up" in spirit.

After recovering, I finished school, saved money, and became an art dealer in Manhattan. I was independent, took care of myself completely, and still managed to make and sell my own art. At twenty-five, I fell madly in love with a well-known comedian named David Brenner, who literally waved a magic wand and made all things possible, including endless laughter. Overnight, my life became a dream of world-class travel and a true soul connection that surpassed anything I'd ever experienced. We had three incredible sons, and lived happily ever after, until, for a variety of reasons . . . we didn't. Part of it was my "growing up" and needing my own identity; the greater part was that raising three boys significantly changed who we were as individuals and a couple.

So . . . what did I do that was so wrong? What's my big confession? Why did I beat the crap out of myself for the entire next decade?

It wasn't really my marriage, or even getting divorced, although that ending was excruciating, as most of them are. It was pretty much everything that happened afterward. I borrowed money to start a business that failed. I borrowed more money to buy a house and the housing market crashed. My ex-business partner sued me and put a lien on the house that was under water. I was in family court, bankruptcy court, and in a lawsuit over my failed business—all in under a year.

I really didn't know what had happened to my wonderful life, only that I must have made some pretty bad decisions to end up where I was.

I began to loathe myself for the mess I was in.

They say we learn more through pain than joy, and my journey of pain had only just begun. "Elizabeth from another land" had really been living in someone else's—at forty years old, I realized I'd given up myself and my needs to another person for a very long time in the name of love, until I couldn't do it anymore. By then, there was not too much left of "me" in there. When I set out on my own, I had no clue as to what I was doing, because I had tossed my "real life" skills, financial and otherwise, right out the window to be a wife and mom.

As women, we do this all the time—but the truth is, self-love can't exist with blind love. The result of that for me was losing everything at forty years old, with two little ones left to raise, and no clear idea of how to carry my part of that responsibility. Having these insights in the middle of debt, bankruptcy, losing my home, business, and soul mate caused me far more agony, grief, and trauma than my accident ever did. Let's just say it felt as if my heart had been ripped out of my chest and handed to me.

I fell into a deep, dark rabbit hole of excruciating pain, with many days and weeks that I really believed dying would be easier than getting out of bed. *I hated myself; I felt such shame, guilt, and loss.* I suffered from extreme insomnia, to the point where the hardest-core sleep meds prescribed by my doctor had zero effect. Between the chemicals, the terror, and the lack of sleep, I lost my grasp on reality, and believed I was seriously losing my mind. I played through the scenario of being locked up forever and never seeing my children again. I envisioned my life in a mental hospital, with my sons being raised by my ex-husband's girlfriend. I thought about who would visit me, how ashamed and humiliated I would feel for not being able to parent my own sons. That scene played over and over in my head—but, having already faced a different kind of physical death so many years before, I had been primed for hanging on.

I discovered the power of meditation, which ultimately transformed my life. Against my doctor's advice, I weaned myself off of all medications. Slowly but surely, my practice guided me into being present in a way that allowed me to safely process my pain. I was able to objectively understand that I had contributed to my situation, but not really caused it, and that there was no shame in anything I had done; I'd created that in my mind. I learned to "own" my mistakes as gifts, rather than grief. I also learned that my younger, independent self was still "in there," and she and I could create a whole new reality, forged in new wisdom and strength.

That was the beginning of my learning self-compassion, which led to forgiveness, which led to self-love. When I learned to extend this compassion to the world around me, everything shifted and my life began opening up in ways I never dreamed possible.

I made up my mind to prevent what had happened to me from happening to anyone else. And not just with my *own* pain— with all pain, from *all* causes. I had no idea how this would happen, but I fully trusted it would.

I continued my path of healing, which began by being the best mom I knew how to be. I worked my tail off at various jobs, did art projects with local hospitals, schools, and veterans' homes. I did my best to balance work that didn't pay with work that did. I volunteered as the room mom for all things "art." I dragged my boys to soup kitchens, shelters, and clothing drives. As hard as it was to say "no," my sons learned that when they were with me, life was different from their time with Dad, and they couldn't have whatever they wanted. We made cardboard forts from boxes, baked a ton of brownies, watched movies at home, and became closer than we'd ever been. In the end, the changes in me were incredibly valuable to them. They learned to appreciate everything they had so much more, including me. Instead of seeing their mom as a woman deferring her life to another person, my sons know me as their devoted, hard-working, self-sufficient (and slightly wacky) mom.

I learned more about myself in those first post-divorce years than I had in my entire life. The most important thing I learned was this: just when I thought I'd lost everything, the truth was, I had *found* everything. I had my kids, I had my health, and I had *me*—with a whole life ahead to plan exactly the way I wanted.

This new realization put my gratitude meter on steroids. I dove even more into personal development, seeking out ways to accelerate my growth in all areas of life. I was fortunate to co-author *Chicken Soup for the Soul: Count Your Blessings,* which shed a little more light on what my real purpose in all this was, although I wasn't quite there.

When I met my *Soul Models* co-author Angela Daffron, a quantum shift occurred: not only did I want to share what I learned from *my* challenges, I needed to get to the bottom of how other people survived their much greater ones, and share *that* with the world. It was partially selfish, because I knew I'd find my own way through their "soulutions." With every single story, I not only got stronger, but also learned more about forgiveness, of myself and those around me. You can't help reflecting more seriously on the topic after interviewing Edith Eger, a Holocaust survivor who forgave the Nazis. Or Mary Griffith, who became one of the greatest gay advocates of our day after her son Bobby took his own life because Mary couldn't "accept" him. Each Soul Model left me in tears and awe. They taught me many things, but the bottom line was this: they survived because they never gave up: they *stepped* up, using their hardship to fuel actions to prevent someone else from suffering. In doing so, they recovered from things that were far worse than anything I could ever imagine.

It was my turn to apply that lesson.

Clearly, I needed to up my ante in the financial arena. Although I had remarried a wonderful man, *there was no way I would ever depend on anyone again.* Call it God or call it grace; one day I landed on the national website for The Women's Institute for Financial Education, *WIFE.org.* When I read their tag, "A Man Is Not a Financial Plan," my heart nearly popped out of my chest. When I learned about the two amazing co-founders, Candace Bahr and Ginita Wall, I was completely blown away. Here were two top wealth managers who had devoted a quarter century of their lives to empowering women financially, offering decades of knowledge, expertise and full-on money management curriculums, all 100 percent free. In that moment, I knew I was home.

I reached out to Candace, and three days later, I was on her doorstep in Carlsbad, California. "Candace," I said, "I know this sounds crazy, but I have to volunteer for you, work with you, and you need to get me on track financially. And (by the way), you are never getting rid of me!"

Over the past several years, it has all manifested exactly in that way, and then some. Candace and Ginita are personal friends and my heroes, and KPBS Heroes to boot. They are Soul Models on steroids, having won more awards for their for-profit and non-profit work than any two women I've ever known. And, they are truly the best teachers I've ever had. We've created "Level 3 for Women," a collaborative community that explores issues like purpose, legacy and heart-centered giving. We are rolling out *WIFE.org's* critically acclaimed "Second Saturday Divorce Workshops" nationwide. I have the privilege of leading the way, helping other women let go of anger, pain, shame, and blame in much less time than it took me. We speak and teach together all over the country, and I am honored to help as many women as possible through sharing my story. *By having a hand in everyone's healing, I have finally forgiven myself.*

In the scheme of things, I'm not sure why we label things "mistakes," "bad," and "negative" anyway. People change and grow, life shifts and moves us in different directions. A situation can be wonderful for a certain time, and then it simply stops working. That doesn't mean it was ever wrong or anyone is to blame. Even knowing what I know now, I wouldn't trade one second of any of it, as it all led me to being exactly where I am today. If I hadn't fallen asleep driving, I would have no idea how precious life is. If I hadn't been madly in love, I wouldn't have my beautiful sons and extraordinary memories. If I hadn't fully depended on someone, I would never know the joy and freedom of being able to take care of myself and my family. As agonizing as it all was, going down that far emotionally led me to helping tens of thousands of women with Candace and Ginita— and, ultimately, to this book in your hands right now.

I loved another person with every ounce of my being, and, through the pain of our parting, I learned to truly love myself.

David left this earth not too long ago. He will be sorely missed, but his legacy continues through his work, our sons, and grandson. When I look in their eyes, I see no mistakes; only perfection. I see their father, and always will—that is a magnificent gift. In his honor and memory, my message to you is to practice forgiveness, on behalf of yourself, anyone you've ever loved, and the world.

Regardless of circumstances, we all come into this world with no limits to what we can achieve. You are extraordinary, and have incredible value. Just sharing your story, your mistakes, your hardships, lending an ear, or opening a door for another human being has great purpose. Your life experiences give *you* great value, because you can use your struggles to help another person. Share something you've gone through with another person who might benefit, and watch out for the magic. Forgiveness is a journey for all of us—remember, forgiveness *is* "for giving."

Elizabeth Bryan teaches and speaks on the spa/resort/corporate circuit and is currently pursuing a master's degree in art therapy.

Embracing Life—
and All That
Comes with It

SOUL MODEL: Dawn Averitt

CHALLENGE: Contracted HIV/AIDS at nineteen years of age.

CHANGE: Became advocate, founded TheWellProject.org, a non-profit providing health resources for women diagnosed with HIV/AIDS globally.

SOULUTION: Take one step every day. Whatever your challenge is, you don't have to heal it, cure it, fix it or make it go away— you just have to keep moving. Figure out who might be the one person you need to talk to, or what will it take to get a good night's sleep, or the one way you can feed your soul in that moment.

Spain sounded so exciting! The winter after my nineteenth birthday, I was offered the chance to model for an agency in Europe. I'd just spent an intense year in an independent study division at NYU, and even though I couldn't care less about the fashion world, I saw modeling as a great opportunity to take time off and travel before returning to school.

In Europe in the '80s, youth hostels were predominantly for young people, and they were relatively safe. The modeling agency sent me to one while I was waiting for an apartment. The people at the hostel introduced me to a man who was another model.

In the middle of the night, he forced his way into my room and raped me.

I did not tell a soul—no one. I didn't speak Spanish and I didn't know anybody. It was some kind of holy week, and no one was even at the agency; everything was kind of "shut down." I kept thinking, *I'm too smart for this; I'm too strong for this. If I tell my parents they'll make me come home, and I will have failed terribly.* So, I just decided it didn't happen—especially to girls like me. I spent about three days recuperating to the best of my ability, and I moved on. Even now, twenty-five years later, it's hard for me to face that this is how I coped. All I can say is that I didn't have the faculties to deal with it at the time, so I had to put it away in a box.

As many as one in three women in this country has experienced some kind of abuse: domestic violence, sexual, or emotional abuse. At some point, everyone is affected on some level. The first couple of times I shared my story out loud in front of a group, I watched the faces of the women in the room; I could immediately see the ones that weren't ready to say anything, and the ones that desperately needed to blurt it out—it was like a hidden epidemic.

* * * *

I was very fortunate to be raised in a strong, stable family with two parents and two younger brothers in a suburb of Atlanta, Georgia. As the oldest and the only daughter, I was often the caretaker for my brothers and all my cousins, a role I loved. My parents were incredibly supportive and encouraging. No matter how low my self-esteem was ,my dad always told me I could do anything, and I believed him.

I started kindergarten early, and always had an enormous sense of adventure. By eight, I was enamored by foreign cultures, languages, and belief systems, and couldn't wait to explore the world. At the same time, I was painfully shy. I was a short kid, and always felt fat and ugly. I went through some really hard stages: at about seven, I started getting heavy. By the time I was eleven, I was 5 feet tall and 165 pounds, with stringy brown hair and a big space between my teeth—I was so awkward! Then I shot up. About eight months later, I was almost 5'8" and 124 pounds! The result was that I had no self-esteem or confidence about appearance and social capacity, and I always felt out of place. Then I got even taller—by the time I was thirteen, I was 5'10" and slim, but never quit seeing that other short, fat kid in the mirror. I relied on my sense of humor, a voracious appetite for reading, *huge* imagination, and an engaged mind.

Throughout high school, photographers and modeling scouts approached me to go to agencies. They wanted to ship me off to model right then, but I was intent on finishing school. My father had been an exchange student, and I desperately wanted to be one as well. The summer before my senior year, I was fifteen. My friends were going to hang out at the beach in New Jersey and try to meet Bruce Springsteen, but I decided I was going to Turkey as an exchange student. It was an incredible, eye-opening experience to live in a mostly

Muslim country where intense poverty was a part of the reality, and guys on every corner carried Uzis on their shoulders!

During my senior year in high school, I took classes at the community college, graduated early, and got into NYU's independent study program, where I wanted to study international law. My first year, I obsessed with getting it all done and graduating at nineteen. I had ulcers and migraines from the self-imposed pressure. My parents suggested I take some time off, so when the chance came to do modeling in Europe, I went. It was so ironic for me to model; I kept waiting for people to open their eyes and realize that I was a chubby, awkward kid. But I wanted to travel, and modeling was a legitimate way I could explore the world, so off I went to Spain.

About seven weeks after I was raped, I got dangerously ill with extremely high fevers. I had lymph nodes the size of golf balls sticking out the sides of my neck, I looked like Frankenstein, and no one could figure out what in the world the growths were. My skin was peeling off my lips, I had chest pains, and I was not lucid half the time. Some friends took me to a Spanish hospital—now I know that that was most likely the point when my body was going from HIV negative to HIV positive.

For most people in that six- to twelve-week period after infection, there is some kind of acute sickness and, for many, it's flu-like. At the time it happened to me, no one had this knowledge. It was 1988, I was this middle-class white girl from the South, and nobody would have ever tested me for HIV. The initial phase lasted about one week; after that I got better, but still had the huge swollen glands in my neck.

I kept modeling for about three more months, heading from Spain to Germany. What an unbelievable world that was! I was around people who smoked hash for breakfast, did coke for lunch, and had ecstasy for dinner. Obviously, not everyone was like that, but my experience was that modeling was a world of fragile, paranoid souls with no sense of self. Everyone wanted to get close to them for the wrong reasons. To be in that world while viewing myself as the fat kid, was a bizarre turn in my life.

I still had big knots on my neck, and if I put my hair up, people could see them. I couldn't continue modeling with those, so in May, I decided to go home. At the beginning of June, I told my mom about the swollen glands. She is a nurse, connected to the medical community, so we headed to the ear, nose and throat doctor, and to a bunch of specialists. I had a battery of tests to figure out what was wrong—I wasn't anemic and everything seemed good. Finally, they gave me a presumptive diagnosis of non-Hodgkin's lymphoma, which in itself was pretty upsetting.

With every test, we were basically trying to cross things off the list. AIDS was getting on the big screen nationally, and I kept asking, "Why don't you give me an HIV test? At least we'll know it isn't that."

The doctor just said, "No, there is no reason to test you. You don't do drugs and sleep around, do you? It's expensive and it will go on your record." He had all kinds of excuses; the more he said, "No," the more I said, "Yes." Finally, he acquiesced.

When the doctor called with my test results, he said, "Your HIV test came back positive. We think it's a false positive, and you need to come back right away and be tested again." *Click!* He hung up the phone! That was HIV counseling in 1988. I thought I was going to be dead before I hung up. I had a repeat test, and on June 28, we went back to the doctor to hear the news. My mom and dad came with me, sat in that cold little room in the office, and waited. The doctor came out and said, "Well, the test is confirmed positive."

Time stopped as our world caved in. I asked, "Where do I find more information; what should I read?

He said, "Oh, don't read anything; there's a lot of bad, confusing information out there. And, don't tell anyone, because you won't get insurance." He suggested I didn't even tell my brothers, because ultimately, it could ruin my family's life.

We were completely stunned. As a parent today, I cannot imagine what that was like for my mother and father. I'm their oldest child and only daughter. Not only were they dealing with a terminal illness, but a horribly stigmatized disease that we couldn't tell anyone about. This moment marked the beginning of a lot of years of secrecy.

On the way home I decided to tell my brothers that I was HIV positive. They'd had some sex education in school delivered by the football coach—like all you need to know about HIV is, "If you're not a drug user, a gay man, or a prostitute, you've got nothing to worry about." Then, he'd moved on to the next STD. When I told my brothers, they stared at me in shock, because I'm not a gay man, and, when did I become one of the other two? I told them I didn't do anything wrong and was not a bad person. They had really different reactions; my youngest brother completely shut down and struggled for many years. My middle brother took off for my mother's bookshelf, where all the medical journals were. Every fifteen minutes he would shout out, "Don't worry, this will be fine!" Or, "It could be worse!" Then he would announce what other malady would be worse than HIV.

Of course, everyone was trying to figure out how in the world this had happened. I had completely blocked out the rape—and no one else knew about it. I was so square; I had never even smoked a cigarette! All I could think of was this horrible experience I'd had in the phlebotomy lab of the hospital in Spain where I had been sitting next to a guy I presumed was a homeless junkie. When they took his blood, he had a seizure and kicked over this old metal table with several vials of blood on it. They all shattered and blood went everywhere. The next thing I remember was the lab tech coming to take my blood, looking a little like one of those wicked scientists, with his blood-covered lab coat. I thought that must have been it; I must have gotten an infected needle. I didn't know that it would have been pretty much impossible to get HIV that way, and obviously I was already sitting in that hospital with swollen lymph nodes.

My doctor instantly said, "I don't think that was it."

I kept saying, "I don't know how else it could be!" I think the shock of the diagnosis made some part of my brain shift entirely into self-preservation mode and said, "You can't deal with *all* of this right now."

At that point, the doctor said I couldn't go back to NYU and deal with the harsh winters. I transferred to Georgia State in Atlanta, where my parents were living, and started pursuing a degree in international political economy taking classes in the fall. My last quarter at Georgia State I got an internship with Senator Sam Nunn in his Atlanta office. I asked about getting a position in his Capitol Hill office and was recommended to transfer there.

Meanwhile, night after night, I had partial, snippet nightmares, where I couldn't figure out what was going on. One night, I was driving home from the Hill, exhausted from the nightmares. There was a song on the radio, and all of the sudden this voice in the back of my head said, "I bet he's dead." And I heard it again. *I had no idea what I was thinking about!* Then the entire rape just flooded back into my brain, almost causing me to drive off the Fourteenth Street Bridge. It was like a whole crazy slide show was running through my head.

I flew home to Atlanta and told my mom everything, making her swear not to tell anyone. Can I say absolutely that's what it was, beyond a shadow of a doubt? The timelines and my history point to that incident. But for years and years, I didn't tell people it was rape—I would say it was heterosexual transmission, even though I knew that would make them think I had slept with everyone in town. I didn't want to tell them about the rape because then they would focus on that, and all of the sudden I would become this "poor victim."

Working on Capitol Hill, I discovered grassroots advocacy. President Clinton had been elected, and kept saying he "would lift the ban on gays in the military." Senator Nunn was a conservative Democrat and didn't agree with Clinton. As a press assistant, I found myself confronted by gay advocacy groups staking out our office and hanging out in the halls, shaking big fake vials of blood in my face saying, "You're a bigot, you hate people with AIDS!" And I was saying, "I am not afraid of you," because nobody knew I had HIV.

I could also see how this was a huge opportunity, because all of these special interest groups were trying to raise their voices. It was so clear how few people had both perspectives. Many government officials looked with disdain on the advocacy groups; many advocates were clearly not part of the government bureaucracy—this created a chasm between the two groups.

After a couple of years in this high pressure environment, I decided I wanted to take what I had learned and use it in a public service model, perhaps within the non-profit world. I was not clued into the HIV/AIDS community and had only let a few close friends know about my status. But my HIV was progressing fairly rapidly, and I was not tolerating treatment very well. I had horrible side effects from the toxicity of the meds, and they didn't seem to be working—I was taking them, they were making me sick, and I wasn't getting better. It was very scary; we were trying all kinds of different drugs, I was trying to hide that I was taking them, and feeling horrible. Plus, they were very expensive. I decided I wanted to be back in Georgia, closer to my family.

One of my dear friends was working for a grassroots organization in Atlanta that ultimately became the AIDS Survival Project. She said, "There is a position open for a Treatment Resource Specialist," which was basically an HIV advocacy, librarian, and counselor job all rolled into one. "It would be awesome to have an HIV positive woman in the role, but you will have to start talking to people about your HIV status." I thought, *Oh my God, that's what I want to do!*

I went home and asked my family if they were ready for me to start sharing my condition in a small way, only with patients, and just begin to take it on. As always, they were incredibly supportive. There was a ton of fear and vulnerability around doing this, and I knew people would judge me, but carrying it around all by myself was getting really heavy. Taking action was something I had to do.

Marching in from Capitol Hill, wearing my pumps and pantyhose, I went into the job interview with five seasoned AIDS activists in their ripped jeans. They're all thinking, *You've got to be kidding me.* One of them said, "What happened, were you sentenced to community service, is that why you're here?"

I had to say it: "I have HIV." They all kind of sat up a little stiffer and looked at me. Then I broke into a litany of opportunistic infection information that I had memorized over the weekend, which was largely useless, but showed that I was trainable. Truthfully, I knew all of about five things about HIV at the time—I knew I had it, and I knew that T-cell levels were the main diagnostic component in people with HIV, and that more T-cells were better than less. I was a total wild card candidate for this job, but I got it.

It was 1993, and the learning curve was incredibly steep. I found myself in a lot of places I had no business being because I was a complete anomaly—a middle-class white girl with HIV from the South with an interest in science. Before I knew it, I found myself on everything from FDA advisory panels to NIH task forces.

At the same time, my immune system was declining rapidly. A normal T-cell count is between 500 and 2,000, depending on your age and the lab used. *In July 1994, my T-cells dropped to 74, and I was officially diagnosed with AIDS.*

Because I was working at the AIDS Survival Project, I knew about the cutting-edge research. I talked my way into being the first woman in a clinical trial in Albany, New York, to get access to a protease inhibitor. At the time, this was one of the new "miracle" drugs, and getting it meant traveling from Atlanta to New York weekly for a month, then every other week for a few more months, and then monthly after that. Almost immediately, I began to respond: my T-cells went up, my viral load went down, and I began to feel better—it was indeed miraculous. I actually had no idea how bad I had felt until I began feeing better. Protease inhibitors ultimately became the main component of my combination HIV treatment regimen, and today, I have a very strong immune system.

As I was beginning the clinical trial, I wrote my first grant overnight like a college term paper (because I didn't know I couldn't), and somehow got funding for my first organization, which I launched in 1995. I called it WISE, which stood for Women's Information Service & Exchange—because no matter what anyone else knows about health and disease, ultimately you know your body better than anybody else—we are all WISE and we need to trust that.

WISE was the first organization in the country that focused on treatment for women, and it was unbelievable the way it took off. The moment I asked for funding, I truly thought, *If I can create a space for women to come together, and we can celebrate our commonalities, no matter how different we are, we can change the face of AIDS.* We could also change the way people viewed AIDS, because everybody has a mother or a sister or a woman in their life in some capacity. I really believed women were the key to changing this country's perception of HIV and AIDS. I still believe that, but it turned out to be a much bigger job than I ever realized!

I knew that in order to create a space where HIV positive women could come and be unashamed of their HIV status, I had to be willing to be "out there," first. As soon as the funding came in February of 1995, I "came out" in living color, on the front of the living section of the *Atlanta Journal-Constitution* for 2 million people and everyone in my family's world. It was a big story about women living with AIDS, and there I was, for the whole world to see. I knew that I had to be okay with being judged—and being vulnerable. But for me, this was the right thing to do.

By 7:30 that morning, my voice mail had 200 messages. That was the day I discovered I was no longer vulnerable! Nobody could do anything to me with that information because I controlled it. By giving it up myself, the message was, "This is it, I've taken away your weapons." It was so intensely liberating, gratifying, and empowering . . . and, I haven't stopped talking since!

It was also an unbelievable experience for my parents and the people closest to us. They had lived for years in secrecy, having to listen to people's crude jokes and comments that we should quarantine all the people with HIV because they were causing problems. What I didn't realize was that not only was I breaking out of my own prison, I was setting them free as well.

My other amazing realization was that the more I helped others, the better I felt! It was very organic. I have no doubt that I am alive today because I took control and had this purpose about fighting for others who didn't have a voice. In doing that, I was fighting for me. I think some of it was pure survival tactics—if you wake up every morning and make a list of what isn't right, will you ever get out of bed? To make it through, you have to get up every day and just keep moving.

Spiritually, I came to the place where I believed that the good and the bad things happen for a reason. The hardest part was coming to terms with not always knowing what the reasons are. Yes, I was raped. But I am no more or no less an AIDS victim than anyone else. If I embraced victim mentality, I couldn't get through the day. I could spend all my time asking, "Why?" or roll up my sleeves and ask, "How?" There were so many things I still wanted to do, and I wasn't willing to give up!

WISE took off like crazy because it filled a huge need. We started a monthly newsletter about living well, and, in six months, we had subscriptions in forty-eight states and eleven countries. My learning curve and trajectory were steep—before I knew it, I was sitting at the table for international committees, boards, and task forces.

By 1998, I was "fried"—I was celebrating the tenth anniversary of my diagnosis and I was about to be thirty. This was mind-boggling, because when I was diagnosed at nineteen, my first goal was to be twenty, then twenty-one. Then I got cocky and went for twenty-five. It was time to figure out who I wanted to be and what I wanted to do.

I realized I had spent all this time traveling around, helping empower people, and trying to make a difference, but I wasn't really taking my own advice. My brother said, "Why don't you do something that shows you are embracing life and you are healthy and well? Why don't you hike the Appalachian Trail?" This was one of our childhood dreams, and my brothers and I wanted to do it together.

In June 1999, my brother, Scott, my future husband, Brad, and my dog, Guinness, and I set out on a journey we dubbed "Trekking with AIDS." It was the early days of the web, we had a site, and people were e-mailing us from all over the world. I did the 2,167 miles from Maine to Georgia with my five-drug combination regimen in tow. On the twelfth anniversary of my HIV diagnosis, all of us completed the Appalachian Trail.

On that journey, I spent a lot of time thinking about why we hadn't been successful in creating a model for women and HIV around treatment information and community resources. Everyone was so focused on the gay male community, even though women really needed access to information at their fingertips too. It was 2001, and I realized the web could make that happen—that was the genesis of The Well Project. I dreamt it up as a hub, a kind of a clearinghouse for women living with HIV and their clinicians and caregivers, where they would find tools to help them communicate with access to reliable, up-to-date information. Today, The Well Project is a global resource, reaching 1.3 million visitors annually from every country in the world.

My main goal has been changing the way people think about HIV, normalizing it as every person's problem. For every 2,500 households, 43 percent of people know someone who has it. The number of people who think they are at risk has gone down, as has the understanding of what constitutes risk. This is where talking about the rape has become useful—helping people understand that it only takes one time to get infected with HIV.

Here in the U.S., 50,000 people a year are being infected with HIV. Yet, if you asked ten of your friends, the likelihood is they don't think it will happen to them. Of new infections among women in the U.S., approximately 70 percent were infected through heterosexual sex and 28 percent were infected through injection drug use.

In the U.S, teen girls account for 50 percent of all HIV cases reported among those ages thirteen to nineteen. Of course, all of these numbers represent what we know or estimate, but there are still many unknowns. The underlying challenge is providing people with information so they can make better decisions—and, everyone should get tested as a matter of principle. HIV is not about being gay, male, bisexual, or having multiple partners. HIV is a *human* disease. My goal is to create a world where there is no more stigma or judgment surrounding it, so we can end this epidemic here and ultimately globally.

In addition to the work I am so passionate about, the other goal and deepest desire in my life was to be a mom. In 2002 and 2004, I was blessed to give birth to two healthy daughters. As the mother of two girls, I have a lot of work to do. As a woman living with HIV, I have a lot of work to do. I would like my daughters to be able to tell their daughters that when they were little girls, there was something called "World AIDS Day," but because of brave women like us, they don't have to worry about that anymore.

One of the great gifts in being diagnosed with HIV is that you realize your own mortality, and you live in the moment. It's about living and loving more deeply, and taking the opportunity to do crazy things once in a while. I feel an enormous amount of gratitude that I have this purpose and such a full life. Am I grateful to have HIV? No. But everybody has an "opportunity" to work with, and, in this go-round, having HIV is mine. I value my days and family and friends and the nuances of completely unplanned events. It has helped to enrich the soil in my life, and with that, I've been able to grow a luscious garden.

When it comes to how much sand has passed through the hourglass, no one really knows. If I assume today's the day, then I am going to live it! We've got to make the most of our time with other people and ourselves. We have to marvel at the trees, find shapes in the clouds, and believe in ourselves. This life is full of all kinds of hurdles, experiences, and challenges, and we *can* get through them—this is the fabric of life.

When you open your heart and see everything as an opportunity to give and share, you will be stunned and amazed at what comes back to you. Giving does not have to be monumental; it is surprisingly easy to help someone—just smile at everyone you see, and watch what happens. If your life is a little better, so is mine, because we are in this together.

There's a Tim McGraw song where he sings that he hopes you have the opportunity to live like you were dying. I'm incredibly grateful to have had this chance.

Dawn Averitt is the founder of The Well Project, which is a global resource reaching 1.3 million visitors annually from every country in the world. Dawn also chairs the Women's Research Initiative on HIV/AIDS (WRI) and serves on the President's Advisory Council on HIV/AIDS (PACHA), among other boards and task forces. Ultimately, Dawn spends her days and nights working on the next step forward to end AIDS in America!

A World
Without Cancer

SOUL MODEL: Margaret I. Cuomo, M.D.

CHALLENGE: Losing too many loved ones to cancer, determined to change the status quo and draw attention to the need for cancer prevention.

CHANGE: Wrote *A World Without Cancer*, in efforts to offer hope, promise and proof that cancer can ultimately be wiped out.

SOULUTION: It is a gift to believe in something greater than yourself—this inspires you and gives you purpose. In the end, we are here to make the world better for each other.

"I'm afraid. Don't leave me," pleaded my patient and friend Nancy, as I turned away from her hospital bed. Her breast cancer had metastasized beyond treatment, leaving her helpless and hopeless.

My sister-in-law Penina's peritoneal cancer took her life at age forty-seven, with little warning other than abdominal swelling. She left behind a daughter and an adoring husband. So many others I have known and loved succumbed to cancer in their forties and fifties, despite the recommendations and regimens of top oncologists.

I have spent most of my life experiencing the horrific effect that cancer has on friends, family and patients. It is unacceptable that one in two men and one in three women will face a cancer diagnosis during their lives. It is unacceptable that cancer is the cause of one in every four deaths in our country, as is the cumulative suffering of its victims and loved ones. Chances are that you have lost someone you know and love to cancer, regardless of how desperately they wanted to survive, and how hard a battle they fought.

In their honor, it is my goal to inspire you to transform your way of life, and improve your health.

My book, *A World Without Cancer* challenges the reader to consider what we could be doing better to prevent cancer. That is part of my heritage as the granddaughter of four immigrants from Italy, who traveled to America with only hope and courage and a desire to create something meaningful in this land of plenty.

My grandparents lived thoughtful, purposeful lives. They ate hearty, but healthful meals, always served with love. They have inspired me to give back to this wonderful country that offered them, and their descendants, so many blessings.

My fearless Grandma and Grandpa Cuomo, Immacolata and Andrea Cuomo, owned and operated a grocery store in Queens, New York, that sold fresh produce as well as Italian specialties. You can imagine that many fresh vegetables, such as broccoli, escarole, carrots and tomatoes as well as pasta and fish or chicken were the mainstay of their diet. It was the so-called "Mediterranean diet," and it has served the Cuomo family well for generations. Charles and Mary Raffa, my other grandparents, were also hard working, and established the Ideal Corporation for the manufacture of refrigeration units and cabinetry in supermarkets and homes. They all lived the American dream.

Grandma and Grandpa Cuomo raised a son, Mario, who was to lead New York with courage and integrity as the first Italian-American Governor of New York for twelve years. My father inspired all five of his children to serve others, and strive for excellence, and to use our gifts for the benefit of our community. My mother, Matilda Raffa Cuomo, dedicated herself to public service by establishing an organization that mentors underserved children and adolescents.

Today, Governor Andrew Cuomo, my brother, is serving New York tirelessly with courage and integrity, and from the very beginning of his term, reached across the aisle to build bridges with Republicans and Democrats alike for the sake of progress in New York.

Collaboration and teamwork are essential in cancer prevention as well, and that is what I am advocating for across the United States. My grandparents lived their lives into their eighties and nineties, and were cancer-free. Shouldn't we expect to live our lives without cancer?

If we fully dedicate ourselves to the prevention of cancer, this impossible dream will become a reality. After dozens of conversations with some of the nation's most accomplished and respected physicians and researchers, I believe cancer can be eradicated just as we have wiped out devastating diseases like smallpox and polio. It begins with the awareness that we are all on one team, because none of us is exempt.

It continues with a conversation about how the current model fails us, by focusing on living with the disease instead of preventing it.

The sad truth is that the "cancer culture" as we know it, is not structured to do what we most need: determine how to prevent cancer and implement our discoveries. The good news is that it doesn't have to be that way.

According to public health experts, we can prevent more than half the cancers occurring in the United States today by simply applying the knowledge we already have. My goal and purpose in writing A World Without Cancer *is to share as many of these important facts with you as possible, and inspire you to change your life for the better.*

Cancer currently claims the lives of over 560,000 Americans each year, or more than 1500 people every single day—and, that number is rising. Yet, scientific evidence tells us that more than 50 percent of all cancers need not occur. At least 30 percent of all cancers are associated with obesity, diet and lack of exercise. Environmental causes, including smoking, exposure to carcinogens in air, water, and consumer products also increase cancer risk.

Although the National Cancer Institute acknowledges that prevention is essential, it allocates 1.3 billion dollars annually for the development of treatments, and only 232 million dollars for cancer control and prevention. That's 460 percent less funding!

In 2010, $2.6 trillion was spent on health care, and it is predicted that by the year 2020, national health spending will reach $4.6 trillion. Despite this, life expectancy in the United States is about fifty-first among the world's nations. The soaring cost of cancer care contributes to the unsustainable overall health-care costs.

Is this the society our children and grandchildren should inherit?

I believe it is our responsibility to leave our descendants a smarter, healthier society.

We have the opportunity to significantly reduce our risk for cancer, heart disease, and diabetes by improving our lifestyles, health and well-being. Public health strategies, including ending smoking, changing diet and level of physical activity, improving access to health care, and regulating environmental and occupational hazards are the first steps. We must galvanize scientists, physicians, the drug industry, advocates, patients and their family members; we must each examine our own lives and understand that unless we become passionate about our participation in eradicating cancer, *we may be its next victims.*

My fascination with medicine began at an early age. I was truly moved by the courage and determination of Madame Marie Curie, who made such a significant contribution to medicine for her pioneering research in radioactivity. Intrigued by pathology, which is the study of diseases and their effect on people, I spent the summer of my sophomore year in high school at a local community hospital in Queens, volunteering in the lab. I was amazed that a malignant tumor, resembling an innocuous gray-white cauliflower, could be an insidious killer.

I was fortunate to be raised in a close-knit family that supported my passion for medicine and inspired a strong desire to serve. We lived very modestly in a middle-class neighborhood in Queens that was a true melting pot of many different cultures where everyone was accepted. My environment was safe and loving, and included grandparents, aunts, uncles and cousins. Everyone was engaged in helping others; our work ethic was strong, and we drew different positive qualities from our parents and grandparents.

As the first daughter born in a family of five children, I had a great deal of responsibility. We couldn't afford a nanny, and my mother always needed an extra set of hands. I learned to multi-task at a very young age, and this gave me many of the organizational skills I have now; it also helped me learn to keep calm during a crisis.

We were raised Catholic with tremendous faith and the understanding that each one of us has a purpose in this world, and an obligation to do the right thing all the time, not only when convenient. I admired my father's courageous position on many issues—he always did what he thought was right, even when it cost him an election.

He was a community activist and a mediator for homeowners' rights—whether it was for people losing their homes or a ballpark that was going to be converted to an office building; all the legal work he did pro bono taught me that we have a responsibility to help those who cannot help themselves, and to make the world a better place. My mother was an elementary school teacher who worked as a substitute while raising us. She dedicated herself fully to being a devoted mother and wife. When my father took public office, my mother embraced her new role, stepping out of her own comfort zone, giving speeches and taking an active role in many of the programs initiated by Governor Mario Cuomo's administration in the 1980s. She eventually founded her own non-profit, Mentoring USA, which pairs underserved high school and middle school students with mentors.

My family's examples of public service were woven throughout my life and career. For me, as a doctor, this translates to the privilege and responsibility of using my knowledge and skills, and mind and heart, to effect positive change.

As a radiologist, I have worked with doctors, patients, insurance companies, pharmaceutical companies, and advocates. After almost 30 years, I realized how backwards the system really is—we spend billions of dollars per year on trying to cure cancer, instead of preventing it. Since 1971, when the "War on Cancer" was declared by President Richard Nixon, the National Cancer Institute has spent more than $90 billion on cancer research and treatment.

This economic model is far from sustainable, and sadly, millions of people continue to suffer and die, and cancer costs continue to rise, with many cancer drugs costing *thousands of dollars per dose.*

From the late 1980s to the year 2000, a "perfect storm" of suffering and loss affected many of my family members and friends. Penina was my husband's younger sister, and was such a vibrant, dynamic woman. My husband's parents had survived the Holocaust; but his mother died of cancer in her forties, likely from the same kind of cancer as Penina. I couldn't stop thinking that something more could have been done. Each death also brought frustration and a sense of failure for me as a medical professional, because I knew we should be light years ahead of where we are, instead of still taking the primitive approach of amputation, which is basically what a mastectomy is. Expensive, toxic protocols like radiation and chemotherapy that date back to the early '80s are still in use today.

Cancer is a brutal disease that takes lives, while its treatments cause pain and suffering. Unless you have a very specific leukemia, or an identified genetic mutation, the therapeutic approach is frequently the same—cut, poison and burn. Cancer patients should be treated with more advanced, sophisticated therapies to turn off the mutated genes, and we should have more definitive information about what is cancer-causing in our environment. *Cancer prevention should be our focus, and our goal.* To continually see your loved ones lingering and suffering under treatment is devastating—and for me, it was life transforming, because I realized that modern medicine didn't have the answers.

I believe we have a choice when it comes to facing challenge: We can withdraw and not think about it, or *do* something. Taking action to help others is the most healing thing—you can't bring back the loved one, but you can enhance the future in their honor. With those thoughts ingrained in my consciousness, there was no way I could sit by and do nothing—it was time to call for positive change and do what I could to transform our approach to this deadly disease.

I began putting thoughts together and met with a publisher. What should have been a two to three year process took only nine months, because I was so compelled to get it done—it was like giving birth to my third child. All of the ideas were on the surface of my consciousness, and began pouring out onto the pages.

I was committed to taking a balanced and fair approach. I have enormous faith in people, even in the pharmaceutical and food and consumer products industries, which can be powerful partners in the effort to prevent cancer.

In the end, I believe we all want to see progress and the eradication—the end—of cancer, because cancer cheats everyone it touches: patients, loved ones and caregivers. It was extremely painful writing about those I lost and the devastating memories of their fight for life, but their memory kept me going. I felt so deeply that they were each with me, moving me forward. Images of them cycled through my brain; I heard their voices and felt their presence. Writing allowed me to recount the impact they each had on me—Caroline, Rosemarie, Nancy, Penina, Peter, Oksana, Irene, Isabelle, Gertrude, Alba, Charlie, Richard, Michael, Bill, Leslie, Sherry, Toni, Joie, Lynne, and so many more, propelled me, inspiring the journey that resulted in *A World Without Cancer.*

My goal is that everyone reading this will join me in creating change, because, armed with knowledge, we can have an impact. The pharmaceutical companies can reinvent themselves by focusing on prevention, and still come out as winners. We can stand up and stop big corporations from selling products that are suspected of being harmful. We can endorse the companies taking action to protect consumers. In 2012, Johnson and Johnson committed to removing harmful chemicals such as formaldehyde, a known carcinogen, from their entire personal care line by 2015. Without government intervention, it is up to us to compel companies like Colgate, Proctor and Gamble, and L'Oreal to follow the good example of Johnson and Johnson in protecting consumers.

Every mother needs to be concerned for her children, because what they consume now can have a grave impact on their future.

The endocrine-disrupting chemicals such as BPA (found in plastic bottles containing water and other beverages), parabens (present in many shampoos, body washes, shaving products, etc.) and others affect the hormones of children and adolescents, and are carcinogenic. To make matters even worse, the harmful effects of these chemicals pass from one generation to the next, ("trans-generational"). Therefore, it is our obligation to choose personal care products that are free of these cancer-causing chemicals, and to choose fruits, vegetables, meats and fish that are free of harmful pesticides, antibiotics, and growth hormones. Our school children can learn how to prevent cancer through good nutrition and physical activity. Of course, smoking is still one of the worst risk factors for cancer, and we must continue to prevent young people from smoking. It's up to us to drive the change.

Writing *A World Without Cancer* has been a life-transforming journey, through which I have met many people who have enlightened and supported me. It has given me new courage that allowed me to focus on the expression of the message, without fear about how it was perceived. What has been especially remarkable is the way people have just come forward, as I needed them—from top policy makers to CEOs of big pharmaceutical companies; everyone was accessible and eager to speak. Through this book I have met many courageous people with whom I am collaborating to change the status quo, and I am grateful to them for enhancing my life as physician and as a person.

I am also extremely fortunate to have a loving, caring, and supportive family. I have a terrific husband and two wonderful daughters and they are my greatest blessings. Everything else—my ability to reach out to others, to be a physician, to ease suffering—those are all privileges that I greatly appreciate. Today, my brother, Governor Andrew Cuomo of New York, continues the legacy of integrity and courageous public service that my father began.

My brothers and sisters and I were extremely fortunate to be raised with my parents' example, but I truly believe that everyone has the ability to improve the world we live in. You need to have faith, follow your instincts and be fearless. Then, wonderful things will happen. Life can be painful and difficult—but when you are engaged in an endeavor that is transformative for others as well as yourself, it is an uplifting experience.

A World Without Cancer has inspired me to consider what we could be doing better. If we truly commit ourselves to the prevention of cancer, this "impossible dream" will become a reality.

Margaret I. Cuomo, M.D., is a board-certified radiologist who has devoted most of her practice to diagnosing cancer and AIDS. To learn more about how you can prevent cancer, read *A World Without Cancer: The Making of a New Cure and the Real Promise of Prevention.*

Accomplishing the Impossible

SOUL MODEL: Ken Kragen

CHALLENGE: Uniting the music industry with millions of individuals globally in efforts to fight starvation in Africa, and hunger and homelessness in the U.S.

CHANGE: Made music history by producing "We Are the World," raising $64 million dollars in just twenty-eight days with an overhead of 7 percent. Followed up with "Hands Across America," a continuous line of 6 million people holding hands from the Pacific to the Atlantic Oceans, raising $34 million dollars to benefit hungry and homeless Americans.

SOULUTION: Everything that happens in life is an opportunity— even the negatives. It's amazing how things work out if you view everything that happens in life as something that was supposed to happen. If you always take that approach you end up turning almost everything into something positive.

Thornton Wilder once said, "Great things balance at all times on the razor's edge of disaster." I have used that quote many times, and "We Are the World" is a great example of it.

The first time I ever worked on the "We Are the World" project was two days before Christmas, 1984. Harry Belafonte called me with the idea to do a major concert fundraiser and have the proceeds donated to help relieve starvation in Africa. The non-profit foundation we ended up founding (USA for Africa) would feed people in Africa, specifically Ethiopia and Sudan, where more than one million people died during the country's 1983 to 1985 famine. I suggested we'd be better off doing a record, and got Lionel Richie, Quincy Jones, and Michael Jackson, plus more than three dozen other artists, involved.

Dick Clark was producing the American Music Awards that January and Lionel was set to host. On the way to Dick's office to talk about Lionel's hosting, I thought, "Wait a second—if we do this event on the night of the American Music Awards, all the artists will be in town and it won't be so hard to get them together!" Dick loved that idea.

Fast forward to the night before the American Music Awards—we were backstage at the Shrine Auditorium rehearsing for "We Are the World." I had forty-five artists lined up, including Michael Jackson, Dionne Warwick, Ray Charles, Billy Joel, Diana Ross, Tina Turner, Stevie Wonder, Cyndi Lauper, and Bruce Springsteen. The manager of one of the big rockers came to me and said, "The rockers are leaving, they're not going to be at the recording session tomorrow night, because they don't like the song that Michael and Lionel wrote; they think it's too pop and they don't want to stand on stage next to the non-rockers." The attitude was, "Gee, we're really hip, we're the rockers. If we stand next to the pop artists, it's going to diminish us somehow."

Lionel Richie has a great line he used all the time. He said, "You are who you hug," and that was the perfect way to characterize what was happening. So here we are, balancing on the "razor's edge of disaster," and I said, "Look, if you leave, you leave. We're recording tomorrow night; I can't do anything about it." The next thing they did was go to Bruce Springsteen, who was the biggest rocker of them all, and asked him to leave with them. If Bruce had committed to go, they all would have walked. Bruce told them, "I didn't come out here to walk away—I came out here to do this song and feed people. I'm going to be there tomorrow night." The minute he said that, they were all going to look stupid if they didn't show, so they all shut up and came the next night. But for that one moment, "We Are the World" balanced on the "razor's edge of disaster."

* * * *

There's a really interesting study, done by the British, that started examining children when they were just seven years old, and checked in with them every seven years of their lives. The study found that what they were doing at that age dictated a lot—in most cases, you could find a parallel to what they were into at seven, and what they were into later in life.

When I was seven, I was building an amusement park in my back yard, with a plan to charge the neighborhood kids twenty-five cents to come in and use the park. The story would be better if the park actually opened, but when I was building the roller coaster with a wagon, I knelt down on an exposed nail that went right into my knee. I had to get it sutured, and my mother cancelled the whole thing! Still, that experience was a great indication of what I would end up doing with my life.

I had one of the smoothest childhoods you could have, and my parents were the most generous and loving people I've ever known. My mother was just beyond belief as a giving person—so much so, that the one time I seriously hurt her feelings was when I was critical of her for being too selfless. I told her she had to think about herself a little more than she did, and that upset her terribly. My mother gave her time and energy in every conceivable way, volunteering at the hospital and working on foreign student committees at the International House at UC Berkeley, even bringing students to our home for dinner. She set a phenomenal example for me and my sister.

My father went to law school at University of California-Berkeley, and ultimately became Deputy Attorney General for the state of California under Earl Warren. After a few years, Warren ran successfully for governor of California and wanted my dad to run for Attorney General, but he didn't want anything to do with politics. We moved to Los Angeles where he became the Senior Managing Partner in the law firm Loeb and Loeb.

It was the 1950s, and my dad represented people who were huge stars at the time like Deborah Kerr, William Holden, Mickey Rooney and Alan Ladd, as well as being the chief lobbyist for all the major movie studios. This was a really high-powered, prestigious exciting job with a six-figure salary. He was also one of the premier tax experts in America. After about ten years, the University of California offered him just $12,500 a year to come back and teach taxation at their law school. He chose to go back to Berkeley. If there was ever an example to set for your kids, it was your father taking one tenth of the salary he was making as a high-priced LA lawyer to go back to the university he loved and take a job doing what he loved to do.

My dad didn't care about material things. We lived a very middle class life, and had a nice home that was average in size. I was always entrepreneurial, and by the time I was thirteen, I was working on all kinds of businesses. In high school I started selling student subscriptions to *Time, Life,* and *Sports Illustrated.* Time Life would give me more than half of the five dollars or so of the subscriptions, and I'd keep around $3.75. In those days, there were no computers, and when people registered for classes at college, they had to stand in long lines. I had the wild idea to go up to the University of California at Berkeley and hand out subscription cards as people waited to register. The cards had my return address, so people could subscribe. The very first week after I did that, I made $1,800 from subscriptions. I was just fifteen, and my mother couldn't believe it!

I was also putting on dances in high school, and by the time I went to college, I was producing concerts. Even back then I was donating proceeds back to causes. In fact, after I did "Hands Across America" and "We Are the World," my mother sent me a picture of myself at sixteen, handing a check to the Red Cross for $64—it was the money we raised in the '50s from a high school dance. This is a huge irony, as "We Are the World" raised $64 million!

The subscription business made money every week, and I continued to build it up. During my time attending Berkeley, I had about fifty salesmen all over California, and had become Time Life's number two top subscription seller in the country for student subscriptions.

I applied to Harvard Business School, thinking I wanted to go into advertising. I was also producing the first couple of concerts for a group called the Kingston Trio, who weren't a big deal at the time. At the first concert I did, they made $360 and I made $82. My dad, the tax expert, informed me that I had to pay an $80 admission tax, so I ended up making two dollars. The Trio offered me a job to become their concert promoter, but my dad said, "If you don't go into grad school now, you'll go into business and never go back to school." I listened to him, turned down their offer and decided to go to Harvard.

The very first day I was in my dorm room, this guy comes in and says, "Oh my God, have you heard this song by the Kingston Trio? It's the number one song in the county!" My thinking at that point was, *I blew it, my career has passed me by; I had that chance and messed it up!* Little did I know.

It was 1959, and a very bohemian time. During the summer of my junior year, another group called the Limelighters was appearing at the main club in San Francisco, the Hungry Eye, and I went backstage to talk to them. The following December, as I was leaving to go home for Christmas break, they called and asked if I wanted to be their executive secretary. My response was probably one of the most significant things I've ever done in my life: I told the leader of the group, "I didn't go to Harvard Business School to be an executive secretary. If you want a manager, I'll be happy to be your manager." Now, I knew nothing about managing, I had never done it, and had no clue. But, after two tough years at HBS, I knew that I didn't want to be an executive secretary.

By the time I got back to school after Christmas, I got a letter from them saying they wanted me to be their manager. I called them and said, "That's fine, but I still have to graduate from business school. I'll go to work for you now while I'm in my last half year, but I won't be able to be your full-time manager until I get out of school." Reluctantly they said, "Okay."

It turned out that reason they wanted me as their manager was that each one wanted to control the group through me, hoping that I was naive enough to go for that. They would each pull me aside, give me their arguments about whatever decision we had to make. Then, the other two would do the same thing. We'd go into a meeting, and as soon as they couldn't agree, they'd say, "Okay let's let Ken make this decision." By that time I had heard all the arguments, so I'd decide. I wasn't always right, but I was thrown into it, and that's how I learned the business.

I always had the mentality that every negative had a positive, and that you just had to get through it, so I applied that to my career. I was proven right about that on a personal level at various times in my adult life, when everything looked like it was falling apart. The first was my first wife running off with another guy eight years into our marriage. Even going through that, I knew there had to be something good that would come out of it, and there was. I became single in the early '70s, which was this amazing time of "free love" that I experienced before meeting my second wife, Cathy to whom I've been married more than thirty-five years now.

Another time, I had this antique 1928 Ford that Kenny Rogers had given me, and a production team doing a Las Vegas show about Chicago in the 1920s wanted to use it. I got pulled in as a producer and then loaned money to cover the production. The show ultimately failed because we couldn't get a decent time slot in Vegas. When it was all over, right before I flew back to LA, I signed paychecks for employees and distributed them. What I didn't know was that when the investors fell through, the company didn't pay payroll taxes. Because I was the only one with any money left, the

IRS came after me. I lost my entire life savings, everything except my house and a car.

Then Jerry Weintraub offered me a job. He was a huge manager with clients including John Denver, the Carpenters, Bob Dylan and Neil Diamond. I made several million dollars for Jerry, and that got me back into business—I signed Kenny Rogers over Jerry's objection, broke Kenny as a solo artist, and eventually left Jerry. Kenny became a superstar—all of that might not have happened if I hadn't lost everything.

In the late '70s, while still with Weintraub, I started managing Harry Chapin, who was a relentless humanitarian and activist. Every week he did concerts to raise money for causes and was always lobbying to get legislation passed to help the homeless and hungry. Harry started waking me up to the injustices in the world, and from that point forward I began to understand how the music industry could have a huge impact. His activism inspired me to encourage all of my clients to give back in some way. I told all of them, "Let's find a charity or cause that you have a reason to be involved in. Maybe you have a parent who died of cancer, or a brother who was killed by a drunk driver. Let's find something in your life that would be meaningful for you to support. I did this for several reasons. First, when you are out there involved in this charity, you have a legitimate reason for caring. Secondly, we will use that to deflect the hundreds of other requests that will come to you every week. And finally, of course, you will help make a difference in people's lives and in turn do well by doing good."

Kenny was a great example of supporting a cause that was personal, because he was virtually homeless at one point. He grew up as one of eight kids living in one room, with an alcoholic father. The most his father ever made in his life was sixty-five dollars, so hunger and homelessness became Kenny's cause. I used to get as many as seventy-five requests for Kenny every day (Oprah probably gets 1000) and we'd say, "Your charity is very important, but Kenny is committed to the issues of hunger and homelessness. He wants to make a true difference in that area." If someone brought us something about that issue, we could see if it merited attention. I did that with every single client, and in my own life too, for a variety of causes. So when Harry Belafonte came to me with the idea of a concert to end starvation in Africa, I was instantly on board.

"We Are the World" was really about accomplishing the impossible, beginning with getting all those artists and their individual egos working together. Very simply, the reason the impossible works is that when you're doing the ordinary, everybody says, "Oh yeah, they're doing the same old thing." When you're doing what seems impossible, they say, "Oh, there's no way; how's that guy going to walk across a rope across the Grand Canyon?" But they perk up and pay attention. Then they start rooting and participating. Then the media covers it. The impossible suddenly becomes possible because of the mere fact that everybody perceived it was impossible when you started!

After producing "We Are the World," I went to New York the following May to pick up a $5 million check for the first proceeds and to do some media. The New York City Ballet was doing a show in honor of "We Are the World." I went to that performance with a guy from the big public relations firm, Burson-Marsteller who was doing pro bono work for us on the project. During intermission, he said, "Now don't laugh, but what if we put people holding hands from

New York to Los Angeles in a continuous line and all at the same time, in one long line, and they sang "We Are the World?" And I said, "You know what, I'm really not laughing. That's just impossible enough to be possible." I've been using that line ever since.

What's interesting is that you don't always realize the impact of achieving the impossible until after you've done it. When you are in the middle of it, you are so caught up in the amount of work it takes to pull it off, and everything else going on. When we recorded "We Are the World," I was doing something every single minute throughout the entire night. By eight the next morning, everyone had left the studio except me, Diana Ross, and Quincy Jones. I remember sitting on the studio floor, just hugging each other and crying because we'd pulled it off. It really hit me again when I went to Africa afterwards on a huge cargo plane to deliver the first shipment of supplies we were donating. It was about 270 tons of food and medicine and various other things. The looks on the faces of the volunteers who were already there, on the ground helping, were so heartwarming and rewarding. The song was a huge inspiration for them, after fighting in the trenches for so long on behalf of literally millions of people who were dying from starvation. And the amazing thing about "We Are the World" was that it wasn't like other charity events that were over at the end of the night—it kept on giving and giving.

When I returned to LA after that trip, a volunteer who worked for us picked me up at the airport. He said, "It's great what you're doing for Africa, but we have a lot of problems in America—you should be thinking of something here like 'We Are the World.'" In that moment, the idea for "Hands Across America" jumped back into my mind. As I look back on that event, it was totally impossible, but we pulled it off. If you fly over the country now, look out a plane window and think that people were standing and holding hands through 17 states, it's mind-blowing! I've seen all kinds of pictures and videos of it, and it's still hard to believe that we did it.

I teach at UCLA now, and the thing I communicate to my students is that everything that happens in life is an opportunity—even the negatives. I use Mothers Against Drunk Driving (MADD) as an example. MADD was founded because Candace Lightner's thirteen-year-old daughter was killed by a drunk driver. That's the most negative thing imaginable, and, even though she was heartbroken, she turned it into an opportunity to save other lives. MADD inspired all kinds of people to take the same concept and say, "I'm going to honor the person who is gone, but also give meaning to my own life, and save other people from the same kind of fate."

My approach to everything is that maybe not every single thing will turn out perfectly. But if you view everything that happens as, "Okay, that was supposed to happen," for the most part, you can see how it does. If you always take that approach, at the very least, you'll take a positive view and that will work to your advantage.

Another thing I teach is the "art of giving." You don't consciously give to get back, but when you give from your heart and put the energy there, it *always* works that way. "We Are the World" and "Hands Across America" cost me about $2 million of my own money; they cost me clients and created all kinds of other issues. Yet nothing has brought me back as much satisfaction and even material rewards as those projects, from which I never took a penny. Those events also gave me more respect and status in the industry than anything else I've ever done. They put me in a different category that has benefited me to this day.

I also teach the art of giving as a general tool. We start with the easiest piece of giving there is, appreciation. The sad fact is that people don't thank other people for doing things. Every time a waiter does a good job, I tell him or her and thank them. It's even more important than a good tip, because hardly anybody does it. There are all kinds of ways to do this, including material ones.

In terms of gifts, I've always found unusual things that related to people in unique ways that would remind them of me for years to come. Probably my most fun ones were gifts I gave many years ago for the two presidents of Warner Brothers Records, Moe Austin and Joe Smith—they were called "The Gold Dust Twins." I had five artists on Warner, and they were all doing extremely well. It was Christmas, and I wanted to get Moe and Joe something special. I happened to go into an antique store and found a beautiful piece of furniture that was actually a captain's commode from a ship—it was a toilet. You opened it up, and inside there was a flower bowl and a pump for water. Closed, it was just a piece of furniture. I had a little brass plaque made for the inside and inscribed, "To Moe Austin—Anyone who takes as much shit as you do ought to have one of these in his office." He kept that in his office for maybe twenty years and showed it to everybody that came in!

Then I went back to the same antique store and got Joe an antique smoking room door from an old train and had a plaque inscribed for it with John Hartford lyrics, because Joe had just signed him as an artist. The plaque said, "It's knowing that your door is open and your path is free to walk." He used that door for the screening room of his house.

Giving is my mantra now for being successful. Anybody who comes to me for anything if I have the time, I always help, because you just can't believe how it comes back. I have speakers in my class who say, "Networking is the most important thing you can do." But what I say is, "The key to networking is 'what can I do to help you?' as opposed to, 'How can you help me?'"

I am grateful to have accomplished the impossible and to be able to share what I've learned. But the most wonderful thing about everything I've achieved was making my parents proud. That is a huge motivator in life, even for people who don't have the most supportive parents. One of the most memorable moments I've ever had was when I was honored by the LA Boys and Girls Club. It was a phenomenal event, held at the Beverly Hilton Hotel. My parents were there, and the next morning I was driving them to a private screening of one the movies I had just finished making. My mother was sitting next to me in the car and my dad was in the back seat. My mother started crying, and I said "Mom, why are you crying?" She said, "Because last night was one of the best nights of my whole life." She probably only lived another year or two. I will always remember that moment; I still tear up when I say it.

Ken Kragen is a nationally renowned speaker, currently teaching undergraduate courses at the Herb Alpert School of Music at UCLA. His "Stardom Strategies for Musicians" class is always sold out. He is also working on an interactive e-book revision of his bestselling *Life is a Contact Sport* and a book on volunteerism in America that he's doing with Tony Robbins. He also runs a series of Mastermind workshops with Sandra and Kym Yancey of eWomenNetwork.

The Calling

"Here is the test to find whether your mission on Earth is finished: if you're alive, it isn't."

—Richard Bach

Marty Gruber is a recovered drug addict who has devoted his life to keeping kids off drugs through his drug awareness program. We can't say exactly how or why Marty "reaches" kids, but he does. He has over 90,000 thank you letters from kids to prove it, and he is out there saving teens every single day.

SOUL MODEL: Marty Gruber

CHALLENGE: As a lifetime drug addict, Marty lost his home, money and family to drugs. His youngest son Christopher died in a drug-related accident.

CHANGE: Has spent the better part of thirteen years providing drug education awareness to over 190,000 students in Clark County, Nevada, high schools and middle schools.

SOULUTION: No matter how much peer pressure you are under, *don't do drugs.* Addiction is for life. People who offer you drugs are not your friends; in fact they don't even like you—friends don't hook friends on drugs.

I was sitting naked on the floor of a filthy, bug-infested hotel room, with blood rushing out of my nose and ears from cocaine abuse, holding the barrel of a .38 pistol in my mouth. I wanted to kill myself because I'd lost everything—my wife, my house, my sons; now the drugs were failing me too—I had become a drug burnout, I couldn't even get high anymore. I changed hands, but still couldn't pull the trigger. I started to cry, got on my knees and prayed for the Lord. I said, "God, if you help me now, I swear to get sober and devote every day of my life to keeping kids off of drugs." One minute later, I felt His presence. I took the gun out of my mouth, stood up, and began my slow, painful recovery.

I was a totally broken man, homeless and deeply in debt. All that was left were my pick-up truck and drugs. I entered a state rehab for thirty days. When I got out, a friend offered to give me a room if I promised to stay sober. Always, in the back of my mind, was the commitment I had made to God.

I was just a baby when I was taken from my mother's arms. My family was very poor, and we all lived in a tiny rented room. My father was an alcoholic, and there were always raging fights going on between him and my mother. Eventually, our neighbors called welfare; they took my brother, sister and me to an orphanage. My parents divorced, and I was sent to a foster home. The woman caring for me locked me in a semi-dark room for two entire years. I was cleaned and fed, but only let out when my parents visited. My foster mother ended up in an insane asylum, and when I turned five years old, I was sent back to live with my mother, who had re-married.

At kindergarten age, I didn't speak, but was rocking and singing because that's all I knew how to do. I couldn't relate to anyone and had severe learning disabilities. I don't have many memories of this time, except for being beaten.

When I was ten and my brother was twelve, my mom kicked us out. We came home from school, and the locks on the door had been changed. There were two boxes with our clothes on the porch, and a note that said, "You don't live here anymore, go live with your drunken father." We found my dad, but he would just drink and beat me unmercifully because I reminded him of my mother, so I wound up being a street kid. Because I had learning problems, I was perceived as disobedient and was beaten even more by my teachers. I was forced to hold my hands out while they hit them with a ruler. My hands would swell up, and the teacher would say, "Cry, damn you, cry!" but I refused to cry.

I failed third and seventh grade, and, by thirteen, was getting drunk on whiskey daily before school. After school, I waited outside the liquor store and begged people to buy me whisky. By eighth grade, I had been in juvenile detention centers three times for stealing food and money. The fourth time I got caught, I was taken to a men's jail in downtown Cincinnati. My cell mate was a huge black man named Mr. Blue, who was a two-time murderer. He protected me and kept the predators away. I'll never forget him saying, "You better hope you leave here before I do."

After thirty days, I was sentenced to three years in a boys' prison. I was accused of being a lookout for two boys who escaped, and the guards almost beat me to death. The only reason they didn't kill me was because a lady who worked at the prison walked in during the beating. They hid my broken body for two weeks so the upper echelon wouldn't find me.

At seventeen and a half, I was released. My mom and stepdad had moved to California and agreed to take me in. The state of Ohio put me on a bus with new clothes and five dollars and shipped me off to stay with them. I stayed there until I went into the Navy at age nineteen. It was the time between the Vietnam and Korean wars, and the military was hard up for people. Even with a seventh grade education, they took me. My commanding officer asked me what I was going to do with my life; I'd never thought about that before. Until he asked that question, I'd only been worried about surviving, but that was a turning point for me. He told me to "learn a trade," and "that's an order." I spent the next four years learning to be an aircraft electrician and was released with the highest rating, as a second-class electrician who trained other people for their jobs.

I did very well and worked in management for several airlines. When I was working at Western Air, I met and married my wife, and we had three sons. At the time, I was a heavy drinker and smoker, but not doing any drugs. I had college graduates working under me whom I was training, and one of the nineteen-year-olds who got hired started riding home with me. One day, he reached into his pocket, lit a joint and offered me some. I took it—less than two years later I was a cocaine addict. The first puff of that marijuana cigarette was a big mistake.

It was the early '70s, drugs were everywhere, and my sons also became addicted. At first, my oldest son was stealing drugs from me.

When you are an addict, you don't care where you get them, and my best source was teenagers. One thing led to another, and I started doing drugs with my sons. My youngest son, Christopher, started when he was thirteen. At sixteen, he went to work at Little Caesar's Pizza. Just one year later, he had his own shop and was the youngest manager in the chain. Management was grooming him to be the west coast rep for Little Caesar's. They would send him into other shops that were struggling, and he'd go in there and clean everything up. He wound up with the largest pizza shop in Southern California, and his future looked amazing.

One night, after drinking heavily and smoking pot, he left work to go home on his motorcycle. He was charging down the street, no helmet, and a van turned in front of him. His head went through the back window, cutting him to pieces. The driver of the van took off, leaving him there to die. Two ladies found my son drowning in his own blood. One of them cradled his head trying to keep him from choking on his own blood. The smell of whisky was overwhelming, because the bottle he'd been drinking from had shattered everywhere.

Chris was rushed to the hospital. When the doctor came out of the examining room, he was crying. He looked me in the eyes and said, "Your son is dead."

In that moment, the bottom dropped out of my world. My middle son Michael was with me. We went into the waiting room that was packed with all our friends and Chris's friends. A little while later a guy from the organ donor association came and asked if I was willing to donate my son's organs to people who needed them. I said, "Of course, whatever is usable from him, you can take."

The worst thing that has ever happened to me in my lifetime was looking down at my son's body in a casket at his funeral. There is no feeling in this world that compares to that. My wife and I were paralyzed and numb. I had Chris's friends crying on my shoulder, just devastated. I tried to support them the best I could and support my wife at the same time. We were surrounded by her family, and that is what made a difference—if it hadn't been for their support and the support of other friends, I don't know what we'd have done.

Weeks later, a letter came in the mail from the organ donor association. I stood in the middle of the living room and read it to my wife. It said, "Because of the unselfish donations of your son's organs, four people are alive today." We locked together, crying like babies.

Even after losing my son, I didn't stop doing drugs. Instead, I tried to bury my sorrow in them until I almost died. I gave up all hope; in many ways I blamed myself for Chris's death. I fought and fought the addiction, lying in bed for days, going through violent withdrawals. I accepted Christ into my life, but it was very hard to stay clean. My body craved drugs, and I craved escape. The withdrawals were brutal, and one day while I was lying in bed, I decided I would go looking for drugs. I heard a voice say, "I will help you, but first you've got to get yourself off drugs." I jumped out of bed in a rage, breaking everything in the room. I felt like nobody loved me, and my life was over. The next morning, I accepted responsibility for my own drug use and began to recover. Finally, my wife and I began digging ourselves out of the sorrow and debt.

Right after my recovery, I tried to get a drug awareness program together, but something was missing. Then, one night when I was alone, something happened. I began thinking about everything that happened in my life. I had spent years trying to push all that down, but that night it wasn't going away. The feelings came over me like a crushing wave, and I cussed every person and the entire world. Then, I sat down and forgave them. I forgave my parents, everyone who beat me, and the guy that killed my youngest son. It felt like a million tons came off my shoulders. I heard the Lord say, "You're ready," and the program fell into place after that.

In November of 1992, I started my first drug program at the West Charleston Presbyterian Church in Las Vegas with two students and a parent. I couldn't imagine going from a broken and homeless old man in a filthy dirty hotel to someone who could make a difference, but I was going to devote my life to trying.

Because I was kicked out of school in seventh grade, I had no writing skills. But I did have a lot of experience developing programs for aircrafts. I got a book on drug programs that had been funded by Hilton Hotels, and contacted them. They sent me information, and I was able to be trained and be certified through the Clark Country School District. I got a certificate, but their program was too long and didn't fit what I was looking for. It provided a great start, but I broke away and developed my own program.

At the first high school where I presented in 2000, I used an easel and flip charts. The teacher liked it so much she invited me back to talk to other classes. I asked for letters of recommendation for other high schools, but for some reason I couldn't get into the middle schools. I wrote dozens of letters explaining my program, and finally got into my first middle school in 2002.

From the beginning, I always asked the kids to write me letters to share how they felt about my presentation. They pour their hearts out, telling tell me things they have never told anyone before. There are kids whose lives I just plain save. Some go home after hearing me speak and help their parents get off drugs. Or, they tell their parents they are doing drugs and need help. I got a letter last school year from a girl whose father had been giving her white powder drugs and sexually molesting her from the time she was five until she was nine. She told a counselor at school and was taken away from him. No one else knew that, but she wrote, "I trust you, Marty."

Each year, I get at least three letters from kids who want to kill themselves. Those require immediate action. I almost always get them on Fridays, when it's too late to do anything. If they sound desperate enough or if there is sexual molestation involved, I call the police. If it can wait until Monday, I e-mail the school a copy of the letter. They get the student in counseling and involve the parents. Because of strict privacy issues I rarely ever find out final outcome.

Getting the kids to open up is the first purpose of the letters—the second is they are my "report card," so I know if the program is doing what it is supposed to and reaching them. I have over 90,000 letters now. To this day, I get numb with disbelief when I read them; I still haven't grasped the enormity of it.

I haven't had too much luck with people supporting the program, because they think they can tell me how to run it. It's a lot of work, but I developed it so one person can do it. The thing to understand is that there are a bunch of strikes against you from the minute you walk into the class. These kids have had so many drug presentations, it isn't funny. At first, they think I am a school spy, and the transformation that happens is amazing to see—first, they don't believe me; then they take notice and the expression on their faces changes drastically. One time when I started speaking to a class, four gang members were asleep. Within ten minutes their heads came up, and within twenty, their hands were up for questions. Two of those kids wrote me later that they quit gangs based on my program.

I connect with the kids because they relate to my story, and I give them the tools they need to put their life together. I tell them, "Don't live in the past—every day you do that, a little bit of you breaks off and dies. If you live in the past long enough, your past becomes your future." Then I say, "Stop beating yourself up for your mistakes—you can't change them, so it's better to learn from them. Take something negative and turn it to a positive by forgiving yourself, and moving your life forward." They listen, because they know I've been there. Through my story they see what happens, and that is my legacy, to inspire others to get off drugs. This program is the best-kept secret in Clark County School District.

I tell the kids to join my army against drugs, called "Marty's Warriors." I teach them to just say, "No," turn around and walk away. If they are approached again after that, it is no longer peer pressure, it is bullying. I have added bullying to my program now to help more kids.

In 2012, I got the Friends of Education Award from the Teacher's Association in Clark County. I am the only person outside their group to have received that recognition, and it made me feel good. That and the letters I get from the kids give me the motivation to keep going. I call it "onward through the fog."

My life's purpose is to help kids stay off drugs. Others can tell you all day what they've done, but I can prove it. I have spoken to more than 190,000 kids so far, and have no plans to stop. Honestly, I don't know what would happen to me if I did stop. Even after all these years, the desire to do drugs does not go away for me—drug addiction is not curable, helping the kids keeps me sober.

I was not a good parent. I did drugs with my sons and their friends. My son died because of drugs, and what I do now helps rectify that, and gives me an overwhelming sense of accomplishment. I have taken that devastating experience and turned it into something positive, so kids don't have to go through what my family did. For the past fourteen years, I have stood in front of thousands of classes telling my whole story, and it's painful every time— but because kids learn from it, I will endure that pain. I have given purpose to my son's life—he didn't die in vain.

Marty Gruber presents his drug awareness classes every single day through the school year. During summers, he presents it at West Care Youth Crisis Intervention Center to homeless and abused teens. He self-published *Searching for the Truth About Drugs: The Life and Calling of Marty Gruber* in 2012.

Passport to Life

SOUL MODEL: Eve Branson

CHALLENGE: Growing up during wartime with very little money or education, having to forge an independent path in a man's world.

CHANGE: Raising independent, successful children; being loving grandparents to their children; improving the lives of the women and girls through her not-for-profit organization in the Atlas Mountains of Morocco.

SOULUTION: Once you realize that helping others is a selfish passport to life, why not be selfish?

I have always loved people, and this kept me in good stead all through my childhood and teenage years. My early years were so different from anything children face today. I grew up in Devon, a rural area in the South of England. From a very early age, my parents taught me the value of money—sixpence pocket money had to be divided four ways: one-quarter savings, one-quarter books, one-quarter sweets, one-quarter yours. This was a small lesson, but it was a good route toward my own, and my family's financial stability in life.

As my family lived in the depths of Devon, I had to be extremely independent to break away and venture out into the larger world. Because I had the security of having a strong family behind me, the courage and desire to seek adventure became part of who I was—fear seldom came into my thoughts. My father always gave me utter confidence, although he also made me aware that I did not know everything. I think the combination of ignorance, love, and faith has kept me safe in situations of potential danger—at least it seems to have done the trick so far!

My mother loved dancing—indeed, late in her life, at age 89, she became the oldest person in Britain to pass the advanced Latin-American ballroom dancing examination. As a young mother, she instilled her love of dance in me from the very start. I was so crazy about dancing that I never even went to high school. Instead, when I was fifteen, my mother sent me to London alone to train in ballet at the Royal Academy of Dance. Dancing gave me the freedom I longed for. I was completely uneducated, but determined to live my life, looking for every different experience I could find! After I completed my dance training, I acted in several West End shows, loving the life of freedom London and the stage afforded me.

But the Second World War was starting—we were being bombed in London—and I felt the desire to sign up. To get some experience, I offered my services as a glider instructor, though I was under age and had never flown a glider before! Flying gliders was an activity that was unheard of for women, who rarely even drove cars at the time. To be quite honest, I didn't care if I was breaking the rules by wanting to learn how to fly. I actually dressed up in a man's pilot uniform to sneak by once, but the men all knew immediately that I was trying to fool them and just laughed about it. Flying was much more dangerous in those days, but I was thrilled to be around airplanes and gliders. I had been so cooped up as a child that I craved adventure!

A year later I was finally old enough to train with the Royal Air Force (RAF) cadets for duty and joined the Women's Royal Naval Service (WRENS). When I had my interview, I told them I wanted to be working out in the open, preferably with ships—I thought that was a romantic idea. So I trained as a "visual signaler" and ended up working at the end of the pier on the Isle of Wight.

Visual signalers were known as "Bunting Tossers." To communicate, we were instructed in the Morse code with hand-held Aldis lamps or with the ten-inch lamp or semaphore with flags for ships farther away. Today's technology has made such signaling outdated, of course, but in those days it was an effective means of communication. Within a few weeks I was issued my uniform—bell-bottom trousers and a saucy little hat—and was sent to Warrington, Lancaster, an inland country town, along with hundreds of other women and sailors for signal training. I have no idea why I was chosen for this job, as I couldn't even spell. Four months later, eight of us were posted to the Black Isle in Scotland, where most of the invasion fleet was based.

One afternoon all the ships left the Basin and only then did we realize that the invasion was imminent. As the majority of ships had left Scotland and gone south, we spent the rest of our duty time on the Isle of Wight.

After the war, being a stewardess was every young girl's desire. We would do anything to see the world and have decent food, as we were so used to rations. But this was in the very early days of flying, and it was absolutely awful when in the sky—we didn't go very high and it was very rough, so the passengers were always feeling sick. You also didn't fly at night, but one evening flying into Rio, we had to make what is called a "box landing," like a helicopter, because we were running out of fuel. We really did think it was the end of us! There was one other time when we were going to Santiago from Buenos Aires and the plane started going down over the Andes. We had to put oxygen masks on the passengers, and if by any chance they rang the bell, we had to get on a temporary mask to look after them. It was terrifying, as we had only two minutes to help them before we ran out of oxygen ourselves!

In 1948, after a year working as a stewardess, I met my Ted, who would later become my husband, at a friend's house party. As I offered Ted a plate of sausages, I said, "The surest way to a man's heart is through his tummy!" It must have worked. He was intrigued, and soon after, we started seeing each other. Before long, given the many flying accidents in those days, he thought, "Well, I better stop her from flying and marry her, I suppose!"

After we were married, Ted was studying to be a barrister, so there was no money coming in. When our first child Richard was born, Ted acquired a sidecar for his motorcycle to carry the three of us; while he drove, I recited legal cases into his ear! My daughter Lindy followed two years later, and Vanessa seven years after that. It was financially essential to work, but I was determined not to leave my children to others. So I was always thinking of ways to make money, beginning with a small industry in our back garden. I would spend most of my time in the garden shed, constructing wooden tissue boxes and wastepaper bins, which I then sold to shops, including Harrods. My little factory was productive, and that gave me the pleasure to press on.

The children were always there on spot so I could keep an eye on them. We couldn't afford nannies or any sort of help, so they had to be self-sufficient, making their own meals and pulling their own weight. One day when Richard was about five or six, he was misbehaving in the car as little boys do. I told him to get out and walk home, that we would meet him at the bottom of the hill in the fields, but he didn't come! We called and called for him. I was feeling awful and terrified, and then a neighbor from a nearby farm phoned and said, "We've got a little boy here with blond hair and blue eyes," and of course it was Richard, who had gotten fascinated watching butterflies instead of coming to meet us.

The girls were very artistic and both were sent to art schools; Richard was educated at a local school until the age of thirteen and then went on to boarding school. He was never one for school. At the time we had no idea he was dyslexic, or even what that really meant, but he excelled at athletics and was constantly off doing his own projects, which we always encouraged, even when it got him in a bit of trouble. The school's restrictions proved too much for him, and he dropped out at age sixteen and began his own business ventures. The first was *Student Magazine,* which became hugely popular, and I believe it was the year after that when he opened the Student Advisory Centre, a charity to help young people.

It was our goal to ingrain in all of our children a sense of hard work, confidence in themselves, and the need to be financially successful. It was so much safer back then to let your children be free and develop as individuals. When Richard was a small boy, he was given a bike from his granny, and he would go off riding all the way from Dorset to Surrey, about 100 miles! It's not as easy today; the world isn't as safe as it was then. I believe the result is that children are curbed too much and not allowed to run free. A sport is imperative, too, but you must give children freedom, while pulling the reins back very gently—this takes courage! The most essential thing in raising children is giving them confidence and never taking it away. And don't give them too many things or too much money! They need to feel the pleasure of accomplishment for themselves.

My greatest achievement has been raising three independently successful children, and now eleven equally successful grandchildren. I have always believed that everyone has the right, and should learn the skills, to be independent. This conviction inspired me to start The Eve Branson Foundation, which began because of Richard. He was always completely daring, trying to break some sort of world record; this time he was set on taking a hot air balloon around the globe. While I was in Morocco, waiting for him to take off, I ran up the hill to see a castle that was for sale. The seller told me that if Richard wanted to buy it, he had to do it within a week, as someone else had an interest. So one morning at breakfast, I showed him the photos of the castle and said, "You have to buy this to make into a hotel!" He said, "With one condition—that you look after the villages and the people there."

The surrounding villages, in the Atlas Mountains, had few resources for young people. Girls left school at thirteen with only perhaps their father's cow to manage. I thought, "Surely that would be a challenge for anyone," and was immediately drawn to help. I knew I could teach them to make and sell things. I don't speak Berber, so I hired an interpreter and created The Eve Branson Foundation, with the goal of teaching the girls lifelong skills they could use to start their own businesses. We hired teachers and set up a carpet workshop and craft house where the girls learn to spin cashmere wool and create other special gifts that are now being sold in the gift shop at the hotel Richard made from the kasbah, Kasbah Tamadot. When I visit the girls now, I get a tremendous welcome; they stand and clap and sing and really appreciate it all!

Every year we have a fabulous event called "Rock the Kasbah" in Los Angeles that raises money for the foundation. Thanks to others helping me, I'm able to take on creating craft houses in more and more villages. This enables me to send out a growing number of teachers to work with the women and girls so they can learn and be independent, with a constructive job at hand.

One can never let challenges hold you back; like Richard, I struggle with dyslexia. This simply means that I see very clearly but tend to get very muddled about figures, dates, and times, which I've learned to work around. I've done so many things and have no intention of stopping; I've been a probation officer, child welfare advocate, and property developer. I take Pilates and play tennis, golf, and croquet to keep myself strong. The key is staying busy and keeping the diary full! I consider myself lucky to have found the mountain girls in Morocco, who have a positive philosophy that shines forth in their faces. They are always laughing and smiling, even with poverty in their homes. When forty odd girls shout out, "Mrs. Eve, Mrs. Eve, will you take us to the sea?"—how can you not love them and want to help?

Once you find the pleasure of giving, there is no need to look for a return—I think this is so terribly important. After I lost my husband of almost sixty-five years, I thought, *Don't feel sorry for yourself for one minute—do well for others.* To make The Eve Branson Foundation successful and help my girls in Morocco is all the satisfaction I ask—as long as my health allows it, my own pleasure will spur me on. Everyone is capable of giving or helping in some way, even by beginning with something very small. Unless you give, you never get!

And one more thing—don't let doubt or fear slow you down or keep you from doing what you love. Throughout my life, writing was my favorite pastime. No matter where I was, I always found time to get up early and write about the events in my life and in the world around me.

In 2010, with the help of my dear friend, writer and editor Holly Peppe, I published *Sarky Puddleboat*, a children's story based on memories of the joyous time Ted and I spent with our grandchildren when they were little. In the book, I'm the magical granny who saves them when they decide to stray from the rules.

And in 2012, after working with Holly for almost ten years to transform my lifelong personal diaries into a book, *Mum's the Word: The High-Flying Adventures of Eve Branson* was published at last. It's the story of my life and a family history too. I think everyone should document their life, as it not only gives you a chance to reflect on your past—it will also help your family understand how your history helped to shape their future.

To learn more about **The Eve Branson Foundation** and to purchase Eve's books, please visit *evebransonfoundation.org.uk/*.

Love Unplugged

SOUL MODEL: Roseanna Means, M.D.

CHALLENGE: Observed that the health-care process is overwhelming for women impaired by exhaustion, mental illness and fear.

CHANGE: Founded Women of Means, a non-profit group of volunteer doctors helping homeless women receive proper health care immediately, without having to navigate the barriers of the system.

SOULUTION: Find an organization to volunteer in—go outside yourself, and give to another person. You will get back so much more than what you give!

My mother was a single parent with a lot of emotional needs, and although I loved her dearly, it was not an easy childhood with her. I was the fourth of five children, and we lived in a very upscale neighborhood in Massachusetts. When I was seven, my parents divorced. Half of us went to live with my father; my brother and I went to live with my mother.

Growing up with a white, upper middle-class background, we didn't suffer financially, but my parents put us through an emotional roller-coaster ride that impacted my self-esteem. People who looked at me from the outside thought I had everything, and it's true; I didn't want for a home or material things. But anybody who has been raised by a needy parent understands that the love from that parent can be very unpredictable. You don't know from one day to the next if you will be loved and accepted. You are walking on eggshells all the time, and that is very difficult.

I did what so many children in that situation do and became an overachiever, trying to win the love and approval that was so inconsistent in my life. Although I stayed in touch with my father, I basically grew up without his presence or influence. He never once told me he loved me, he wasn't in my daily life, he didn't come to any of my school events—I've always missed that, and felt like there was a big hole in my upbringing.

When I was thirteen, I started working as a candy striper (a volunteer assistant), in the local hospital. I took specimens down to the lab and brought in hospital mail. I knew how to "play the game," and look like I knew what I was doing, even though I felt very insecure and lonely inside. People saw me as very strong—but underneath that, was actually a shy, painfully self-conscious person.

I was part of the sixties generation and spent a lot of time demonstrating against the Vietnam War and the invasion of Cambodia. Everything that happened during that era of our country's history really stayed with me. I went to Washington to demonstrate against the war with other young people but felt frustrated because our message wasn't getting through.

For my first year of college I went to Vermont and then transferred to MIT. I found out when I got there, that I was dyslexic—I hadn't realized that before, and I really struggled. I also took training to be a respiratory therapist because I wanted to find out what it was like to be in the hospital. That work helped pay for my college education. I carried a beeper and was doing things like running to the community hospital in the middle of the night if they needed to put someone on a ventilator. Being a candy striper and respiratory therapist helped me understand what it was like to take orders from doctors and be part of a medical team, but not be the person in charge. This really told me I wanted to *be* the person in charge!

After college, I got into Tufts University School of Medicine. I loved learning how to take care of people, talk to patients and listen to their stories. It was exciting to come up with a diagnosis and treatment. I had found my niche and was really good. I had these overachieving qualities and was "multi-tasking" before the word was invented. I remember being very proud that someone could be admitted in the evening, and by the next morning I'd have their entire work-up done for the morning report.

My role as a patient advocate was strong; I was always "schmooz-ing" with the nurses, orderlies, and techs, leveraging those friendships to help me do my job. This was back in the late '70s, before MRIs were invented, computers weren't being used, and nobody had e-mail. Patients would come in and just be so scared; they wanted answers right away, and I felt compelled to help them.

I was accepted into an internship and residency at Brigham and Women's Hospital in Boston, one of the best in the world. That was a huge deal; a classmate and I were the first women ever to be accepted into that program. I was terrified, because I didn't want to "mess up," and went through a period of "imposter syndrome." I thought, *They are going to discover I am this dyslexic overachiever and don't know what I'm talking about!*

During my second year, one of the faculty doctors talked about how, since the war in Vietnam had ended, Cambodian refugees were pouring across the border to Thailand, looking for safety and asylum in other parts of the world. These Cambodian refugees were survivors of the Khmer Rouge genocide. They were swarming into Thailand, which had set up refugee camps to process individuals who desperately needed medical help. This faculty member knew I had been an activist and encouraged me to go there and help. No one *ever* left the Brigham and Women's Hospital; it had been a tough competition to get in there, but I took a three-month leave. I had also gotten married, but nothing was going to stop me.

I signed up for three months with the International Rescue Committee and worked at the border of Thailand, giving medical relief to Cambodian refugees. This period was really the defining time in my life—I had come from a Harvard teaching hospital where there is more money than God, all the resources and high technology you can imagine, and I was in a primitive outpost in the middle of the Thai border, taking care of refugees with only my compassion and clinical skills—no fancy equipment. The people were so inspiring and had such compelling stories! Every single one had survived genocide, and many had devastating medical conditions. Dealing with orphans and family members who had witnessed the horrendous executions of their families was a huge eye-opener.

The lesson for me and for everyone reading this is how important it is just to show up. I had nothing fancy, no X-ray machines or vaccines, just myself. The message to the Cambodian people was, "Here is this doctor, willing to drop everything, leave her husband, and fly 10,000 miles to come into the jungle and help us." That was really powerful for them. I was in total awe of these people who had overcome a level of adversity that, as an American, I would never see in my lifetime. I had such respect for how they had survived; their resilience was astonishing—they held so strongly onto their beliefs and cultural norms, teaching dances, basket weaving, making costumes and music. There was an incredible will to keep it all alive, despite having gone through what they did. I was so impressed and honored just to observe and be part of this—it completely changed my path and sent me back a different person.

I decided that instead of becoming a cardiologist as I had previously planned, I was going to go into primary care and not specialize. Around the same time, my husband and I started our family. I gave birth to one healthy son, then lost my baby girl, Katharine, in the third trimester. This was so incredibly devastating; there was no medical reason for what happened.

Determined to have another child, I soon became pregnant again. Halfway through my pregnancy, my husband discovered a mole on my back. Having just lost Katharine, I was terrified to have the mole removed until after I gave birth. It wasn't the smartest thing to do, but the fear of losing another baby outweighed common sense.

I gave birth to a second healthy son, had the mole checked out, and was diagnosed with melanoma, the deadliest form of skin cancer. I was extremely lucky that it hadn't spread and was able to be removed in outpatient surgery. I was advised not to have any more children because of the possibility of the cancer's recurring, but I got pregnant with my third son, who was born perfectly healthy.

As a full-time working mom, my days began at 4 AM, so I could work before making the kids' breakfast and getting them off to school. My husband had more flexible work hours and was able to help. We never had anything fancy for dinner—I think we lived on mac and cheese and frozen peas, and the kids really didn't care. Not having had a father in my life, I made sure I was a total presence in theirs, going to every single game and every performance.

Because of my experience with the Cambodian refugees, I wanted my boys to understand how blessed we were to live in one of the wealthiest suburbs in the country, and to know the world didn't look like that. We decided to take off a year and live in a country where they would be exposed to different people in a completely different culture. My boys were six, nine, and eleven years old. The lesson I shared with them was this: "The sun is going to rise tomorrow and we will still be a family. It doesn't matter if the people next to you don't speak your language or look different or practice different customs—we are all human beings on this earth together."

We made no plans other than that we were going. I had a lot to do to wind down my practice, but still needed to work. I took an interim job at Mass General Hospital in their walk-in unit, where some of the walk-ins were homeless patients. I began caring for people whose lives had been trashed; many had alcohol/substance abuse problems and mental illness. Suddenly, the light bulb went on. I thought, "I'm home . . . this is what I am supposed to do—it is why I was a candy striper and why I was led to Thailand. I was led to be a caretaker of those who have lost everything. There but for the grace of God go any of us."

In that moment, I knew I was going to take care of homeless women.

We rented our home and sold our cars, bought one-way tickets to Costa Rica and took a faith-based leap into the unknown, believing it was the right thing to do.

Once we arrived, I started a free medical clinic for women. The kids went to school, became fluent in Spanish and had playmates from all different backgrounds. I volunteered as the school doctor, so I was with them every day. After almost a year, Boston Health Care for the Homeless recruited me to be part of their inpatient program for homeless people who are too sick to go back to the streets after the hospital. We moved back, and I became the medical director of the program.

After several years, I realized that even with all the services this program offered, there were many homeless women who just weren't coming in. I started asking "Why?" I learned that life as a homeless woman is very violent, with a high chance of being assaulted. Many women become homeless because of economic disaster—they worked part-time, left work to care for kids, or were abandoned by their mates and got stuck raising the kids alone. They did not have the financial resources to ride out a major life calamity. Many were forced to flee their homes because of domestic violence, and urban hospital and government homeless clinic waiting rooms made them feel exposed. These women needed to focus on survival needs like finding food or a bed; they couldn't afford to wait for long hours in an emergency room. More importantly, women's health issues span our lifetimes. For women to not feel comfortable or safe in health-care settings meant their health was at risk.

If they were in pain and needed painkillers, chances are they would wait for the prescriptions, then be targeted and robbed. Many times they were too proud to say they were homeless, and they didn't always look like the stereotype of "bag ladies." Most of the time the mainstream primary care physician wouldn't ask about their living circumstances, and the women would go back to the shelter and miss out on basic medical care.

The problem with the shelters was that they needed to empty out at 6:00 AM. There is a whole sub-culture there: how long you can stay, which ones are day shelters, which ones will take you when you are drunk, which ones don't, which ones offer showers, and so on. I could see that the women were just falling through cracks all over the place.

The more time I spent with the women, the more I learned about the role of trauma in their lives. So many women said, "I don't want you to come near me or touch me. I don't want you to take my blood pressure because you are putting pressure on my arm, and it feels like when I was beaten up." These women needed their own safe place to go, where there weren't any men. I decided to go directly to the shelters and give them care in a way that felt safe for them.

I called a friend who was a podiatrist, and explained that I had a population of women who didn't want to be touched, and that we needed to do something that took away the threat of being so close. So I learned podiatry skills—how to cut toenails and shave calluses. For the women who were really suspicious and mistrusting, I sat on the floor, put their feet in my lap, cut their toenails, shaved their callouses and did a foot massage—obviously this is a very biblical, meaningful message, that says, "You can lean on me; I am here to serve you and make you feel better."

No insurance company was going to pay me to do a foot massage, but it was and is incredible in helping me build trust—it might lead to a woman talking about who beat her up, or the pimp who had been threatening to kill her, or how she got pregnant when she was raped.

It was clear that the things I was doing actually got the women to come in and stay. They liked the fact that I wasn't filling out forms and asking a lot of questions; I didn't care if they gave me an alias; to them I was just a doctor giving direct healing—it was "health care unplugged!"

This went on for about a year, and I was having regular gatherings at my house with friends who were supportive of the issues. My colleagues "got it," and that's when Women of Means was born. We filed for 501(c)(3), and I built the model based on doctors who were volunteering in shelters where the women felt safe. We didn't ask them to negotiate the health-care system or come to some strange place—we came to them, offering care with no time limits.

I went to the shelters, and said to the women, "Here I am, you guys know me, I'm going to be here every Tuesday with my blood pressure cuff and my stethoscope, so why don't you think about coming back?" They started signing up to get their blood pressure taken. Or, they opted for foot care if they were too scared for me to get too close at first. Then they started asking for aspirin and cough drops because when you are homeless, getting in the car to buy these things is not an option, so I started bringing in over-the-counter supplies regularly.

After several months of paying for the supplies myself, I started buying in bulk from the medical supply house. This all came out of my pocket for the first four years of the organization, and I received no salary.

The women used the ER for tests that I could perform faster and less expensively myself, such as tests for strep throat, urine infections and pregnancy. I applied to the state Department of Public Health, and got permission to bring in little kits that diagnose these things in five minutes. Soon I was bringing in asthma nebulizers to treat asthma flare-ups, as another way to prevent them from going to the ER.

All during this time, my personal life was really challenged. One of my sons had emotional issues from the time he was a toddler that were a huge strain on my marriage and family. I did everything possible to help him, including taking an entire year off to tend to him, but his illness had become unmanageable. Sadly, my husband blamed me for my son's problems. There were some extremely painful issues bubbling up to the surface of our marriage, and a lot of emotional starvation. About eight years after founding Women of Means, it finally all fell apart and we divorced.

I also had severe arthritis in both knees, and right after my husband moved out, I had double knee replacement at Brigham and Women's, where I was the senior attending physician. This is an extremely painful surgery, and the recovery is lengthy and difficult. This period was an extremely horrible, lonely time in my life, filled with so much pain. Every support that I had come to believe was there for me, was gone. My pastor, members of my community, and many of my former best friends were nowhere to be found. Perhaps they assumed I "had it all" and didn't need them. It's wrong to make stereotypical assumptions about people who are rich, educated, white and accomplished. Those people suffer too, and I suffered plenty.

The physical disability of having both knees replaced at once was devastating. I couldn't walk, and there were times I would crawl through the day because I had no choice, then go home and cry into the pillow all night long. Through it all, the homeless women *saved* me; they were my guiding light. I would go to the shelter on my shift, get a cup of coffee and sometimes just sit with them. Just going in and holding their hands, their holding mine, and our simply being women together, was very empowering. They comforted me, telling me, "It's going to be all right, Dr. Roseanna." *These were words that I had said to them in their darkest hours.*

When no one else was there, the women were my sole comfort, and I knew that the bond we share as women was far more powerful than the economic differences that separated us. How else could a white woman raised in comfortable economic circumstances be able to understand and walk in the shoes of someone whose pillow is the cold sidewalk? Women go through all kinds of life experiences—what brings us together are common hurdles, like abandonment, growing up too fast, or not having a mother or father figure. These commonalities and the strength we draw on to overcome our challenges is what creates our sisterhood.

Through it all—losing my child, having cancer, being divorced and having my knees replaced, the only thing that kept me going was knowing that caring for these women was where I was led and what I was supposed to be doing.

At our peak, Women of Means had twelve shelters; now we have eight, because four were closed by the state to make room for biotech expansion, but we are growing again. In 2001, we brought in our first nurse. We can only afford to pay them half the market rate without benefits, and the doctors all volunteer because they love just "being a doctor." You go in, have face-to-face time with the women and scribble a few notes. We do things like handing out medical supplies, foot care, asthma treatments and testing for diabetes. We have very popular electives for medical students and residents from across the city who work with us and are affiliated with two nursing schools. We do about 10,000 visits a year, all free. If you estimate that just walking through the door of a Boston hospital and having a nurse take your vitals costs about $1,000, we are probably saving about 30,000 ER visits a year, with a cost savings of about $3 million a year to the hospitals. And, the patients are getting much better care.

Day after day, we provide huge value that is so meaningful to the women. The world they live in is very lonely and isolated; sometimes we are their only human connection. We are "huggers"—sometimes it is the only time they've been touched without being beaten. People come up to me and say, "Dr. Roseanna, I just need a hug," and I give it out—because I know they've lived from the last time they saw me without any single person touching them in a nice way. That is something I can't bill an insurance company for, but it's what everyone deserves!

Roseanna Means, M.D., is re-married to the love of her life, whom she met as the result of volunteering at an orphanage in Nepal, where she went to "nurture herself" by taking care of poor people. For more inspiration, visit *www.WomenOfMeans.org.*

Life is good

SOUL MODEL: Steve Gross

CHALLENGE: Struggled through some lonely, frightening times during childhood.

CHANGE: Helping children overcome life-threatening challenges—such as poverty, violence, and illness—through the power of play and optimism.

SOULUTION: Helping other people—provided you do it with an authentic spirit of joy and love—is the best way to help yourself.

L ife is good, but it certainly isn't easy. There are a lot of things about life that don't make much sense. How can anyone understand acts of terror that destroy the most innocent of lives? How does anyone make sense of the fact that we have the abundant resources and technology to transmit all forms of media across the globe instantaneously, but we haven't yet figured out how to provide all people with clean drinking water? How can anyone make sense of the fact that in one of the wealthiest countries in the world, some children go to sleep hungry and others without a roof over their heads? It's enough to make you go crazy if you let it. Personally, I always knew that the sadness, pain and injustice in the world would be too much for me to take unless I was doing something to make things better. Life is short. Even if you live to be a hundred years old, you get less than 40,000 days. I knew early on that I didn't want to waste my time wallowing in a sea of despair, when I was lucky enough—as we all are—to be able to swim ashore and do something positive.

I was the youngest of three kids and grew up with a lot of love. My father was a math professor at Bunker Hill Community College, and my mother stayed home and took care of us. They were a great "one-two-punch." My father was, and still is, "bigger than life." As our resident humanitarian and philosopher, he was our moral compass—always sharing worldly wisdom and imparting big picture life lessons, while my mother was the grounding force that made us all feel taken care of and loved. She knew me better than anyone and could sit and listen to me for hours. If I had to compare, I'd say that my dad was always interesting and my mom was always interested.

I was an outgoing, funny, and athletic kid (if I do say so myself). On the outside, I appeared supremely confident (some would go so far as to describe me as conceited and cocky), while on the inside I was overly sensitive and insecure. While I was not aware of it at the time, my older brother was struggling with serious mental illness, and my dad was working three or four jobs to keep our heads above water financially. If we lived in a poor town, we would have been one of the wealthiest families, but the reality was that we were one of the poorest families in a wealthy town. As my dad likes to remind me, everything is relative. Not surprisingly, there was plenty of stress at 171 Gould Street in Needham, Massachusetts. In an attempt to bring light and levity into my home, I would do just about anything to get a laugh.

I could imitate both my parents perfectly, was always good for an impromptu joke or prank, and would delight my parents, especially my dad, with my athletic achievements (in my family, taking the stairs instead of the escalator is considered an athletic achievement).

Despite growing up in a nurturing environment filled with advantages that most of the world's children only dream of, including a comfortable home in a safe community with two adoring parents and a great school system, I worried a lot. A lot a lot. My biggest fears always centered around losing the people that I loved the most. Come to think of it, the fear of loss was always with me. If not front and center, it was lingering somewhere in the background. If my parents were late coming home from dinner, I'd worry that they were in a terrible accident. I couldn't even make it through a sleepover party without eventually breaking down and insisting that my dad pick me up and take me home (1:15 AM was the closest I ever came)!

Strangely enough, when I was nine, I begged my parents to send me to sleep-away camp. My next-door neighbors, whom I admired and were quite a bit older than I, went every summer, and I wanted to do what they did. My parents didn't think I was ready to be away from home for a month, but I convinced them otherwise. I could be damn convincing when I wanted, and usually figured out a way to get my way.

As usual, my parents were right. I wasn't ready—not even close. At camp, all of my insecurities surfaced. Instead of my comfy, cozy middle-class community cocoon, I found myself *alone* in the woods, cohabiting with hundreds of other boys—all of whom seemed older, bigger, stronger, and more savvy than I. To hide my insecurity and loneliness, I tried to grab center stage as I did at home, hoping to get others to love me like my family did. My parents found my antics adorable, but the kids at camp didn't. I was rejected, teased, and beaten up a lot. I could handle the punches, but not the rejection.

Don't get me wrong; summer camp wasn't exactly "Lord of the Flies." I mean, there were counselors there whose job it was to take care of us and make sure we were having fun (at least that's what the brochure said). But what I needed most was a caring adult to comfort me, guide me, and help me adjust, and I didn't get that at all. In fact, the camp's counselors were immature and insensitive at best—cruel at worst—and responded to my struggles with harsh discipline and ridicule. Instead of, "Hey, I know how you must be feeling, let's see if we can figure this out together," it was, "Hey 'Oh, How Gross' (the nickname they gave me), you think you're tough? Let's see how tough you really are. Go sleep outside in the woods alone." Sadly, most of the counselors had no training or insights into soothing frightened, lonely, sensitive little boys.

My overnight camp experience went on for four long summers. At first, I told my parents that I loved camp. Looking back, I'm not sure why. Perhaps I just wanted them to think I was strong enough to handle it. They responded by saving up and signing me up the following summer for the whole summer. That winter, as the thought of going back to camp hit me, I was overwhelmed with fear about having to go through it all over again. I had nightmares. I worried obsessively for the entire six months leading to summer, pleading with my parents not to send me again. They were confused as to how I could go from seemingly loving camp, to being terrified of it overnight. They consulted with a child psychiatrist who urged them to be firm and make me "fight through it." He believed that if I gave into my fear, it would haunt me for years to come. Having perhaps lost some confidence in their parenting instincts due to the difficulties they experienced trying to manage my older brother's mental illness, they went against their intuition, and followed the expert's advice.

As soon as I was old enough, I got a summer job as a counselor and always tuned into the kid who was the underdog and didn't have friends. I did that every summer all throughout high school, kind of helping myself heal from my experience.

When it was time for college, I went to UMass, Amherst, to study business. I'm not sure why I chose that as a major; I had no idea what I wanted to be, and everyone told me that I couldn't go wrong with business. After all, in a capitalist society, isn't everything some form of business? None of my classes excited me. What did excite me were my extracurricular activities. I coached basketball in downtown Springfield, worked with mentally challenged adults at a group home, and spent my summers working with kids at camp. It felt good to be of service to others. A job that didn't enable me to be of service to others would feel empty to me. Instead of changing my major, which would have required another semester of school, I decided to add a minor in education.

I enjoyed the education courses that I took. They inspired me to explore ways in which for-profit-business could be used to help kids learn, grow, and reach their full potential. The only capital investments that excited me were human capital investments, and I quickly became the "bleeding heart liberal" of my group of friends.

In my junior year of college, the owner of the camp where I worked asked me to consider taking a semester off from UMass. He wanted me to work with him at an after-school counseling program for children called The Academy of Physical and Social Development. To do so, I would have to postpone my senior year at UMass. I believed that this was an incredible opportunity to jump start my career, and I went for it.

The Academy wasn't your typical counseling program. It began as a gym that used boxing as a vehicle to help kids develop self-esteem and social skills. Over time, boxing became a less predominant part of the program—instead, the staff started to use sports and cooperative play as the primary treatment modality. So, instead of sitting in an office talking about their issues with a counselor, children at The Academy played with other kids and a counselor in the gym, in a way that was designed to help them feel good about themselves, their abilities and their relationships with others.

To give you an idea of the types of activities at The Academy, I'll share one of my favorites—a game we called Banana Mountain. It was played in a totally matted room with a huge crash mat leaned against one of the walls. The angled crash mat was Banana Mountain, and it was the children's job to get the group to the top of it. I—or one of the other counselors—would get on our hands and knees at the base of the mountain and try to stop them from getting to the top. We would block, wrestle, and tussle with them. The only way they could win the game would be figuring out how to get the entire team to the top of the mountain. Such joyful, rough-and-tumble play served as an excellent vehicle for helping children learn how to work together, trust adults, take risks, and begin to view themselves in a strong and positive light. It was amazing how simply playing in a joyful, connected, creative, and empowering environment brought out the best in children, helping them resolve an array of social and emotional challenges. The parents would tell us, "I don't know exactly how you guys are doing it, but my kid loves coming here and he has never felt better about himself!" For kids with serious psychological issues, The Academy served as a form of inexpensive therapy. For more well-adjusted kids, who simply needed a positive outlet to play and burn off steam, The Academy served as an expensive after-school sports program. It taught me that play, when used right, was incredibly powerful medicine.

While at The Academy, the Better Homes Foundation approached my colleagues and me about bringing a group of homeless children to the gym as part of a pilot program. We agreed to help—the moment this group of homeless preschoolers came squealing into the gym, I was hooked. These kids were starved for safe, loving, joyful play. The cramped quarters of the shelter did not provide this outlet, nor did the drug-addicted and gang-infested parks nearby. Sure, the "regular" middle to upper class kids at The Academy needed our help, but if we couldn't do it, there were many other care providers ready to step in. The children from the shelter, who were all desperately poor, didn't have these same options. I thought, *If I'm going to work with kids, I want to work with the ones whose needs are greatest.*

It was then that I found my calling. I was inspired to start a program dedicated to providing joyful play opportunities to all homeless children in the Boston area, and called it "Project Joy." Over twenty years later, Project Joy became "The Life is good Playmakers." Many of the parents of the children with whom I worked at summer camp and at The Academy helped me get the project off the ground. They believed in the power of play, because they experienced it first hand. I was so young and green at the time, you could have mistaken me for baby spinach. Without the help of lawyers, accountants, educators, and experienced entrepreneurs, I couldn't have done it. We put together a board of directors, got our 501(c)(3) nonprofit status, found an old gym to renovate and started raising money—one dollar at a time.

In the early years we drove from shelter to shelter in our old, barely serviceable van, picking up preschoolers and their teachers and bringing them to our renovated play space in the basement gym of a local YWCA. While at the gym, children and adults spent time joyfully playing together. The positive impact of this weekly playtime was quickly noticeable to all involved. Children who had been withdrawn and frightened were now engaging with confidence, while children who had acted angry and aggressive were now playing together harmoniously.

Project Joy's vision was a world where all children could grow up feeling safe, loved and joyful. However, we soon realized that there were real limits to the amount of good our small team could do. What was most discouraging was the fact that we only got to spend an hour or two each week with the kids. Could such a short amount of "playtime" really make a difference, given that most of the kids were returning to some real rough living situations? In addition, we found it sad that the young children we served needed to hop on a van in order to find a safe place to run, play and just be kids. We realized that to transform the lives of the poorest, most vulnerable children, we would need to help transform the environments that were built to care for them—namely the homeless shelters, preschools, and day care centers, where children were living and learning every day.

Transforming these environments began with supporting the men and women on the front lines who dedicated their lives to helping their community's most vulnerable children. We worked with community leaders to identify these local heroes and provided them with intensive training, follow-up coaching, play materials, and lots and lots of love and respect. With this new focus, our small team began to have some big impact.

Coincidentally, or as fate would have it, I had grown up down the street from two brothers who had their own vision of making a difference in the world by spreading the power of optimism. Bert and John Jacobs are great friends who supported our work from the very beginning, even before they started their successful company, "Life is good." In the early days, they made us fundraising T-shirts, played in countless basketball/softball tournaments, and chipped in whenever they could to help our young nonprofit. John actually created Project Joy's first logo. Their support for Project Joy grew as their company grew. Every year beginning in 2004, "Life is good" held a festival to help kids. The more they witnessed the power of our program, the more committed they became to advancing our work. "Life is good" signaled that commitment in early 2010 by officially joining forces with us, and Project Joy officially became the "Life is good Playmakers."

This partnership has provided a tremendous boost to our movement. Our community of teachers, social service providers, counselors and medical professionals has now grown to over 5,000 throughout the U.S. and Haiti, where we established a team in 2010. These unsung heroes use the power of play every day to build joyful, loving, life-changing relationships with over 100,000 of our most vulnerable children.

They say that overnight success in the nonprofit world takes ten years. Well, we're on year twenty-five, and we've barely gotten started (I've always been a little slower than the norm. Why do you think I stayed back in kindergarten?) The Centers for Disease Control and Prevention has called exposure to childhood trauma the single greatest health crisis facing our children. Thanks to "Life is good" and our huge community of optimists, we're poised to face this crisis head-on by helping transform kids sidelined by trauma into enthusiastic players in the game of life.

I have my own amazing family now, and my best advice to parents is to make time to be with your children. I mean REALLY be with them (no cell phones or other distractions). Follow their lead. Get down on their level and play with them as equals. Let them be the teachers and instructors. Kids would rather have parents who are interested in them than parents who are interesting *to* them.

The other thing is that parents seem to always want is to prep kids to be better in the future (for example, "He's going to have to learn to be more responsible when he gets to high school") instead of valuing where they are today. If we pay attention to giving our kids what they need in the present moment—without evaluating so much—then a bright future will emerge in its own sweet time. And, because what you focus on grows, it's important to "catch" them being good. Like, "Wow, I saw you sharing! Did you notice that you shared? Are you proud of yourself?" Kids want to be recognized for the good in them. The other thing I've learned is that I'm better off not being home physically if I can't be home emotionally. My son can handle my being away at work, but he has a real hard time with me being home, but inattentive. I believe that children would rather have 100 percent of your attention for one hour than 25 percent of your attention for the whole day.

The greatest source of joy that a person can have is by making a positive impact in the lives of others while doing something that they love doing. There is no "one size fits all." Some people will never be social workers or community activists, but there are many other things they can do to make a positive impact. My dad taught math—it was simply his vehicle to share love. If you're a great chef, you can share love through food. If you're an accountant, you can share love by helping a person learn to budget or help them file their income taxes. If you're an electrician, you can share love by lighting up somebody's home. Love is never just an emotion, it is an action. Sharing love in whatever way you can gives you a greater sense of well-being and purpose. Once you start connecting with other people who are doing the same thing, you become part of a community that is spreading the power of optimism.

There is a great quote in the book *Field Notes on Compassion* that says, "Be kind to everyone you meet, because everyone you meet is in the midst of a struggle." If you live long enough, you are going to experience tragedy. Some struggles are visible; some aren't. If we can feel and empathize with someone else's suffering and help alleviate it in some way, that helps *us*. Even folks who aren't interested in spreading positivity can make great contributions to the world simply by not spreading negativity. It's not so difficult to do. Sometimes it's as simple as putting a smile on your face and checking your tone of voice when your server forgets to bring you more water, or not leaning on your horn because somebody in front of you is driving too slowly.

My parents still wonder if they made the right decision in listening to the "expert" advice to send me back to camp. None of us will even know for sure—life doesn't give us the opportunity to see the results of taking a different path. I wouldn't to change a thing—I'm really happy with how things worked out, because it led me to who I am and what I do today. I'm almost embarrassed to put my bad summer camp experiences into the same paragraph as the life-threatening traumas that many children are forced to endure. However, when it comes to fear and suffering, there is no absolute hierarchy. Pain is pain—it hurts—and my challenges led me to my life's purpose.

I get so much more than I give from my work. It's given my life so much joy, love and meaning. My dad taught me, "We have no control over our birth or death—but we do have control over helping to make someone else's journey from birth to death better by being there to help." No one ever needs to say, "thank you" to me—I don't act out of obligation. I do it because I want to. In that sense, I'm a pretty selfish guy. Because when you are serving others—with joy I might add—you are really serving yourself.

Steve Gross, M.S.W., is the Executive Director, founder and Chief Playmaker of the Life is good Kids Foundation, a 501(c)(3) non-profit organization that uses play to srengthen and heal children whose lives have been deeply impacted by trauma. He has devoted his career to serving our most vulnerable children. Steve lives in Boston with his wife Kerrie and his children, Mookie, Ben, and Daisy.

The Real Life
of Lieutenant Dan

---

*"The nation which forgets its defenders will itself
be forgotten."*

—Calvin Coolidge

SOUL MODEL: Gary Sinise

CHALLENGE: Supporting all veterans, including the more than
three million disabled, who have suffered injuries that they will
endure the rest of their lives on our behalf.

CHANGE: Founded the Gary Sinise Foundation, with a mission
of serving our nation by honoring our defenders, veterans, first
responders, their families, and those in need. Travels the world
with the Lt. Dan Band, raising funds and spirits on behalf of our
wounded warriors.

SOLUTION: If you see someone in uniform, just know that taking
the time to thank them will mean a lot. They don't ask much at
all. They are just doing what they signed up to do. But that little
gesture of gratitude from a stranger will make their day.

I was a little worried the first time I was asked to visit our wounded at Landstuhl Medical Center in Germany, in 2003. But as I had played a wounded soldier in the '90s and had been involved with some of our disabled veterans through the Disabled American Veterans organization, I reminded myself, *Think of what they've sacrificed for me. Now it's my turn to show my support for them.*

The first ward I walked into was full of banged-up guys who weren't severely injured, but there were plenty of bandages to go around. They would be patched up and likely return to the battlefield soon. The room was quiet, and I was unsure of how to get started. So I just went up to a soldier and held out my hand. "I'm Gary. How are you?" Another soldier hobbled over. "Hey, Lieutenant Dan, pleased to meet ya." Soon there was a group around me, chatting about themselves and their families. I kept reminding myself, *Remember, it's not about me. It's about them.*

Then I went upstairs to visit the patients in their rooms, those who'd lost arms or legs, had been badly burned, and some who were in comas and did not know I was there. But family members were there by their bedsides, and I could tell their spirits lifted when I came in the room. There's no way to see that and not be moved. What happens is you get so wrapped up in their stories, you forget about yourself and the fear of seeing some pretty tough things. They were so happy I was there—I could see how important it was to their healing that anyone would take the time to visit and show them they cared.

Leaving the hospital, I felt like I'd made a difference, if only for a few minutes, in the war-torn lives of those guys and their families. It felt like I was being used by a power bigger than myself to give these people hope and to bring a little joy where there was so much fear of the unknown future that lay ahead. It was a humbling experience to say the least.

Since then, I've visited wounded service members many times, returning to Landstuhl three or four more times—and at National Naval Medical Center San Diego, Walter Reed National Military Medical Center, San Antonio Military Medical Center, and others. Each time, the selflessness of our defenders reminds me that our country—vulnerable as it is—is served by noble men and women willing to make the ultimate sacrifice.

My awareness of what that sacrifice really means began in my twenties. I was born in Blue Island, Illinois, and we eventually moved to Highland Park, where I went to high school. My dad was a film editor who worked constantly, but my mom was there for me all the time. Academics didn't come easily for me; it was always difficult to sit in a classroom and listen to a lecture by a teacher. I think part of the problem was that I didn't learn proper reading skills early on. And of course, if reading is hard for you, then studying is going to be miserable.

I struggled all the way through school. I lacked self-confidence, so what I didn't have in academic skills, I made up for in other ways, by just getting my hands dirty and doing things like organizing the local kids in the neighborhood into a baseball team or a football team or a rock band or whatever. I somehow developed these "do it yourself" sort of leadership skills. I think part of the reason was that I felt intimidated by kids who were smart in school, so I would make up for it by bossing them around, and somehow, that made me feel stronger.

I was a teen during the Vietnam War, and, while kids just a few years older than me were off fighting in that brutal conflict, I was growing up in suburban Chicago, playing bass, singing in bands with my friends. When I was a sophomore in high school, on a lark, I tried out for "West Side Story," and by closing night I was pretty much hooked on acting. It was good fortune, luck, and perhaps a little of God's plan that, when standing in a hallway in the school, the drama teacher Barbara Patterson walked up to me and told me I should audition because I looked like I could play a gang member. So I did, and she cast me in the play. After that, all I wanted to do was act in the plays at school and she had a big influence over my early life, encouraging my do-it-yourself and do-it-your-way attitude.

I was in high school in the late '60s and early '70s. I saw the news reports about the Vietnam War on TV, and joined an antiwar rally once at my high school—really just to get out of class. I didn't have much of a clue about what was going on over there.

I turned eighteen just as the war was ending. Since I was never into school, I wasn't about to go to college. I wanted to do theater, so I got together with a high school friend, Jeff Perry, and his college friend, Terry Kinney, and we started the Steppenwolf Theater Company. I contacted the local Chamber of Commerce about finding a space for our little group, and they told me about a vacant Catholic school basement that used to be a teen center. I went there to check it out, and the priest who ran it told me he would lease it to us for a dollar a year. After that, things started falling into place; we built an 88-seat theater in that space and slowly developed a following. The early group was the three of us plus six others, four who are still members, John Malkovich, Laurie Metcalf, Alan Wilder, and Moira Harris whom I married five years later.

The primary goal and focus of our group was building a strong ensemble and the reason it succeeded was because it was always about the group, and not one individual. Through that experience, I learned a lot about listening to other people.

When I was twenty-five, I was in Los Angeles and saw a play called *Tracers*, in which real Vietnam vets relived their experiences on stage. It was one of the most powerful things I'd ever seen, and, sitting in the audience, I was mesmerized. Later, I thought about what I'd been doing at eighteen and nineteen, and how oblivious I had been to what guys my age were going through. I decided to direct a production of the play at Steppenwolf.

I had only two vets in my cast and wanted to get a better understanding of the Vietnam experience, so we visited the local VA hospital to talk to vets struggling with post-traumatic stress. The battles they described, the haunted look in their eyes—I couldn't get them out of my mind. The worst part was hearing about how they'd been treated by some people when they came home. One actually said, "I was afraid to wear my uniform in public."

This made a tremendous impression on me. I realized how lucky I'd been to have so many opportunities while guys and gals like them had made huge sacrifices, only to be treated with contempt instead of honor. I began getting involved with vets groups and causes, and felt great compassion for their ongoing plight. My wife, Moira, had brothers who were Vietnam veterans, and I would talk to them about their experiences. I was really inspired by my brother-in-law, Boyd McCanna (Mac) Harris, a West Point graduate, who was a great leader, and I have no doubt he would have become a four-star general if he hadn't been struck down by cancer at a young age.

Time and again I thought, "We have not been grateful enough for our soldiers." After *Tracers,* one of the first things we did at

Steppenwolf was create "Vets Night," a program offering free dinners and performances to veterans, but I knew I had to do more.

So I stayed active with a few of the Chicago area veterans groups who had attended performances of *Tracers* and even had the privilege of helping to build a veterans memorial in Lansing, Illinois. As a thank you they included my brother-in-law's name on the wall of heroes.

I continued directing and acting in plays, had some success in New York, and eventually was offered a film directing deal in Hollywood at Columbia Pictures. In 1987 we moved to Los Angeles where I pursued my film directing and acting career.

By the time I read the *Forrest Gump* script in 1993, having spent so much time with Vietnam veterans, I understood immediately the feelings of bitterness and hurt that Lieutenant Dan's character wrestled with. He was angry and mad at God—but I believe this character was the first time a Vietnam veteran was portrayed in a film as someone who could overcome his challenges and move on from the Vietnam War. He goes through anger and despair, yes, but in the end, he is standing tall. Playing him felt like something I was meant to do, like paying a debt of gratitude—and, that role ended up changing the course of my life.

About a month after the movie opened in 1994, The Disabled American Veterans reached out to honor me for playing Lieutenant Dan. I didn't know anything about them at the time, and they wanted me to attend one of their conventions. I flew out to Chicago, and when I arrived I was brought in the back way through the kitchen. I could hear my voice coming through speakers in the ballroom. They were playing clips from *Forrest Gump* on the screens. They told me that when I heard my name being announced, I should go through the door to the stage, which I did.

When I looked out into that ballroom, I saw upwards of 3000 people; nearly 75 percent of them were disabled veterans, from WWII to the present day. Many were in wheelchairs. Any of those who could stand gave me a standing ovation for playing a disabled veteran in a way that they believed was honorable. I was so moved and caught off guard by my emotions. I'm an actor—I play parts. These people lived the part that I played. They were severely wounded, and they were applauding *me*. From that point on, I stayed very involved with their organization.

On September 11, 2001, when we were attacked by nineteen terrorists, I realized how vulnerable our country really is. Now we were going to war and I wanted to do something to support our troops, so I signed up for the USO shortly after our forces landed in Afghanistan. The first time I called the USO, they had no idea who I was, but they recognized the name Lieutenant Dan.

My first overseas USO trip was to Iraq in June 2003. More than 180 people were on that tour—actors, comedians, football players, rappers, you name it. This was my first encounter with so many active-duty military members. I must have shaken thousands of hands—there'd be a petite woman from the Philippines, a huge guy from Georgia, a man from Colombia, a woman from Korea, a New Yorker—all of them serving proudly as Americans. I can't think of a better example of what our country is all about, having so many incredible people serving us voluntarily.

My second visit to Iraq was in November 2003, with a smaller USO tour. We went to Camp Anaconda in Balad, north of Baghdad. One afternoon the troops took a few of us—including me, Wayne Newton, Chris Isaak and Neal McCoy to a local school.

Our troops had helped to make repairs on the school, like pouring concrete floors and adding windows and doors. Even after being fixed up, it was just a tiny room filled with tables and benches, and nothing on the walls but flies. Yet, to them it was a great improvement and it struck me that the kids were just the same as American kids—goofy and giggling and excited about the distraction we provided. They also seemed genuinely fond of our guys and gals, hugging them and calling them by name.

The kids sat four at a desk, and I saw one of them scribbling something in a small, beat-up notebook. Then he handed his stubby pencil to the kid next to him. The second child scrawled something and passed the pencil to the next boy. I realized that was all they have to write with! Three kids were sharing a pencil so small that most Americans would have thrown it away. I asked one of our guys about it, and he said, "There aren't enough school supplies. They'll be using that pencil until it won't write anymore."

Back in the states, I couldn't shake that image. Our troops had done so much good at that school already, but maybe I could help them do more by sending donated school supplies. Someone at Camp Anaconda suggested I get in touch with author Laura Hillenbrand, who was getting Arabic translations of her book *Seabiscuit* for the kids, who were fascinated by the story.

Laura and I spoke by phone, and Operation Iraqi Children (OIC) was born—a charity to help our troops spread much-needed supplies and goodwill to Iraqi schoolchildren. After nine great years OIC has recently come to an end, having delivered more than 300,000 school supply kits, thousands of toys and blankets to the children of Iraq and Afghanistan. With our great partner Mary Eisenhower and the folks at People to People International, Laura and I have been amazed at the generosity of the American public in supporting OIC, and it was something really positive for our troops.

By that time, I had started a band with Kimo Williams, a Vietnam vet pal of mine. For the first year I was doing USO tours, it was just handshaking and taking pictures, which I did pretty much every month. I could see that, to our soldiers, having somebody they see on television or in the movies coming over to say, "Thank you," really boosted their morale. But the idea of entertainment; a show, is a whole different thing. So I kept telling the USO that I had musicians I played with for fun, asking if they would let me bring them on a tour to perform for the troops—and sure enough, they let me take me a band overseas.

That began the very active effort to get out as often as possible and play for our troops—we do forty to fifty shows a year, and it keeps me on the road most weekends. It's a big show where we play all hits, and it's very popular with the military. I've been on bases all around the world, and played hundreds of concerts for our military men and women.

Since 2003, we've entertained over a quarter million troops and their families, boosting morale and raising money for our wounded warriors. For me, interacting with our military community and our wounded puts everything else in perspective. These are our freedom providers and they give so much for all of us.

So from 2003, after going all around Iraq, Kuwait, and visiting bases in Italy, Germany, and back to Iraq, and all around the states, I was hooked. I could see how someone like me could make a difference, and eventually I would realize that I could do even more by starting a foundation of my own. It was the next logical step for me to provide financial support, as well as to encourage people who want to help to learn about the best military charities.

In 2010, The Gary Sinise Foundation was created with a mission to serve our nation by honoring our defenders, veterans, first responders, their families, and those in need. We do this by creating and supporting unique programs that entertain, educate, inspire, strengthen, and build communities.

We've partnered with The Tunnel to Towers Foundation and created our Building for America's Bravest™ program to build custom smart homes for severely wounded veterans. All of our warriors encounter difficulties returning to civilian life, but, like Lieutenant Dan in *Forrest Gump*, these heroes face unimaginable life changes. Each home is customized to ease the day-to-day challenges they now face with features like retractable cook-tops, cabinets, and shelving; elevators; roll-in bathrooms; automated doors and lighting; intercom systems, and more—all controlled by an iPad, to help restore their independence in countless ways.

We've created "Dining with Defenders," to serve good meals to deploying troops at LAX, and other festivals to boost the morale and spirits of the patients, their families and the medical staff at military hospitals. We've also created an Emergency Relief Fund dedicated to assisting those in urgent need, and partnered with GE, which donates the appliances that go into the smart homes, on *GetSkillstoWork.org*, a program that helps veterans put their military experience to use in civilian jobs.

The band folds into the overall mission of lifting spirits, boosting morale, raising money and awareness, and building support. Let's say we build a smart house—what happens then, if you have no arms and no legs? Where's your job? Are you going to stay in the house and hide? You need community support if you are going to make it. Going to towns around the country and playing music in support of our wounded helps the community understand what is going on. The fact that someone who is on TV every week comes to help this wounded warrior who lives among them; that raises a lot of awareness.

I have veterans in my family whom I respect and am proud of. I have way too many friends who are Vietnam veterans and came back to an ungrateful nation that treated them badly. It was shameful, and we can't ever let that happen again. Every president sends the troops somewhere to defend our country, and we are lucky that we have volunteers to do that duty.

When you go overseas and see the caliber of people fighting for us, and the courage of people who are injured and have to live with a disability for the rest of their lives, it's very humbling. It reminds you that there is a lot more out there than in your little world. There's so much to be said for service above self.

I'm blessed to live in the United States of America and have the freedom I have. Many people have paid the price for that freedom by giving up pieces of their bodies and minds. Paying tribute to them is the least we can do, and a healing and positive thing for our country.

I've played a lot of characters in my more than 30 years as a professional actor, and I'm proud to say a fair number of them have been members of the military. Not a week goes by that someone doesn't refer to me as Lieutenant Dan. On *CSI: NY* I played Detective Mac Taylor, an emotionally wounded ex-Marine. Mac was named after my brother-in-law, who was such an exemplary leader. Every day I am reminded of his inspirational qualities.

Knowing so many extraordinary people in the military community, people who willingly sacrifice each day, has certainly taught me to be more grateful—grateful for so many things, not the least of which is that I married Moira and that we have been able to raise our three children in this great country. And, most grateful that there are so many men and women who put their lives on the line to defend it.

When I first got into this business, I never thought of myself as anything that special. It wasn't until I played Lieutenant Dan that I realized the impact that a movie character could have on people, in this case our wounded warriors. When I walk into a service member's hospital room and realize that his or her body is broken, maybe missing legs, or arms from a blast, I am humbled. And, when they wait in line for me to sign a picture because they relate to me because I played Lt. Dan, well, wait a minute, I am the one who is inspired, and I want them to know there is a grateful nation behind them.

So, if you see someone in uniform, just know that taking the time to thank them will mean a lot. They don't ask much at all. They are just doing what they signed up to do. But that little gesture of gratitude from a stranger will make their day.

Gary Sinise serves as spokesperson for both the American Veterans Disabled for Life Memorial Foundation and Disabled American Veterans, and was instrumental in raising funds for the Pentagon Memorial in Washington, D.C. and The Brooklyn Wall of Remembrance in NYC. He serves on the board of Snowball Express, on executive councils for The Medal of Honor Foundation and the USO, and is an advisory board member for Hope for the Warriors. In recognition of his humanitarian work on behalf of our troops and veterans, Mr. Sinise has received many distinguished awards including The Bob Hope Award for Excellence in Entertainment from the Medal of Honor Society, the Spirit of the USO Award, The Ellis Island Medal of Honor, and in 2008 he was a recipient of the Presidential Citizens Medal, the second-highest civilian honor awarded to citizens for exemplary deeds performed in service of the nation, only the third actor ever to receive this honor. In 2012, Sinise was presented with the Spirit of Hope Award by the Department of Defense and was named an honorary Chief Petty Officer by the Navy.

Turning Broken Bones into Dancing

"What is to give light must endure burning."

—Victor E. Frankl

SOUL MODEL: Edith Eva Eger, Ph.D.

CHALLENGE: Incarcerated in the death camp Auschwitz during the Second World War, lost her parents and most of her friends and family.

CHANGE: Discovered hope; became a world-renowned speaker and psychologist with a practice in La Jolla, California, where she uses her experiences to help others cope with trauma and lead full lives by moving beyond their problems, no matter how insurmountable they seem.

SOULUTION: The real concentration camp is in a person's mind—that one is built from shame and regret, which makes us unable to forgive. It's not "I forgive you" or "You forgive me." If you are going to blame someone for your feelings, you are not taking responsibility. Forgiveness is a gift that you give to yourself.

I spun around dizzily, trying to stay focused on the dance I was performing. *But I was so hungry.* We were given soup and bread to eat once a day; the bread was like eating sawdust. But if I finished, I would get a few bread crusts. My audience was made up of a few Nazi officers . . . one of them could flick his wrist and order me to be immediately executed if I didn't do what he said.

He was called the "The Angel of Death," because of the terrible experiments he performed on live humans, particularly twins. His name was Dr. Josef Mengele. I had to keep going; there were so many others like me who were also starving, and I knew I would share my bread with them. I closed my eyes, twirling and spinning. My body was in Auschwitz, but my mind was in Budapest. There, I was all dressed up and strong, performing onstage in front of an audience of thousands who were applauding me under the bright lights as I danced "Romeo and Juliet" to Tchaikovsky. After what seemed like forever, Dr. Mengele ordered me to stop and gave me the bread crusts. I went back to the barrack where I slept with the other girls and women, sharing my bread with them.

As long as I could remember, I had been dancing. When I was very small, my mother took me to ballet school in Kosice, Czechoslovakia, where we lived with my parents and two older sisters, Magda and Clara. Clara was the superstar violinist, Magda was the pretty one, and I was the "runt." I was very shy, and although I was a good student, I didn't have much of my own identity.

My ballet instructor was a spiritual man. On the first day we met, he picked me up, and I did a full backbend over his arms. He said, "God built you in such a magnificent way that all of your power, all of your ecstasy, has to come from inside out." I had no idea what he was talking about . . . until later on. I devoted myself to gymnastics, practicing over five hours a day for many years.

In March of 1944, during the Second World War, the Germans invaded Hungary. My sister Clara was the only Jew to be accepted to a musical conservatory in Budapest. A Christian professor managed to smuggle her out of Kosice and hid her at his home.

I had a boyfriend named Eric, whom I loved dearly. Before he was taken by the Nazis, he said, "Edie, I will always remember your beautiful eyes and hands; that is what I will think about in the camps. When we are all free, I will find you, and see those eyes and hands again."

In April of 1944, my family and I were rounded up, put into a cattle car, and taken to the death camp at Auschwitz in Poland. I was sixteen years old. My mom hugged me and said, "We don't know where we're going; we don't know what's going to happen." She pointed to her head, continuing to speak. "Just remember, no one can take away from you what you put here, in your own mind."

When we arrived in Auschwitz, my father was immediately taken away. My mother, Magda, and I, were put into another line. Then, Dr. Mengele split Magda and me into one line, and my mother into another. I tried to follow her, but Dr. Mengele grabbed me, pushing me back with Magda, telling me I would see my mother soon. "She's just going to take a shower," he said.

I never believed my life was in Dr. Mengele's hands. I felt that God was with me, and I could turn to him. Right then, I was able to turn hatred into pity, and I began to pray for the Nazi guards.

Magda and I were taken to the women's section of the camp. I asked one of the inmates when I would see my mother again. She pointed toward a chimney billowing smoke, and said, "You'd better start referring to your parents in the past tense."

We were given gray uniforms and our heads were shaved. Magda held a clump of her hair and was crying. Through her tears, she asked me how she looked. I realized in that moment that I had become Magda's mirror. And, that we have a choice to focus on what we have lost, or pay attention to what we still have. I said, "Magda, you have got such beautiful eyes, and I couldn't see them when you had your hair all over the place!"

We were given barely any food and were forced to sleep two or three together on straw mattresses stacked in bunks, sharing pieces of a dirty blanket. We used communal toilets. Every single time we showered, we never knew what would come out—water or gas. The water wasn't filtered, so if you drank it, you could get a disease and die.

I made up my mind that no matter how badly they beat and tortured me, they could never, ever, murder my spirit or take away my hope. If I fought, I would be shot. If I ran, I would die on the electric fences surrounding the camp. I learned the third alternative—how to "flow" with what was. I kept repeating to myself, "If I can survive this day, tomorrow I will be free." I thought about Eric and his love and the hope of a future with him. I imagined our lives when we were all free again. This is how I kept the Nazis out of my head.

After about seven months, instead of being sent to the gas chambers, Magda and I were moved and sent to work on ammunition trains as slave laborers. I think it was December. Bombs were falling and we were taken further and further away, toward Austria. We were led to a German village, housed in a community hall, and told not leave under the threat of death.

At that point, we were deteriorating physically; the little food we were given had something in it that stopped our periods. Magda weighed almost nothing and was dying from starvation. I went outside, hopped a fence and picked carrots from a garden. As I climbed over the fence to head back, I turned around to find a German soldier, pointing a gun at me. We made eye contact, and I began to pray, not for me, but for him, so he wouldn't pull the trigger.

He turned the gun around and pushed me inside, and I still had the carrots. The next day, he burst into our prisoners' room, demanding to know which one of us had left the building for the carrots. I crawled out on all fours to beg forgiveness. He gave me a loaf of bread and said, "You must have been very hungry to do what you did." I wish I could meet that man again and thank him for not following orders.

In April of 1945, Magda and I were marched from Mauthausen in Austria to Gunskirchen, with thousands of other Jews in the "death march." If you fell down from exhaustion and starvation, you would be immediately shot. I was very sick and broken from being beaten and not having enough food, and I collapsed. The girls with whom I had shared my bread crusts formed a human bridge and carried me the rest of the way to Gunskirchen.

On May 4, 1945, we heard that the camps had been liberated. A Nazi took us to the middle of a forest. He had dynamite, and the plan was to execute us. He fled, leaving us there in a pile of bodies. We were all on top of each other, sick and emaciated—we didn't know who was dead and who was alive. We knew the Nazis were gone, and I saw people leaving. Then, after a while, they came back. We were so brainwashed; we fell into that "learned helplessness." Even though we were free, we didn't know what do with freedom. I was very ill with typhoid fever, and didn't know how anyone would know I was alive among all the corpses. When the Seventy-First Infantry of American soldiers arrived to liberate Gunskirchen, I was able to slightly move my hand. They saw that and pulled me out from the pile of dead bodies. It was almost one year since we had been imprisoned, and Magda and I were free.

I was taken to a hospital, where I became suicidal. Both my parents were gone, and I was only starting to come to terms with everything that had happened. God spoke to me there and said, "If you die, you're going to be a coward. But if you live, I'm going to show you that you're going to be here for something special." I realized that I was going home, and that the biggest concentration camp was in my own mind.

When I finally returned to Kosice, everyone who survived was seeking out others to see who had made it. I searched far and wide for Eric, asking everyone for any information. I found out he had been shot and killed one day before liberation.

After the war, I got married to be "normal." I didn't love my husband, but was honored that anyone wanted to marry me, and I wanted to be the best wife I could. He had inherited his grandfather's business, and his father was mayor of the city. His family was one of the wealthiest in Czechoslovakia, and our home took up an entire block.

After our first child was born, the Communists confiscated my husband's business and threw him into jail. I packed up my daughter and my big diamond ring, went to the prison, and bribed the warden to let my husband out. We fled to Vienna, and then onward to America. When we arrived, I had to borrow six dollars to get off the boat. We moved to Baltimore, where I worked in a sweatshop and was paid seven cents for every dozen boxer shorts I could sew. I will never forget being sent to the "colored" bathroom at the factory. That was very hard to see, after experiencing Nazi Germany and Communist Russia.

My husband and I had two more children, and for years, I struggled with survivor's guilt and shame. Because I never thought I deserved to live, I pushed myself to be a high achiever. In my thirties, I decided to go back to school and become a psychologist. In 1969, I received my degree from the University of Texas, El Paso, and later went on to get my doctorate. I became a psychologist, a sexologist, and later, a diplomat. Today, I have five grandchildren and three great-grandsons. To me, that's the best revenge against Hitler!

My experience during the war was the best education I ever had. It taught me about compassion, faith, and survival. The people who lived were the ones who helped each other—not the ones who were out only to save themselves. Magda and I were so fortunate to have each other the whole time, and I think that is a bigger lesson for humanity; a sense of belonging is one of the biggest parts of resilience.

I also learned that "giving is getting." Relationships are about give and take and tolerating each other's differences. We can't give what we don't have, and we must find ways to cooperate, not dominate. Dominating is about debasing a person into an object, like saying, "Jews are a cancer to society." You can kill Communists and Fascists, but you can't kill the ideas behind any of them. Our job is to think of better, more beautiful ideas.

I have lectured all over the world. Someone in the audience once asked how I could forgive what was done to me. I said, "The Nazis cannot hold me hostage or prisoner of the past. I was victimized, but I am not a victim. People have only the power over you that you allow them to have. The real concentration camp is in a person's mind— that is one built from shame and regret, which makes us unable to forgive. If you are going to blame someone for those feelings, you are not taking responsibility."

Forgiveness is not my forgiving you or forgiving the Nazis; it's a gift that I give myself. When I returned to Auschwitz many years after I was liberated, I was able to begin doing that. I want to have joy and passion—that's impossible when you hold low-level chronic anger. It is not an overnight process, and I have yet to fully arrive.

I have been so fortunate in my life. I am freer now, more than I ever was, and I am so grateful to be a role model for others. Acknowledging the truth of life is not easy, but I am thankful to do it and teach others the same thing. I tell my patients, "Don't cover up your pain and don't medicate it—you have to 'feel to heal.'"

I believe the soul is taking residence in our bodies, and that tremendous loss can become something wonderful and completely unexpected; you just have to take the responsibility of your own feelings and liberate your mind. I am in my eighties now and still don't know what I'm going to do when I grow up. Hardship creates a wonderful opportunity to become more appreciative of life. I'm here, and I'm still dancing!

Edith Eva Eger, Ph.D., has a busy clinical practice in La Jolla, California, and an extensive speaking career. She holds a faculty appointment at the University of California, San Diego, and has appeared on numerous television programs, including *Oprah*. Her sister Clara passed away of Alzheimer's Disease, but Magda is alive and well. She is a Life Master in bridge and teaches piano in Baltimore, Maryland.

Soul Selfie

We've all done it. Held up our camera and snapped a selfie to share with others. Rarely do we get it on the first take. We sift through five or six images to get the photo that makes us look right: *This one makes me look fat . . . This one makes my nose look huge . . .* (until we finally take) *. . . THIS one! I look awesome!* Send.

I wrote "The Awesome Anthem" to have that same effect on my spirit; to show me the mightiest version of myself. When I perform it, I hit "the Awesome Pose," in which I call out "I am awesome!" while holding up my hand like I'm taking a selfie. But this selfie takes a snapshot of my soul. Not of how I look on camera, but of how I live on purpose. Not to share with others but with myself.

It caught on. Folks began hitting this pose whenever they did something awesomfied. So I shot a video for the poem showing people from all walks of life—from celebs to scientists to seven-year-olds— taking this Soul Selfie to declare their place in the Global Community of Awesomeness. I share with you here an excerpt of the poem to remind you what your selfie should show you. Because on our most difficult days, when our vision has no flash, we all sift through five or six dark images of ourselves to get the one that is right: *This one makes me look weak . . . This one makes my despair look huge . . .* (until we finally embrace) *THIS one! I AM Awesome!* Send.

THE AWESOME ANTHEM (EXCERPT)

By Sekou Andrews

"AND I AM/NOT PERFECT
BUT I'M PERFECT AS I AM
I'M NOT BEAUTIFUL/LIKE I USED TO BE
I'M BEAUTIFUL/LIKE I AM
LIKE THE SCAR WHERE A BREAST ONCE WAS
LIKE SURVIVAL WHERE A DEATH ONCE WAS
LIKE THE BETTER WHERE A BEST ONCE WAS
EVERY GRAY HAIR A TROPHY
EVERY WRINKLED FOLD A STORY
EVERY POUND OF FAT A CHALLENGE
REMINDING ME/THERE IS ALWAYS SOMETHING TO PURSUE
AND ALWAYS SOMETHING TO CELEBRATE!"

Read the full poem and watch the awesomnacious video at TheAwesomeAnthem.com